POISON PILLS

POISON PILLS

The *Untold Story* of the *Vioxx Drug Scandal*

TOM NESI

Thomas Dunne Books
St. Martin's Press ❦ *New York*

THOMAS DUNNE BOOKS.
An imprint of St. Martin's Press.

POISON PILLS. Copyright © 2008 by Thomas Nesi. All rights reserved. Printed in the United States of America. For information, address St. Martin's Press, 175 Fifth Avenue, New York, N.Y. 10010.

www.thomasdunnebooks.com
www.stmartins.com

Library of Congress Cataloging-in-Publication Data

Nesi, Thomas J.
    Poison pills : the untold story of the Vioxx drug scandal / Tom Nesi.—1st ed.
       p.   cm.
    Includes bibliographical references and index.
    ISBN-13: 978-0-312-36959-0 (alk. paper)
    ISBN-10: 0-312-36959-X (alk. paper)
    1. Rofecoxib—Side effects.   2. Merck & Co.   I. Title.
 RA1242.R64N4   2008
 362.17'82—dc22

                          2008019633

First Edition: September 2008

10 9 8 7 6 5 4 3 2 1

In Memory, Susan Nesi

CONTENTS

Dramatis Personae

David Anstice   President, Human Health—The Americas; member of the Management Committee, Merck & Co.

Francesca Catella-Lawson, M.D.   Assistant Professor, Department of Medicine, University of Pennsylvania

Garret A. FitzGerald, M.D.   Robinette Foundation Professor of Cardiovascular Medicine, Department of Medicine, University of Pennsylvania; Chairman, Department of Pharmacology, University of Pennsylvania

Kenneth C. Frazier   Senior Vice President and General Counsel; member of the Management Committee, Merck & Co.

James Fries, M.D.   Professor of Medicine, Stanford University

Raymond V. Gilmartin   Chairman of the Board, President, and Chief Executive Officer; member of the Management Committee, Merck & Co.

David J. Graham, M.D., MPH   Associate Director for Science, Office of Drug Safety, U.S. Food and Drug Administration

Peter S. Kim, Ph.D.   President, Merck Research Laboratories; member of the Management Committee, Merck & Co.

Philip Needleman, Ph.D.   President, Searle Research and Development, Monsanto Company

Bruce Psaty, M.D., Ph.D.   Professor of Medicine, Epidemiology, and Health Services, University of Washington

Alise Reicin, M.D.   Senior Director, Pulmonary-Immunology Group, Merck Research Laboratories, Merck & Co.

Edward M. Scolnick, M.D.   President, Merck Research Laboratories; member of Board of Directors; member of Management Committee, Merck & Co.

Deborah Shapiro, Ph.D.   Director, Biostatistics and Research Division Sciences, Merck Research Laboratories, Merck & Co.

Gurkipal Singh, M.D.   Adjunct Clinical Professor of Medicine, Department of Medicine, Division of Gastroenterology and Hepatology, Stanford University School of Medicine

Eve E. Slater, M.D. Assistant Secretary of Health, U.S. Department of Health and Human Services (2001–2003); Senior Vice President, Corporate Public Relations and Regulatory Liaison, Merck & Co.

Eric Topol, M.D. Chairman of Cardiovascular Medicine, Cleveland Clinic Foundation

John L. Wallace, Ph.D., MBA Professor of Pharmacology and Therapeutics, University of Calgary, Alberta, Canada

Frank A. Wollheim, M.D. Editor, *Rheuma 21*; former Chairman of the Department of Rheumatology, University of Lund, Sweden

Today . . . [we] are faced with what may be the single greatest drug safety catastrophe in the history of this country or the history of the world. We are talking about a catastrophe that I strongly believe could have—should have—been largely or completely avoided. But it wasn't, and over 100,000 Americans have paid dearly for the failure.

—David J. Graham, M.D., MPH, Associate Director for Science, Office of Drug Safety, U.S. Food and Drug Administration, testifying before the U.S. Senate Finance Committee, November 18, 2004, on the harm caused by Vioxx

POISON PILLS

The Widow

The very essence of civil liberty certainly consists in the right of every individual to claim the protection of the laws, whenever he receives an injury. One of the first duties of government is to afford that protection. The government of the United States has been emphatically termed a government of laws, and not of men. It will certainly cease to deserve this high appellation, if the laws furnish no remedy for the violation of a vested legal right.

William Marbury v. James Madison, Secretary of State of the United States, **Supreme Court of the United States, 5 U.S. 137, February 1803 Term, opinion of the court delivered by Chief Justice Marshall**

Carol Ernst remembers with vivid clarity the death of her husband, Bob, on May 6, 2001. After a sentimental dinner at the Olive Garden restaurant in Keene, Texas, the same spot where the two had gone on their first date, the couple returned home and went to bed. The meal had been healthy as usual because Bob was a triathlete, and though he was fifty-nine, was in better condition than most people half his age. The only health problem he suffered from was pain in his hand that was being treated by a new drug called Vioxx. The pill seemed to work well—and had few side effects—or so it appeared.

When Carol Ernst tells the story of her husband's death, her eyes are sad, voice soft, words pensive. She still blames herself for Bob's fatal heart attack. "I feel very guilty at times. I feel like if Bob had never met me, he might still be alive because I was the one who told him to ask about the Vioxx."[1]

This was the second marriage for both Bob and Carol. Ms. Ernst had been alone for fifteen years after her first marriage had ended, and considered herself blessed that she had met and fallen in love with this tall, well-built man who could bike-ride sixty-two miles in the Fort Worth, Texas, heat, barely breaking a sweat. He worked at the local Wal-Mart and led a fitness class called "Young at Heart."

An hour after the couple sank into bed, that May 6 night, Carol was awakened by Bob's labored breathing. "At first I thought I heard him snoring," Carol says, but her experience working in medical offices warned her otherwise. "When I woke up more, I realized it wasn't snoring. It's what's called agonal breathing, those last few breaths."[2]

Paramedics arrived minutes later. They started vigorous cardiopulmonary resuscitation. No response. Twenty minutes later, Bob Ernst was dead from cardiac arrest, brought on by an irregular beating of his heart.

Carol's daughter, Shawna Sherrill, was with her mother later that night when the fifty-six-year-old woman broke down. When an Emergency Room doctor said her husband was dead, Ernst said she was devastated. "How can this be?" Carol cried. She thought her husband was the image of health.[3] It was a question she asked over and over, to everyone from her doctor to the pathologist who performed an autopsy on her husband.

Carol found information on the Internet about the potential of the pill Vioxx to cause heart disease and contacted an attorney who agreed to take the case. The lawyer, Mark Lanier, a top trial attorney as well as a part-time Baptist minister with a down-home folksy style, finally put Carol on the witness stand in August 2005. Her calm, sincere, and convincing story of her marriage and Bob's death deeply struck the jurors. They also expressed deep anger at the secret memos about Merck's knowledge of Vioxx and heart disease revealed during the trial.

Less than a week later, the twelve men and women delivered a stunning verdict that sent shock waves through the drug industry. Vioxx, the pharmaceutical giant Merck's most popular pill, which the company had pulled off the market a year earlier because of a study linking it to heart disease, was responsible for the death of Carol Ernst's husband.

The still grieving widow thought she had won the case. In fact, her fight and that of tens of thousands of others had only begun. Merck immediately appealed the verdict and said it would fight each case one by one.

. . .

The future and safety of medicine will be determined, not only by laboratory work and drug safety testing, but by the results of jury trials, legislation regarding drug company liability, and other complex judicial and regulatory decisions. The 2004 removal of the bestselling and highly touted pain pill, Vioxx, by Merck Corporation, and the resulting litigation, has involved at least 27,000 patients, and countless state and federal fraud probes. These investigations have generated controversy, made headlines, changed physician prescribing habits, and caused anyone who has ever thought of taking a pill to question whether it is free from causing disastrous harm. The clashes will continue for years, if not decades, as the most critical issues in medicine flare in public.

Even the Supreme Court is now involved and justices are staking out their positions for one of the most important medical opinons of the new century. In a related case Justice Stephen Breyer asked who should make the decisions that will determine whether a drug is on balance going to save people or, on balance, going to hurt people. "An expert agency on the one hand or 12 people pulled randomly for a jury role who see before them only the people whom the drug hurt and don't see those who need the drug to cure them?"[4]

The Vioxx legal battles involve the collision of two titanic forces. On the one side is the pharmaceutical giant Merck, which has spent close to two billion dollars on legal fees to try cases and limit financial losses. On the other side, patients, their lawyers, and a grand jury are still poring through millions of secret corporate documents and listening to testimony, attempting to decipher the odd and tumultuous events surrounding the development of Vioxx and other pills in a similar class of drugs.

Despite proposed legal settlements with injured parties of $4.85 billion and Merck's agreement to pay the government $671 million to settle claims it overcharged and bribed doctors for a number of medications, the Vioxx story continues with just as much passion and zeal as ever, with many astonishing new revelations yet to come.

"Merck still has Vioxx lawsuits coming from all directions, including

Canada—from patients in eighteen foreign countries, from health providers and consumers who paid for Vioxx and want their money back, and from stockholders looking to recoup their losses," reports Linda Johnson of the Associated Press.[5]

Furthermore, thousands of former Vioxx users who claim other injuries—dangerous chest pain, abnormal heart rhythms, and similar conditions—are excluded from the settlement and many of their cases continue.

Scientists and attorneys are also looking into the frightening possibility that Merck never fully revealed the dangers of Vioxx with regard to patients with memory loss (cognitive impairment) and cases of mild Alzheimer's disease.

Predicting what will happen next in the serpentine tale of Vioxx is impossible. The story of this drug, which began in laboratories in the early 1990s, has all the earmarks of a medical *Godfather* story—a virtual war between the largest drug companies in the world, threats to investigators, manipulated research disputed by the very medical journals that published them, "incomprehensible" press releases, and endless lawsuits—one involving an attempt by Merck to censor a Spanish medical bulletin. Careers rose and fell and billions of dollars hung on the words of investigators worldwide.

Dr. Jerry Avorn, professor of medicine at Harvard Medical School, who has studied the deceptions and dangers of the pharmaceutical industry for years, was surprised by Merck's secret e-mails and memos presented at the Ernst trial. "Even as a seasoned observer of drug company affairs, I have been surprised by the way Merck handled the emerging evidence about cardiac risk," Dr. Avorn said.[6]

Nonetheless, Carol Ernst's lawyer, Mark Lanier, was blasted by everyone from physicians to newspaper columnists for winning the trial by twisting the facts and relying on nothing but "an ignorant jury of hicks," despite the fact that his witnesses included some of the best-known physicians and scientists in the world. Even as the Texas jury was deliberating, Merck's lead attorney, Gerry Lowry, said, "If he [Lanier] had any evidence Vioxx causes arrhythmia, this case would have been over three weeks ago."[7]

A few months after the trial verdict, CNBC broadcast a debate between Lanier and Richard Epstein, the James Parker Hall distinguished service professor of law at the University of Chicago and a senior fellow at the

Hoover Institute. The professor had written an op-ed piece for *The Wall Street Journal* and said that "physicians lamented" the fact that they could no longer use the drug.[8]

Many leading newspapers, including *The Washington Post,* also mocked the Ernst trial. In an editorial entitled "The Vioxx Hex," the *Post* wrote that the "Texas jury in that case awarded $253.4 million to the widow of a man who died of a heart attack triggered by arrhythmia, which is not a condition Vioxx has been proven to cause." The *Post* said the jury was confused about the medical evidence.[9]

On September 12, 2006, a year after the trial, *The Journal of the American Medical Association* issued a public health bulletin and published a study from the Harvard School of Public Health, Brigham and Women's Hospital, and Harvard Medical School clearly demonstrating that Vioxx "increased risk of renal [kidney] events and arrhythmia events [heart rhythm disorders]."[10] Eric Ding, a coauthor of the study, noted that the evidence of kidney damage was evident by the year 2000, one year before Bob Ernst died. The Harvard study further showed a link between Vioxx and arrhythmia by the year 2004. This evidence had been verified one year before the campaign by many connected with the Ernst trial as peddlers of "junk science."

Eric Ding says that the evidence about the Vioxx/arrhythmia association "should have been disclosed much sooner . . . because publication is very slow."[11] The study authors stated that Vioxx use was associated with increased risk of arrhythmia and damage to the kidneys. Higher doses and longer duration of Vioxx treatment contributed to the adverse effects." Among Lanier's expert witnesses were Dr. Benedict Luchessi, M.D., Ph.D., inventor of the heart pacemaker and one of the world's best known authorities in cardiovascular pharmacology and professor at the University of Michigan Medical School. Luchessi actually helped train some of the Merck researchers working on Vioxx. Also among the experts for Carol Ernst was Dr. Isaac Wiener, cardiologist and co-director of the Cardiac Arrhythmia Center at UCLA Medical Center in Los Angeles.

The way many media reports came out, Carol Ernst was not a victorious widow; instead, she and the jury that heard her were portrayed as menaces to pharmaceutical innovation and the scientific method itself.

Wrote Professor Epstein, "[I'm] a scared citizen who is steamed that those 'good people' have imperiled [my] own health and that of [my] family and friends. Nobody of you have ever done a single blessed thing to help relieve anybody's pain and suffering. Just do the math to grasp the harm you've done . . . Your verdict says you think that the American public is really better off with just hot-water bottles and leftover aspirin tablets."[12]

Americans have hardly returned to hot water bottles, and it seems odd that one of the nation's leading attorneys would be frightened by a sixty-year-old widow and a handful of Texas citizens. But Merck was just beginning to fight and had in its employ some of the largest law firms in the world, and a war chest of over a billion dollars. The company's tactics in the trial and subsequent statements made it clear Merck was playing "hardball" and would fight each case brought against it, one by one. Nor did the pharmaceutical company ever concede any wrongdoing.

Contradicting Dr. Avorn and others, Merck argued that it gave adequate notice of the heart risks of Vioxx in the drug's label or product description that accompanies the drug. Somehow, the warning never made it into any of the thousands of television commercials for Vioxx that blanketed the United States. Since these advertisements are monitored by the Food and Drug Administration, it should cause great concern about giving so much power to this federal agency, as Justice Breyer suggests.

Senator Charles Grassley, (R) Iowa, former chairman of the Senate Finance Committee, who conducted hearings on Merck, summarized: "The FDA was also negligent in the Vioxx case . . . those running the nation's public safety agency repeatedly dismissed the concerns of their own scientists and seemed to do everything possible to keep the public in the dark about emerging problems with Vioxx."[13]

Despite Merck's power and finances, many lawyers and physicians still press on, perhaps inspired by the sentiment of Carol Ernst after her trial victory. She felt the fight was not just for her, but that every man and woman deserved a right to know what a medication could do to them. Her husband, Bob, would never have touched Vioxx if he had known about its true risks.[14]

PART I

CHAPTER 1

Shooting Stars

Just one small pill let me resume my life. I could get up in the morning without pain. I could take my daughter to the park, lace up my skates and perform again. It was a miracle.
    —Dorothy Hamill, Olympic champion and America's Sweetheart[1]

Pharmaceutical analyst and managing director of Deutsche Bank Barbara Ryan was sleeping soundly in her Connecticut house when her phone rang a little after seven on the morning of September 30, 2004. She was *supposed* to be wide awake and already writing research notes, but she'd seen nothing newsworthy the night before and decided to take a small break from her normally hectic and pressure-filled job.

The phone call snapped Barbara awake. It was from one of her associates, Billy Mathews, who sounded perplexed and worried. "We got this really weird news bulletin from Merck," Mathews said.

Barbara listened as her partner gave a quick summary. "They announced a press conference at nine with the CEO, Ray Gilmartin, and their head science guy, Peter Kim. They don't say what it's about, except that it involves 'new information on a currently marketed product.'"

By now Barbara was out of bed, simultaneously trying to get presentably dressed and do some quick mental calculations. Mathews continued: "Merck won't say a word and the trading desk is going crazy." It didn't take Barbara more than a few seconds to figure out what was happening, although even as she did, she did not quite believe it. "Vioxx," she said. "They're yanking their biggest-selling drug."

There was a slight pause on the other end of the line. "What are we looking at?" Mathews said, trying to stay calm.

Barbara was still running all the facts through her head. "A very great deal of money and a lot of angry investors," Barbara said, already assessing Merck's losses.[2]

At 8:08 A.M., nine words appeared on the screens of every brokerage and newsroom in the world. From the Dow Jones wire: "Merck Announces Worldwide Withdrawal of VIOXX."

Barbara Ryan was already at her office on the squawk box as members of the stock exchanges and frenzied traders were trying to calculate Merck's opening price. "We don't exactly know what Merck's going to tell us at the press conference," Barbara said. "But my best guess is fair value of around 31 dollars a share." The stock had closed the previous day at $44. The monetary loss Barbara was predicting was in the neighborhood of $26 *billion*.

Shortly before 9:00 A.M., September 30, 2004, Raymond V. Gilmartin, chairman, president, and chief executive officer of drug company giant Merck & Co., stood amid a small army of scientists and public relations professionals reviewing his three-page outline of meticulously prepared remarks. He was impeccably dressed in a dark charcoal suit and red tie, his gray hair neatly combed and gelled. Gilmartin watched almost absentmindedly as a team of technicians adjusted the microphones and lighting in the hastily decorated Bijou Room of New York's Hilton Times Square hotel.

Only a few members of the assemblage knew the carefully guarded specifics of this press conference, but no one had any illusions as to just how grim the reaction would be.

Next to Gilmartin was the recently appointed president of Merck Research Laboratories, Dr. Peter Kim, examining notes and conversing intently with members of his scientific staff. Both he and Gilmartin had thoroughly rehearsed for this moment, knowing that every word they spoke would be videotaped, examined, reexamined, and undoubtedly litigated.

The vice president of Merck's public relations department, Joan Wainwright, who had been virtually locked up in a hotel room with crisis communications experts for the prior three days, tried to maintain a sense of decorum among the roomful of anxious reporters, financial analysts, Merck employees, and government officials. Ever since her office had issued the

Vioxx withdrawal press release before dawn, Merck had been bombarded with media calls—but the company simply would not comment.[3]

With cameras rolling, Gilmartin came to the podium and started reading his speech to announce the voluntary withdrawal of Vioxx. "We are taking this action because we believe it best serves the interests of patients," the Merck chairman said.[4] The company's decision was based on the results of a large study of patients that showed that Vioxx, the company's bestselling drug to treat pain and inflammation, caused an increased risk of heart attack and stroke.

The background noise of clicking text messages barely distracted the CEO. Never a man known for charisma, Gilmartin continued calmly. The APPROVe (Adenomatous Polyp Prevention on Vioxx) study had been designed to learn whether Vioxx could prevent colon cancer, Gilmartin said. But scientists monitoring the results discovered that in the Vioxx group, as compared to the group receiving no medication, patients were significantly more likely to experience heart attack and stroke.

Vioxx was no ordinary drug, and Merck was no ordinary company. The pain medication had been approved for use in over eighty countries, hailed as one of the world's major medical advances, and taken by at least 20 million patients in the United States alone. Its annual worldwide sales were $2.5 billion, which accounted for 12 percent of Merck's revenue. The pharmaceutical giant was certainly not a fly-by-night corporation.

Merck was among the world's oldest and most prestigious pharmaceutical companies, tracing its roots back nearly four hundred years to an apothecary in Darmstadt, Germany, near the bustling city of Frankfurt am Main. In the previous fifty years, Merck scientists had participated in numerous medical breakthroughs, including the development of cortisone and penicillin, the cure for tuberculosis (streptomycin), and the discovery of a new class of cholesterol-lowering medications, called statins, all of which led to Nobel Prizes for medicine.

Throughout the 1980s, Merck had invented and sold one blockbuster pill after another—and the corporation's stock price had soared along with its reputation as the gold standard in the pharmaceutical industry.

However, while Gilmartin continued to speak, the glory decade of the 1980s seemed a distant memory. As Deutsche Bank analyst Barbara Ryan had predicted, Merck stock, which had started the day at $44 a share, plummeted to $33, effectively wiping out 27 percent, or $30 billion, of the company's value. The share price now hovered around an eight-year low, selling for what it was worth in 1996, only two years after Gilmartin had started with the company.

The CEO's carefully prepared words were the foundation of what would be called the "Merck Vioxx defense," and became the basis of official future communications on the subject. The story: Merck had no reason to believe until September 25, 2004, that Vioxx was harmful to the heart. The instant the company had proof that this was the case, it took immediate steps to protect patient well-being by pulling Vioxx off the market. "Putting patients first" became the public relations slogan.

In fact, even as the September press conference was starting, a huge staff within Merck's worldwide headquarters in Whitehouse Station, New Jersey, was already contacting the regulatory authorities in the eighty countries where Vioxx was available, informing them of the company's decision and asking them to remove hundreds of thousands of pills from doctors' offices, hospitals, and pharmacies. The largest drug withdrawal in history was now under way.

So sudden and unexpected was the Merck announcement that most physicians learned about the event only *after* they had received calls from distraught patients. One of these doctors had more than a passing interest. Dr. John Braun, an internist from Oradell, New Jersey, who himself took Vioxx, had been in practice for more than twenty years. Widely respected in his community, Dr. Braun appeared to pride himself on the compassion he showed to his patients, his comprehensive knowledge of medicine, and his scrupulous attention to detail. Following the advice he tirelessly rendered to patients, Braun kept himself in excellent physical condition and paid particular attention to keeping his risk of heart disease low. He had been both mystified and depressed when, at the age of fifty, he had had a near-fatal heart attack. It happened in August 2004, just a month before Vioxx was withdrawn.[5]

Dr. Braun had good reason to be worried. A year before the Merck announcement, one of his older patients, John McDarby, had suffered a debilitating heart attack that left him partially paralyzed and in need of almost constant medical care. McDarby had seen him for more than eight visits and had taken Vioxx for three years.

Was Vioxx related to Dr. Braun's own heart disease—and if so, how many others both in his practice and around the globe had suffered as a result of taking the pill? The brief Merck announcement did not give him much to go on and provided scant information to reassure his patients.

Only a handful of researchers knew the closely guarded results of the APPROVe study and thus, like Dr. Braun, the world's doctors were as much in the dark as the panicking patients. Merck information hotlines were jammed for days after the press conference as health care practitioners sought to learn more details behind the giant drug company's decision to withdraw the drug.

That extraordinary decision began on September 24, 2004, when Dr. John Baron, professor of medicine at Dartmouth Medical School, personally called Merck's Dr. Peter Kim to inform him that the data and safety monitoring board (DSMB) of the APPROVe trial was recommending that the study be halted for safety reasons after eighteen months.

The study was a randomized, double-blind, placebo-controlled trial that involved 2,600 patients. Randomized, double-blind, controlled trials (RCTs) are designed so that neither the patients *nor* the physicians in the study know who is getting the inactive (placebo) pill and who is getting the active (in this case, Vioxx) treatment (double-blind). Every patient who enters the trial has an equal chance of being given either Vioxx or placebo (randomization).

In order to insure the safety of the trial participants, however, a small committee of medical experts is allowed to take periodic looks at the side effects in the two groups. These experts, the DSMB, are not allowed to communicate with any other researchers, *unless* they spot either something alarming or something unusually positive. It is imperative that, along with other members involved in the clinical trial, they are "blinded." They remain so throughout the trial unless they spot an extraordinary trend—in which case they have the obligation to "unblind" the study.

One of the most significant pieces of evidence against Merck was an article published in *The Journal of the American Medical Association* that linked Vioxx with the *potential* of cardiovascular damage.[6] And then there were matters only a handful of top Merck executives knew about: data manipulation, withholding crucial information from the medical community and the U.S. Food and Drug Administration, damaging e-mails, the possibility of the cardiovascular risk of Vioxx by Merck's own scientists—and an immediately upcoming meeting with the FDA concerning deaths in a group of patients taking Vioxx in Alzheimer's disease trials—all time bombs set to go off.[7]

The Alzheimer's data showed not only an increase in deaths with Vioxx, but the unsettling suggestion that Vioxx accelerated the development of Alzheimer's disease in a clinical study coded 078, the cognitive impairment trial. Dr. John L. Wallace, professor of pharmacology and therapeutics, and a Food and Drug Administration panel expert on Vioxx and Celebrex, states: "Assuming that there was a statistically significant difference between the Vioxx and placebo groups [in the *JAMA* Alzheimer's study] . . . I think you could make the point that the results are suggestive of harmful effects of Vioxx on the brain, possibly even a neurotoxic effect (just as there are toxic effects in other organs, including the GI tract, kidney, cardiovascular system, etc.)."[8] These mortality analyses were not made public in a timely fashion.[9]

Merck had steadfastly maintained Vioxx's safety—and vigorously fought to keep the pill's miracle image intact. However, the APPROVe study would now open the floodgates. Merck had major decisions to make that might well affect the future survival of the company. Kenneth Frazier, Merck's chief counsel, calculated that those decisions would have to be made within days, if not hours.

Lawyers within corporations have one enormous advantage over other employees. They are protected by attorney-client privilege from being subpoenaed. Therefore, Frazier and his legal team could shape a response to the APPROVe study and other allegations against Merck without being subject to later legal scrutiny. Frazier initiated phone calls with key Merck executives and consultants, careful not to either leave notes or communicate by e-mail. This would be the pattern of the next days' whirlwind meetings.

Sharp divisions of opinion emerged among executives, researchers, outside consultants, and legal experts. One group favored leaving Vioxx on the market. Merck would take the results of the APPROVe study to the Food and Drug Administration and negotiate new warnings to be placed in the drug's information packet (label) to doctors. Vioxx had survived label changes before and would likely survive another.

On the other end of the spectrum were those who argued for immediate voluntary withdrawal. Maybe—this group believed—Vioxx would survive, but at what sales level and legal jeopardy? The APPROVe trial data did not distinguish which people in the research group might, or might not, be at risk for heart attack. Thus, only a very tiny portion of patients would be willing to stay on the drug—and even fewer doctors would prescribe it.

A third group fell somewhere in the middle. A withdrawal of Merck's largest selling drug and a linchpin of the company's strategy for the next decade seemed too great a step to contemplate.

Unspoken among the company's executives was that either way, they stood to lose millions of dollars in personal holdings of Merck stock.

Kenneth Frazier and his legal team aligned with the second group. If Merck acted quickly and voluntarily took Vioxx off the market, a defense could be formulated that the company was acting in the best interests of its patients. In fact, the story had a nice ring to it. Merck had always abided by scientific evidence, and the minute that new data showed Vioxx to be harmful, "patient concern came first." Furthermore, Merck had diligently shared all its information with the FDA. Therefore, the company could use the FDA as a legal shield for its decisions.

Recent state laws such as those in Texas and federal regulations bolstered this defense. A 2006 FDA ruling asserts that if a drug had received FDA approval, the pill's manufacturer could not be held liable in state courts. In other words, injured patients would not have the right to seek compensation from the drug company no matter how negligent. This would be an invaluable boon to the pharmaceutical industry.

The APPROVe data *appeared* to have another silver lining. The clinical trial had not been halted until after eighteen months, and therefore Merck could confidently state that patient harm took at least a year and a half to occur. In addition, because the patients had been monitored closely, the company could say that damage did not occur unless patients took the drug exactly as they had in the study: *every day.*

The Merck legal team quickly calculated that they could show that many patients missed their doses and thus would not win a lawsuit. They also decided that there would be no quick monetary settlement offered to any of the victims. Frazier vowed that Merck would fight each lawsuit "one by one." With a multibillion-dollar legal war chest, Merck would retain an army of lawyers and scientists, slam expert witnesses, hire detectives to track down drug receipts of any patient who tried to sue them, and fight every case as if the life of the company depended on it—as indeed it did.

None of this made it into the press conference, but Frazier got the word out quickly behind the scenes in the weeks that followed. The message was clear and the financial community liked it: Fighting Merck would be like attacking an armed fortress that defended itself with every lethal weapon at its disposal.

Dr. Baron and his colleagues saw something very alarming when they looked at the data at the eighteen-month interval. The patients, in what they now knew was the Vioxx group, had experienced *twice* the number of heart attacks and strokes as the group on the inactive treatment.

Dr. Kim was shaken. He wanted to personally see the data as soon as possible. For years he himself had assured the medical community that there was no link between Vioxx and cardiovascular disease. Now the Merck chief scientist was being told that this wasn't true.

Kim received the results on the morning of Friday, September 25, and began to examine the complex pieces of the report. By that afternoon, he informed Raymond Gilmartin that there was a very serious problem. Gilmartin wasted no time in contacting Merck attorney Kenneth Frazier. Frazier knew exactly what kind of firestorm was likely to envelop the company—and that he would be the point man in any future proceedings. Already, a number of lawsuits alleging that Vioxx was harmful to the heart were under way, and several company employees had been sharply questioned by attorneys.

But Merck had a secret weapon in Frazier, an African-American, who grew up in a less than genteel neighborhood in Philadelphia, studied at Harvard, and fought his way to the top of his profession. Frazier was as tough as he was charming. While most corporate attorneys would rather face a firing squad than appear in front of the press, Frazier loved the limelight. He had actually spent a few years as head of Merck's public relations department, cultivating both his and the company's impeccable image. Now he had the challenge of a lifetime, for the evidence against Vioxx was considerable.

By September 28, two days before the Vioxx withdrawal was made public, a press release was crafted that would, in essence, be the script that every official at Merck would follow. At first, neither Gilmartin, nor any other executive, would deviate from the basic story: the withdrawal was voluntary, the drug was safe for eighteen months, the actual risk was slight, and the company was acting as they always had—in the public interest. At least from the company point of view, the Merck CEO's bland, unflappable manner was perfect for the press conference.

Indeed, as the news event unfolded, Gilmartin read the prepared statement without deviating by so much as a word. "Although we believe it would have been possible to continue to market Vioxx with labeling that would incorporate these new data, given the availability of alternative therapies, and the questions raised by the data, we concluded that a voluntary withdrawal is the responsible course to take."[10]

Speaking to the audience after Gilmartin, Dr. Peter Kim would only acknowledge that "the new data provided [Merck] with information on the cardiovascular profile of Vioxx. While the cause of these results was uncertain at this time, they suggest an increased risk of confirmed cardiovascular events beginning after 18 months of continuous therapy."[11]

For an hour, the audience of press and financial analysts peppered the speakers with questions, trying to get more definite responses. But Kim and Gilmartin stuck to the script. Over and over, they emphasized the voluntary nature of the recall and that they regretted that patients would no longer have access to the medication. "While we recognize that Vioxx benefited many patients, we believe this action is appropriate," Kim stated.[12] He reiterated the company's belief that Merck had never doubted, until a week before, the general safety of its leading drug.

"We now know that by November of 1996, Merck scientists were seriously discussing a potential risk of Vioxx—association with heart attacks," Gurkipal Singh, M.D., Adjunct Clinical Professor of Medicine told the Senate Finance Committee after analyzing internal Merck documents.[13]

These documents were many of the same memos presented at the Vioxx trial involving the death of Bob Ernst.

The dangers of Vioxx to the heart had been learned early during the time of the drug's human studies. The first evidence appeared in 1996, when a classified Merck document noted more heart problems among people being tested with Vioxx at high doses than those treated with a placebo. States the memo: "The treatment period was six weeks vs. placebo. The initial dose of MK-966 [Vioxx] was 175 mg, but in mid study, the dose was lowered to 125 mg . . . Adverse events of most concern were in the cardiovascular system, e.g. MI [heart attack], unstable angina [chest pain], rapid fall in hemoglobin and hematocrit [dangerous blood problems] in some subjects."[14] Note that these serious side effects showed up in a matter of weeks at a dose that was a little more than twice the approved amount for treatment of acute pain (50 mg).[15] (While Merck recommended that this dose not be used for more than five days, patients with excruciating pain often don't suddenly stop their treatment, nor do they limit the dose.)

As Dr. Wallace points out, "it is normal to test at least 10-times the effective acute dose (I would say this is particularly important when the maker of the drug is very publicly making claims about the extraordinary safety of the drug—I recall very clearly many occasions where Merck scientists and doctors working with Merck were claiming that Vioxx was 'safe as placebo.' ")

Had Merck been testing Vioxx at 10 times the "acute dose," it would have been giving patients 500 mg of the drug! As it turned out, severe problems developed at a far lower level. (Some very valuable drugs are very toxic at a dose just above a normal range, but they are almost always used for serious diseases and require careful monitoring, sometimes in a hospital.)

This was certainly not the case with Vioxx.

In the mid-1990s, Dr. Garret FitzGerald, professor of cardiovascular medicine at the University of Pennsylvania and one of Merck's own consultants, warned that Vioxx had the potential to harm the walls of the blood vessels protecting the heart. He suggested that Merck set up a series of experiments to test this theory. Few of them were ever performed.[16] Other scientists cautioned that Vioxx was related to kidney damage and an increase in blood pressure that could be linked to heart problems.[17]

Dr. FitzGerald also found similar problems with a drug in the same class as Vioxx called Celebrex, made by rival drug company Pfizer. Like Merck, Pfizer denied the finding of any cardiovascular problems with its drug, but cleverly began its own campaign to portray Vioxx as the "more dangerous" of the compounds.

Dr. John Braun, like most family physicians, knew little of the incriminating data about Vioxx. All he could recall were the hundreds of visits by Merck salespeople offering drug samples and reassurance; the glowing reports in medical journals and the lectures from enthusiastic researchers. And despite his medical training, neither Braun nor his patients could fail to be impressed and inspired by the stunning image and astonishing story of Olympic ice-skater Dorothy Hamill. Hamill's public appearances on behalf of Vioxx, and the seemingly endless commercials in which she was featured, had made Vioxx a household name.

There was a certain irony here. Dorothy Hamill's life story seemed to almost parallel that of Vioxx: instant and premature fame, crises, world renown, and ultimately burnout.

Even as Dr. Braun's patient John McDarby was struggling to recover from his heart attack, he could never forget the stunning vision of Hamill twirling around an ice-skating rink to the tune of the hit song "A Beautiful Morning." It was an image seen over and over again—from 2001 almost until Vioxx was pulled from the market three years later.

The Dorothy Hamill marketing campaign for Merck and Vioxx was one of the most astonishing for *any* corporation and will probably never be surpassed in sheer impact.

It is a fact that companies large and small spend enormous sums to get product endorsements from celebrities. Nike granted Michael Jordan a minor fortune to endorse its sneakers—and Tiger Woods flashed his American Express card to impress upon viewers the wisdom of running up debt. Pfizer enlisted presidential candidate Bob Dole to endorse its impotence pill, Viagra. Over the years, movie stars, athletes—even astronauts—have touted countless products, many with great success. Both academic and industry studies leave no doubt about the potential influence of a celebrity endorsement.

Nonetheless, the public seldom takes the endorsements completely seriously. Whether or not Tiger Woods charged his trips to American Express had little effect on either his life or his golf game. Michael Jordan really did wear Nike sneakers during his amazing basketball career, but no one believed that Jordan's skill was the result of shoes. As to whether Viagra really improved Bob Dole's sex life . . .

Dorothy Hamill was different. She really *had* taken Vioxx. It really *had* (at least in her own mind) changed her life. She did go from invalid to near-Olympian and said so sincerely to audiences large and small. What's more, the images on the television screen backed up her words. Without Vioxx, Dorothy's lithe body would not have been able to defy gravity and fly with elegance and style around the ice.

Yes, the Vioxx marketing campaign known as "Everyday Victories" involved the hallmarks of previous celebrity product endorsements. But rarely had the celebrity, in fact, believed and actually *shown* the near-miraculous effects of the product to an eager audience of tens of millions of people. Life and marketing blended seamlessly.

Dorothy Hamill had been a star most of her life. Barely out of her teens, hadn't she already won the National Novice ice-skating championship? While other kids were still asleep, she was practicing her spins and jumps at a local rink in upstate New York that now bears her name. By the time she was seventeen years old, Hamill had already placed second in the World Championships, and with her graceful movements, dazzling athleticism, and engaging beauty, she had been thrilling crowds whenever she performed.

She came into the 1976 Innsbruck Olympics as an underdog. Most commentators thought she was too young and inexperienced at nineteen to win the gold. But in a spectacular display of skating that included the invention of a new and thrilling maneuver, the "Hamill Camel," she captured the championship and the hearts of the world.

Time magazine put her on its cover, dubbing her "America's Sweetheart." The business press published stories saying that she now could command the highest price for a commercial endorsement in advertising history. Hamill was besieged by agents and promoters.

She quickly entered a high-powered world of celebrity and money. Hamill married Dean Paul Martin, son of movie star and singer Dean Martin. She drew enormous cheering crowds at professional ice shows. The public listened to her every word. She was now a figure of inspiration—and Hamill quickly found that even when she talked about things she knew little about, millions took notice. Her magnetism on ice translated immediately into magnetism in the media.

So the storybooks had it.

But there was another side. Hamill was unprepared for the demands of fame and money. Her marriage to Dean Paul Martin quickly collapsed. A year after winning the gold medal, she was involved in a bitter dispute with her once revered coach. Dean Paul Martin died in a plane crash.

Hamill used her money to purchase the Ice Capades. However, the stress of performing and managing drove her to the hospital with a bleeding ulcer. She married a second time. In 1990, Dorothy Hamill found her world falling apart. Her second marriage turned into a bitter personal and monetary dispute and she was forced to file for financial relief in the U.S. Bankruptcy Court of California. Twenty years after becoming a superstar, Dorothy Hamill moved to a modest house in Baltimore with her nine-year-old daughter, away from the crowds and spotlight. The years of skating had taken a terrible toll on both her body and mind. Her joints were swollen and her mornings were wracked with pain.[18]

Physician after physician attempted therapy, but nothing worked. Until one day she was introduced to a new miracle medication: Vioxx.

Executives at Merck simply could not believe they had found a figure whose life story so paralleled the history of their own product. Both Vioxx and Hamill had the potential to inspire and give new hope to a worldwide audience. Merck therefore came up with the brilliant idea of actually incorporating Hamill's life story in the Vioxx marketing campaign. (Each story was carefully edited. The dark side of both Hamill's life *and* Vioxx were omitted so that nothing would ruin the fairy tales.)

Dorothy Hamill made her national debut for Vioxx on August 29, 2000, on *Larry King Live,* where she, along with fellow Olympian Bruce Jenner, were given almost an hour of airtime to tell their stories.[19] As she had at age nineteen, the plucky athlete struck gold. Using the winsome manner that had endeared her to millions of Olympic viewers, Hamill made one of the best appearances of her life. She told about pain and depression. She spoke about her inability to get out of bed in the morning—in fact even her inability to take care of her daughter. Until Vioxx:

Hamill: For me, it was—I was getting to the point where, you know, I could barely play with my daughter. And I was still trying to make a living ice-skating, and I was getting to the point where I thought, you know, I might have to give this up and not just from a performing standpoint, but just from a—something that I love to do for me, for fitness.

My biggest problem has been my neck and my back. I would get up in the morning and I'd sort of shuffle to the bathroom, and think, oh, if I could just spend the rest of the day in bed. And it has taken me, I would say, three years until I actually got to the bottom of it.

I just—I felt old, I felt depressed, tired all the time. I mean, having chronic pain is exhausting. And I got to the point this year, I was on tour and I couldn't skate. And so, I went to a doctor, and we finally got to the bottom of it, and my doctor prescribed Vioxx for me, and it's as if I've been given a new life, it's just—it's been amazing. I feel twenty years younger, I don't look it and I don't skate it, but I feel that way.

The day after Dorothy Hamill's appearance, even Merck's CEO Raymond Gilmartin was smitten. He had received heartrending letters from arthritis sufferers saying that they were going to immediately ask their physicians for Vioxx. Gilmartin personally congratulated the public relations department, and one marketing executive wrote that "with Dorothy telling our story" Vioxx sales were going to soar and overtake Celebrex—an obsession within the company.

Patients poured into doctors' offices, the doctors wrote prescriptions, and drugstores filled them.

Hamill rarely mentioned that Vioxx had any side effects. In fact, she said on *Larry King Live* that even though she had experienced a bleeding ulcer, Vioxx had been proven safe with her. Nor did she speak about the large black WARNING in the physician insert, *informing of the extreme risk of prescribing Vioxx to patients with a history of bleeding ulcers.*[18]

Officials at the Food and Drug Administration were furious and threatened Merck with a warning letter for violating advertising rules. This wasn't the first time Merck had broken the regulations, and the FDA finally wanted the company to own up to its actions. A top-level phone conference was set up among the senior legal and marketing executives of Merck and the senior officers at the FDA. On the call were Thomas Abrams, the FDA's Director of Drug Promotion Marketing, Advertising, and Communications (DDMAC), and Joanne Lahner, Merck managing counsel. They were joined by a number of high-ranking Merck marketing and public relations executives.

The pharmaceutical company pleaded that they had "taught" Dorothy Hamill what to say, but that the star "went off the script and said things completely on her own." (Merck would never have dreamed of Hamill claiming that Vioxx had saved her from a life of pain and despair!) Nonetheless, Merck promised that they would immediately cease the Hamill public relations appearances pending retraining by Merck. That was September 12, 2000. Among those listed on the Merck memo summarizing the promise to the FDA was Joanne Lahner herself, the Merck lawyer responsible for reviewing and clearing some of the most sensitive material in the company.[20]

No FDA warning letter was ever issued.

The day after Merck promised to cease the campaign, on September 13, Hamill and Jenner appeared on WAGA television in Atlanta, via satellite. Now Hamill had even more extensive training to stay on message. Her words were strictly scientific:

> **Hamill:** I got to the point where I realized I had to give [skating up]. I didn't realize what was wrong. . . . Everything hurt. I'd shuffle to the bathroom in the morning and want to spend the whole day in bed. Having chronic pain like that is exhausting. I got to the point where I would drive my daughter to the playground, instead of walking her to the park. I thought I would have to give up skating. . . . I was diagnosed with osteoarthritis and my doctor prescribed VIOXX. . . . I'm skating two hours a day, I go on rides with my daughter, it's changed my life a lot.

So blatant was this "infomercial" that the *Atlanta Constitution* wrote a story accusing the television station of pandering to the pharmaceutical industry. Even the broadcaster WAGA was embarrassed and promised to "review its policy." No one mentioned that providing information about Vioxx without identification of the sponsor (Merck) appeared to violate federal requirements—although WAGA kindly provided a number that viewers could call to get more information about the pill.[21]

The FDA never knew that the Hamill campaign was continuing. DDMAC, chronically understaffed and underbudgeted, simply never found out—or worse—didn't care. As a result of Merck's Vioxx marketing, to use FDA safety officer Dr. David Graham's words, "the public paid a terrible price," as did Robert and Carol Ernst.

At 10 A.M., September 30, 2004, Raymond Gilmartin and Dr. Peter Kim finished the press conference announcing the results of the APPROVe study and the Vioxx withdrawal—and then began another meeting with financial analysts. Reporters were already writing stories and gathering quotes. The news was studded with words like "disaster," "shocking," and "calamitous."

Barbara Ryan spent the day appearing on television business programs and writing research notes. She stated rather caustically that "Merck had a run of bad luck, but it can't stand up and say it ain't broke anymore. It is, and it needs to be fixed."[22]

The announcement, as devastating as it was, signaled even more than the end of Vioxx. It led to a complete reassessment of the entire class of "super aspirins," and within a year similar products made by Pfizer— Celebrex and Bextra—encountered severe difficulties. In December 2004, a colon cancer trial involving Celebrex was halted because of the drug's safety issues, and six months later, Bextra, known as "son of Celebrex," was pulled from the market, not only because of increased heart risk but because it sometimes caused a fatal skin disease.

By the evening of September 30, the Bijou Room at the Hilton was almost empty. In brokerage offices, Barbara Ryan and other analysts were still working figures, trying to calculate how much the Vioxx withdrawal would really cost. Not only was there the immediate loss of revenue from the drug's absence, there were also lawsuits to consider. Estimates ranged as high as an additional $60 *billion* in liability.

Could Merck bear that cost and survive? Many doubted it. The celebrity financial analyst James Cramer predicted that Merck would be devastated within a matter of years. The stock picker came up with a typically flamboyant quote: "When the juries hear that people died because they took a drug meant to relieve shoulder pain, they will destroy Merck, sure as shinola."[23]

No one mentioned the name Dorothy Hamill. The celebrity remained silent in her Baltimore home, not uttering a single word about the product whose fame she had helped propel.

The greatest pharmaceutical marketing campaign of all time ended the same day that Gilmartin and Kim made their announcement. Dorothy Hamill disappeared along with Vioxx.

Two shooting stars faded—at least temporarily—and vanished from public sight that day.

CHAPTER 2

Super Aspirin and Poison Pills

The immediate history of Vioxx begins with the 1990 discovery of a chemical in the body known as cox-2. Scientists believed this enzyme was responsible for causing the stomach distress and potentially serious ulcers initially associated with popular pain medications such as Motrin, Advil, and aspirin. Researchers speculated that if a pill could be designed that blocked cox-2, the resulting compound would be a safe and superior alternative to these drugs. Such a pill would have incalculable value, because pain medications are the best-selling drugs in the world. Roughly 50 billion tablets of aspirin alone are consumed every year, and it has been sold continuously since 1899. A pill that could replace it is considered the holy grail of the pharmaceutical industry.

The Vioxx story gathers momentum in June 1994, when Raymond Gilmartin, a Harvard MBA with no prior pharmaceutical industry experience, became the new chief executive officer of the world's largest drug company, Merck & Co. He took over from a much admired medical scientist, Dr. Roy Vagelos, who had helped put Merck on the *Forbes* list of most admired companies in America, seven years running. Gilmartin and then chief scientist Dr. Edward Scolnick championed a crash program to race Vioxx to market.

At almost the same time, Dr. Philip Needleman, research chief of G. D. Searle (a division of Monsanto Chemical Company) began an all-out program to gain approval of Celebrex, also a cox-2 inhibitor. Not long afterward, the pharmaceutical giant Pfizer Inc. took a stake in Celebrex and eventually purchased Searle. Much of the development of Celebrex took place amid complex corporate maneuvers, but it was Pfizer that ultimately put up the huge amount of money and resources that led to a blistering war with Merck for control of the cox-2 pain market.

Both Merck and Pfizer quickly realized the enormous stakes involved with developing a cox-2 inhibitor. Early laboratory results suggested these compounds were a godsend. Not only did they seem to have the potential to treat pain and arthritis without injuring the stomach, but scientists believed the drugs could also dramatically cut the risk of Alzheimer's disease and prevent colon cancer.

In 1998, about a year before Vioxx was approved for marketing in the United States, Dr. Jerome Groopman of Harvard Medical School became convinced that he had found a new class of wonder drugs. A regular contributor to *The New Yorker*, Dr. Groopman was just as influential as Dorothy Hamill in creating the phenomenon of Vioxx and its rival drug, Celebrex. His reporting added an enormous amount of credibility to some of the seemingly astonishing stories about the pills' therapeutic powers.

Groopman, while not a sports celebrity, has become an extremely powerful force within the fields of both medicine and journalism. He holds the prestigious Dina and Raphael Recanati Chair of Medicine at Harvard Medical School and has served on the Advisory Council to the National Heart, Lung, and Blood Institute. Groopman prides himself on being at the epicenter of the modern medical complex, having held several high-ranking positions at the Food and Drug Administration, sitting on the advisory boards of the world's most influential medical journals, and authoring more than 150 scientific papers. He has published three well-received books, one of which was turned into a television series (*Gideon's Crossing*) for ABC. Even among top-level physicians who are generally known as opinion or thought leaders, Groopman stands out.

It was no small matter, therefore, when he wrote a lengthy article for *The New Yorker* in June of 1998 entitled: "Super Aspirin: New Arthritis Drug—Celebra."[1] Celebra was the name for the drug later known as Celebrex, and very close in composition to Vioxx. They comprised the same class of "wonder compounds," according to Groopman. Remarkably, Dr. Groopman's writing went beyond what even Dorothy Hamill might have claimed.

All who read the article, whether Dr. John Braun, the New Jersey family practitioner, or the millions who suffered from chronic pain and arthritis, could not have been blamed for believing that the world of pain treatment and perhaps treatment of many other illnesses was about to be radically transformed—for not only did Dr. Groopman put forth his own conclusions about super aspirins, he quoted world-famed authorities. Furthermore, the article had been carefully authenticated by the famous fact-checking department of *The New Yorker*, which has had an almost perfect record of verifying every piece of information the magazine publishes.

Like Hamill, Groopman began his discussion of super aspirin with a personal story. He himself had suffered debilitating pain brought on by arthritis developed while training for the Boston Marathon. Despite years of searching for relief, he had found no satisfactory remedy. Now a remarkable new class of drugs was offering hope for people like him and millions of others. These compounds were far more powerful than mere aspirin and far safer. Groopman portrayed common drugs like aspirin and Motrin as almost lethal.

By contrast, discussing human studies being conducted for Celebrex, Groopman wrote that more than ten thousand people had been tested and none had experienced any side effects.

Groopman relates the story of Rich Dillon, a fifty-three year-old firefighter from Lincoln, Nebraska, who had experienced the pain of severe arthritis of the knees for a considerable period. Dillon's affliction became so terrible that it was difficult for him to support the heavy fire-fighting equipment needed to enter a burning structure. He also had to decrease many of his leisure activities.

This changed when the firefighter began to participate in an experimental study to evaluate super aspirin. After taking the medication, Dillon was ecstatic. "It's been tremendous." He had no side effects from the treatment and enjoyed sustained improvement in his knees. "He could now do his job without pain," Dr. Groopman reported.

Dorothy Hamill could not have said it any better on *Larry King Live*. But this was not the Larry King show, this was *The New Yorker*. The world's best physicians backed Dr. Groopman. For example, Groopman spoke to Dr. Lee Simon, who was not only a professor at Harvard but an authority who sat on the Arthritis Advisory Committee of the Food and Drug Administration. Simon was also conducting clinical trials for Searle, the manufacturer of Celebrex, and being paid significant fees to do so.

When the FDA sees that a drug researcher has a conflict of interest, that scientist is not permitted to serve on the advisory board that will help evaluate the compound (except by special exemption). But Simon, only months before the Groopman article was published, had sat on a special FDA panel set up to evaluate the criteria by which super aspirin was to be approved. No conflict of interest had been declared.

In *The New Yorker*, Simon described Celebrex (at least as Groopman quotes him) in a way not usually heard in the halls of the Rockville, Maryland, FDA offices—for he characterized the drug as "*incredible*." In his Celebrex study, Simon had not only achieved outstanding efficacy, but no side effects. "None," Simon emphasized. FDA experts never hear the word "none" when doctors describe the side effects of new drugs—or if they do, they immediately have serious concerns regarding the investigator's credibility, if not sanity.

Groopman's description of the problems with many common pain control pills was a serious exaggeration, which eager marketers were happy to exploit. There is no question that aspirin and drugs like Motrin and Aleve may cause stomach upset and sometimes lead to ulcers. These pills are generally known as non-steroidal anti-inflammatory drugs or "NSAIDs." NSAIDS, such as Motrin and Advil, work by mobilizing chemicals in the body that dampen inflammation and soreness. But newer NSAIDs, about which Groopman made no mention, were already proving themselves safer to the stomach and doctors had learned to better control dosages to lessen medical complications. In addition, certain pills such as Prilosec and Nexium can dramatically lower ulcer risk when used with these pain relievers.

Dr. James Fries, professor of medicine at Stanford University Medical School, upon whose data many of the scare stories about NSAIDs were erroneously based, said that much of the information taken from his world-renowned arthritis health study, Arthritis, Rheumatism and Aging Medical Information System, or ARAMIS, was either distorted or out-of-date.

"Many NSAIDs were incorrectly used at first and some of the initial ones developed were more toxic than those we have now," Dr. Fries says. "Many of the people who developed serious problems with these drugs were elderly, with underlying illnesses, and were also taking other medications or alcohol that worsened their health."[2]

(Ironically, the makers of naproxen, an NSAID that Merck said was more dangerous to the stomach than Vioxx, are now running television advertisements showing various people "springing to life" in just the same way as those portrayed in the Vioxx and Celebrex ads.)

But control of pain and swelling were only two of the uses that Dr. Groopman thought possible for super aspirin: "Not only does the drug represent a quantum leap forward in the therapy of arthritis, if some promising research is borne out, it may even play a role in preventing or treating a host of other conditions, from cancer to Alzheimer's disease."

Dr. Groopman interviewed a fellow scientist, Dr. Clifford Saper, professor of neuroscience at Harvard. Dr. Saper expected that super aspirin would slow the progression of mental deterioration by at least half. Saper believed that inflammation occurred when neurons in the brain were injured. This swelling started a cycle that caused even more brain damage.

Dr. Saper said that Celebrex promised to "break open the vicious cycle of inflammation in Alzheimer's." Quite an astonishing statement in and of itself, and even more so since he did not cite results of a single human study. Yet the claim is part of an age-old school of medical thinking that holds that "logic" and "what makes sense" or "rational therapy" should dictate the practice of medicine. But rational therapy needs to be buttressed by randomized, controlled human trials to determine what is—and is not—effective treatment.

In the case of preventing Alzheimer's disease, as with so many other ailments, the difference between theory and actual clinical results was enormous.

Groopman never mentions an alternative possibility than what is stated by a Harvard expert, a fatal assumption. The alternative explanation: perhaps a chemical that affects the delicate balance of the brain might make neurological disease, such as Alzheimer's, worse.

Pain relief, possible arthritis cure, Alzheimer's treatment. What about cancer?

Dr. Groopman continued: "Excitement about super aspirins is growing even among cancer researchers. Several studies published during the past decade have indicated that patients taking drugs like Motrin, Advil and Aleve have a fifty per cent lower incidence of colon cancer. But only recently have scientists figured out why this might be. Most colon cancer is *believed* to arise from two sequential mutations. The primary mutation causes . . . excessive growths called polyps. A second mutation can then cause a polyp to become cancerous. It stands to reason that super aspirin would block the first step of this process." *Stands to reason* are perhaps the three most dangerous words in medicine, when the reason is not supported by experimental evidence.

In fact, some *laboratory* experiments did show that the new wonder drugs prevented colon polyps from forming in mice and therefore this type of cancer might never get started—however, the experiments were far from definitive. But promising enough to investigate more fully?

Certainly, scientists at Merck and Searle thought so. Their own animal studies exhibited the same promising results and the companies decided to spend tens of millions of dollars to develop and execute tests in humans to find out if their compounds could indeed prevent colon cancer. When the start of the trials was announced, company and academic researchers alike thought it possible that these cancer prevention studies, like the Merck APPROVe trial, would be among the most significant in pharmaceutical history. In 2004, when the APPROVe trial was halted because Vioxx caused excess heart disease, these statements proved ironically prophetic.

In 1998, some financial analysts believed the cox-2 inhibitors would eventually earn more than $10 billion a year, maybe a great deal more. After Celebrex and Vioxx were made available in 1999, the battle between the two companies that manufactured them became one of the most brutal and expensive the drug industry had ever witnessed.

Almost immediately after the launch of Vioxx and Celebrex, however, scientific reports surfaced that the pills could cause heart disease and death. Merck and Pfizer denied the allegations and waged huge advertising and public relations campaigns to affirm the safety of their drugs. The

Food and Drug Administration took only minimal steps to publicize and enforce the warnings. Drug salespeople brought slick brochures to physicians, assuring them how safe the pills were. As a result, cox-2 inhibitors became the fastest-selling drugs in pharmaceutical history.

Then one day it all stopped.

The rest is medical history.

CHAPTER 3

Cox in Paradise

There's no business like show business.
—Irving Berlin

D r. Philip Needleman, the tall, enthusiastic, and ambitious head of science for the G. D. Searle/Monsanto pharmaceutical company (soon to be acquired by Pfizer), sprinted to the podium of Salon 4 of the Ritz-Carlton Kapalua Hotel in Maui, Hawaii. It was about 8:00 P.M. local time, July 28, 1998, and the drug company executive was in top form. Only about a month before, the noted medical author Dr. Jerome Groopman had canonized him in a *New Yorker* article that was sure to earn him a Nobel Prize for medicine.[1]

The weather in Hawaii was perfect, a soft breeze blowing in from the ocean. The hotel was as magnificent as its promotional brochure suggested: five-star dining, a professional golf course, tennis, sea-view rooms, and native island entertainment.

The reception, with Hawaiian hors d'oeuvres and tropical drinks, had already put the jet-lagged scientists into a mellow, if not soporific, mood. But Needleman, in his booming, Brooklyn-accented voice, took the crowd's weariness in stride, as a challenge to be overcome—just like finding a new drug, convincing the world it is your own discovery, and making sure everyone understands its revolutionary place in medicine.

On March 24, 1998, a little over four months before the Maui scientific symposium, an FDA advisory committee led by Dr. Michele Petri of Johns Hopkins University had assembled to assess how to *scientifically* prove the value of super aspirin. The committee dealt both Pfizer and Merck a severe blow.

Members suggested that before the drugs could be approved, they had to demonstrate that they could prevent *serious* ulcers in *humans*. Neither Merck nor Pfizer had such data. Now it was all up to Needleman. He was one of the world's finest scientists in the field of pain research, and he and his team had to prove at the Hawaii meeting the unquestionable scientific reasoning behind the magic of the pill they had invented: Celebrex. Every researcher and physician would have to logically conclude that it was a pill that could relieve inflammation and pain without harming the stomach.

Further, Needleman needed to convey the excitement and importance of this discovery both to the FDA and the advisors who would eventually vote on whether to approve the drug. And what better place to undertake such a momentous scientific display than in the sumptuous Ritz in Hawaii?

Since not only were the best-known and influential pain researchers in the world present, but also both the former and future heads of the FDA Arthritis Advisory Committee, Dr. Michelle Petri of Johns Hopkins and Dr. Steven Abramson, professor of medicine at New York University. Dr. Lee Simon (Dr. Groopman's doctor and a Harvard professor, now a *former* member of the committee) was also in attendance. Simon had recently completed the final clinical trials for Celebrex, whose subjects, Groopman noted, had "no side effects."[2]

Most important of all was the presence of James P. Witter, M.D., Ph.D., medical officer of the FDA's Anti-inflammatory, Analgesic and Ophthalmic Drug Products division, and the person responsible for the team reviewing the super aspirins for the government. Witter was usually based in FDA headquarters in Rockville, Maryland, where his staff had just started to analyze Pfizer's Celebrex approval submission. It had been submitted to the FDA only a month before the Hawaii meeting. Steven Geis, M.D., Ph.D., executive director of Searle, was also at the Ritz. The following December, it would be Geis's job to present the Celebrex data in public to both Witter and Abramson, whose job it would be to assess the drug with strict objectivity. Maui was the perfect place for a rehearsal.

Not that the FDA was failing to do its job. In the cramped confines of their offices, statisticians, chemists, doctors, and clinical trial experts were racing to assess the validity of Searle's Celebrex submission, which ran into the thousands of pages. E-mails and correspondence flew back and forth between the FDA staff and Pfizer's scientists, who continually updated and answered questions about the experimental findings. It was no small job, for the application ran 452 volumes, each 400 pages long, for a total of 180,800 pages.

The Ritz-Carlton meeting was underwritten by five major pharmaceutical companies: Searle Pharmaceuticals and Pfizer Pharmaceuticals (actually the same company by this time); Merck, Roche, and Johnson & Johnson. Merck planned to sell Vioxx on its own, but Searle and Pfizer were using the technique of combining resources, pioneered in the early days of the pharmaceutical industry by German drug companies. Although Searle had invented Celebrex and performed the experiments necessary to get it ready for FDA approval, it wanted to use the much larger resources of Pfizer to develop a world-class sales and marketing campaign.

Pfizer was considered the ideal partner in the 1990s mostly because of its history of innovative and aggressive drug marketing and advertising that stretched back at least forty years and was perfected under the leadership of chief executive officer William C. Steere, Jr. Steere was a Stanford University graduate who joined Pfizer as a sales representative directly after college. Although he rapidly moved up through the executive ranks, Steere never lost the wit, humor, or charisma that personified his sales career, nor did he lose touch with the Pfizer sales organization.

In some ways, Pfizer and Merck could not have been more different companies—despite having some common German roots—and the contrast between them set up the conditions for the largest and most bitter pharmaceutical marketing battle of the twentieth century. Since 1668, Merck grew as a tightly controlled family business and partnership. It remained faithful to the business philosophy of the "ethical" industry, and although it entered alliances, the company had built its power using its own resources. In contrast, by the late 1990s, Pfizer was more akin to a drug conglomerate that grew by extremely clever mergers and acquisitions of an array of drugmakers.

The company name derives from German chemist Charles Pfizer, who arrived in America with a partner in the syrup business in the middle 1800s. The company's fortune turned on the manufacture of citric acid, which was made from the juices of oranges, limes, and lemons. It was used in a popular purgative or laxative called citrate of magnesia and as a flavoring in soft drinks.

Pfizer's involvement with the main-line pharmaceutical industry did not begin until the 1940s, when the company was able to use its chemical expertise to aid in the development of penicillin. Although the venture was a success, Pfizer remained a manufacturer, not a distributor, and quickly saw its profits drop as more chemical makers entered the drug market.

Pfizer executives were determined to keep control of their next medical product, an antibiotic called Terramycin. Under new aggressive chief executive John McKeen, Pfizer created its own pharmaceutical sales force that became known for its highly aggressive tactics of targeting and selling to doctors—the so-called Pfizer Blitz. The most remarkable feature of the Terramycin launch was the huge advertising campaign, which included ads that ran in the widely read and esteemed *Journal of the American Medical Association.* Pfizer spent $7.5 million on the campaign and in the process became *JAMA*'s biggest advertiser. It proved to be an enduring relationship.

Pfizer also had some close friends in the Food and Drug Administration. Henry Welch, director of the FDA's antibiotics division, was one of the most powerful men in pharmaceutical development throughout the 1950s. It was revealed in 1960 that Welch had pocketed $260,766, derived, in one way or another, from the interests he was sworn to regulate. According to a May 30, 1960, *Time* article titled "A Profitable Sideline":

> Welch hooked up in 1952 with a Manhattan publishing outfit called MD Publications Inc. to put out a series of medical journals puffing new drugs. As editor he got quite a deal: 7.5% of the net advertising income, plus 25% of the income from the cost of adding "extra" late-closing papers, plus 50% of the net income from sale of reprints. Most lucrative of the journals was *Antibiotic Medicine and Clinical Therapy,* which was passed out free to as many as 60,000 physicians. With guarantees of a big professional audience, leading drug-makers took acres of ads—spurred

on by articles mostly favorable to new antibiotics and often written by researchers working for the companies themselves. The drug-makers bought plenty of reprints of the articles to deluge doctors with publicity for their newest products. . . . The wonder was that Welch got away with so much for so long. He carefully told his superiors before making any deals, but never told—and was not asked—about the details.

Welch was forced out of the FDA in 1960. By then, the art of creating medical journals that were actually more akin to "advertorials" was at least a hundred years old. One of the most famous was the *Therapeutic Gazette*, published in the 1880s by George Davis, principal of drugmaker Parke, Davis & Co., now owned by Pfizer. Independent journals took notice of the *Gazette*'s marketing techniques, particularly the revenue and popularity to be gained from the distribution of reprints and "ghost writing" (publishing articles written by pharmaceutical companies, but bearing the names of prestigious academic medical professors).

Throughout the 1990s, William Steere turned Pfizer's marketing into an art form. As a young salesman, and later a pharmaceutical executive, he was personally affronted by what he considered the arrogant attitude of the drug industry's leader, Merck. He made it both a personal and professional goal to overtake Merck and make Pfizer number one, any way he could. Steere would accomplish this by personally galling both Merck employees and the company's leadership.

One of Steere's greatest accomplishments was forming a co-marketing agreement with Warner-Lambert for their blockbuster cholesterol-lowering drug, Lipitor. Merck was the original American inventor of the class of drugs to which Lipitor belonged and considered itself the undisputed leader in cholesterol medication. As Lipitor rapidly overtook Merck's competing drug, Zocor, it was clear that a simmering battle between the two companies was taking on the aspects of a war.

Steere shook up the industry in many ways. He gave approval for the development of a kind of drug that no other main-line drug company would touch: a pill for male impotence—Viagra. (The huge pharmaceutical company Glaxo thought so little of a similar compound it virtually gave it away to a small biotech company called Icos.)

Viagra was a triumph of both medicine and marketing and Steere enjoyed every minute of the campaign to sell it. Pfizer literally invented a new disease, "erectile dysfunction," and sent emissaries to the Pope to make sure the Catholic Church would have no objection to the pill. Pfizer emphasized in all its literature that the pill was strictly medicinal—pleasure and sexual arousal were purely optional.

Viagra jokes proliferated in the media and at Pfizer headquarters itself: *Did you hear about the first death from an overdose of Viagra? A man took twelve pills and his wife died.* Even Steere got into the act. He once stood in front of a group of suited Wall Street analysts while holding up the famous blue pill. When asked how to use Viagra, the story often repeated is that Steere said, "You pop one in your mouth and hope you get lucky an hour later."

As Pfizer had done with Terramycin, the company created a unique, aggressive, and unorthodox sales campaign. Pfizer salesmen developed relationships with urologists to cure "erectile dysfunction." This proved to be a brilliant strategy. By focusing on the physical component of impotence, Pfizer got away from the arcane explanations and attempted ministrations of psychologists (who usually provided no cure anyway) and shifted the focus to physiology: blood vessels, dilation, and impaired nerve function. Now a *real medical problem* could be addressed by *real medical specialists* with a *real* pill.

The 1998 launch of Viagra was the most successful in modern pharmaceutical history—until Celebrex and Vioxx. (Viagra was associated with a few deaths in the first months of its launch, but it was determined by Pfizer and the FDA that it was not the fault of the drug, but excessive physical exertion, among other causes unrelated to the actual pill.)

With Lipitor and Viagra, Steere was well on his way to overtaking his Whitehouse Station, New Jersey, rival and making Pfizer the world's number one drug company. What he needed was one more product. One more blockbuster pill. Pfizer scientists believed they had discovered it when they looked at early clinical studies demonstrating a new pain medication being developed by G. D. Searle: Celebrex—an inhibitor of cox.

The term was not lost on the Pfizer marketing managers who were working on Viagra. At meetings, quips such as "*We're going to license a drug that inhibits cox?"* nearly dissolved the participants in laughter. *"For years we've done nothing but help cox, now we're going to inhibit them? Cox are going to drive our sales numbers straight up!"* It was said that Steere had a ready answer. *Just make sure you spell it right.*

The ambitious CEO knew from all the cox hype being generated at scientific meetings that Merck was now in his sights. All he had to do was hire prominent doctors to support the drug, get the FDA on board, and have a major opinion leader, preferably a journalist, to give something called a "cox-2 selective inhibitor" a reputation everyone would envy.

Dr. Frank A. Wollheim is one of the world's leading authorities on arthritis. Until 1998, he was chairman of the Department of Rheumatology at the University of Lund in Sweden and an esteemed clinician and lecturer. Professor Wollheim is also a talented writer, who has written hundreds of scientific articles and a number of books on subjects related to arthritis. After retirement, Dr. Wollheim decided to augment his income by accepting freelance assignments from an Internet medical journal, *Rheuma 21st.* The site was extremely popular among both specialists and general practitioners worldwide and Wollheim liked the idea of being able to reach so many physicians, so rapidly. It was almost like having the world as your classroom.

Rheuma 21st is devoted to keeping doctors up-to-date by covering and presenting excerpts and commentary from cutting-edge medical meetings. Wollheim was thrilled when he was offered an all-expenses-paid trip to Maui to write an online report of the proceedings. "It was first-class, all the way," Wollheim says. "I mean no luxury was spared."

He came up with the catchy headline "Cox in Paradise," although he never quite grasped, even with his excellent English, that the title might have a different connotation to the not so high-minded. Wollheim took photographs, interviewed participants, and joined in the general enthusiasm for the wonder drugs that just shortly before his arrival in Hawaii had been dubbed super aspirins.

After the meeting, Wollheim posted his report. It began: "A recent issue of the *New Yorker* contained an enthusiastic medical dispatch by Jerome Groopman entitled SUPER ASPIRIN. It was an appraisal of the new Cox-2 inhibitors . . . which are now in late phase III development, or are being filed for licensing as treatment in arthritis. . . . The 60 participants had 3 full days of science and intensive work, in a beautiful environment and good sunshine."[3]

Although Wollheim admitted that the meeting was sponsored by "several drug companies," the report he wrote was complex, detailed, and highly selective. While there was much written about "molecular side chains," "confocul microscope technique," and "antisense oligonucleotides" (none of which was of particular interest to busy practicing doctors), a few sentences stood out: "Selective Cox- 2 inhibition exerted by celecoxib [Celebrex] is as effective as conventional NSAIDs but devoid of gastrointestinal toxicity." This quote came from Dr. Phil Needleman, the purported inventor of Celebrex and chief scientist of the drug company that had developed it. He was assuring his elite guests and the world that he had found the holy grail of pain medicine.

Needleman's optimism was clearly supported by the data. "Some 10,000 patients have already been studied and have shown no stomach problems," the drug company executive stated. More detailed data was presented by Dr. Geis, who again stated that no gastrointestinal toxicity had been found and that the drug was highly effective.

Dr. Paul Emery, professor of rheumatology at the University of Leeds, England, was responsible for presenting Merck's Vioxx data, which was just as impressive as Searle's on Celexa. Like Celexa, Vioxx did not show any instances of stomach trouble. "The data was very impressive," Wollheim reported. Although he mentioned a "shadow," that 5 percent of the people taking Vioxx had edema, or swelling, a potential sign of kidney problems, this was common to many pain control drugs and seemed of little concern.

The meeting covered all the potential miraculous uses for the cox-2 drugs that Dr. Groopman had written about in *The New Yorker*: prevention of cancer, halting of Alzheimer's, arresting arthritis, and relieving pain. But, most important, it gave all the regulators the chance to join the general acclaim and revelry. In case none of the attendees was sufficiently excited, ample time was given for "pause and reflection." On the second day of the meeting, the lectures ended at 1:00 P.M. and a stupendous array of resort activities was arranged for the guests. During this time, they got to interact with doctors and marketers of the drug companies who were in attendance, including Roche and Johnson & Johnson. Many enjoyed the world-class greens at the Plantation House Golf Course, where the PGA-Mercedes Championship is held each year.

At six, the assemblage gathered for cocktails, heard a quick lecture, and then attended a spectacular event: the Ritz-Carlton Hawaiian Luau. It was a stupendous show. The luau was held on a grassy area next to the beach. From this spot, the researchers, regulators, and marketers could gather with their mai-tais and watch an almost mystical sunset over the island of Molokai while torchlights illuminated the stage. All stops were pulled out for the elaborate festival: native Hawaiians, hula dances, folk music, singing. A master of ceremonies stood to the side getting the crowd into the rhythm of the performance, inspiring them to take part.

The loud beating of drums echoed along the beach as the MC continued his exhortations. He took the crowd through a historical pageant of Tahitian and Hawaiian folklore, finally bringing the event to a climax with fire and knife dancers. Many in the crowd were sporting their "Cox in Paradise" green T-shirts. This was a true celebration of the birth of a new era in medicine—a spectacle of dance, fire, and speeches.

Not that scientific debate failed to take place. Dr. Wollheim recalls a walk along the beach with one of the academic organizers of the meeting, Dr. Peter Lipsky. Wollheim was worried. He had read some new research that questioned whether a cox-2 inhibitor could prevent cancer. The paper said that more that just cox-2 molecules would be needed.

"Oh, that's rubbish," Lipsky said.

That was about the end of the talk.

The Second International Workshop on cox-2 concluded with a gala dinner at the Banyan Tree restaurant, featuring some of the world's finest cuisine served in a glass and wood-beamed setting overlooking the Pacific. "It was a dream," one of the participants said. "The seafood tasted like it was just caught—vegetables just picked . . . and the setting just magnified the excellence of the cuisine."

Professor Wollheim looks back at the meeting with some wistfulness.

"It wasn't all paradise, not as far as the science was concerned. The warning signs were there. We all heard them. Dr. Catella-Lawson from the University of Pennsylvania presented data linking the cox-2 inhibitors with heart attack risk. Her warning seemed to get lost in all the excitement."

Six months after the meeting, Dr. Francesca Catella-Lawson and her colleague Dr. Garret FitzGerald published their findings in the *Proceedings of the National Academy of Sciences*.[4] A University of Pennsylvania Medical School press release came out with the headline: "How Super Are the 'Super Aspirins'? New Cox-2 Inhibitors May Elevate Cardiovascular Risk."[5] This was the first time that such an association was publicly reported in humans. The article was published three days after the approval of Celebrex for widespread public use. Animal experiments and other data had pointed in the same direction, and Professor John Oates, an advisor to Merck and also an attendee at the Hawaii meeting, had warned the company early on of this danger.

None of this appeared in Wollheim's "Cox in Paradise" Internet report. However, the consequences of the meeting were far greater than most of the participants could imagine. Despite the "few minor caveats" (as one prominent participant put it) revealed about super aspirins, the leaders of arthritis medicine were now on the cox-2 bandwagon and they would be quickly spreading the word of the miraculous compounds far beyond the confines of Hawaii. The drug executives present were able to use their newfound friends to start speakers' bureaus—groups of hired experts who would barnstorm the country lecturing to other doctors about the advantages of the new cox-2 inhibitors.

The experts themselves would have wonderful new careers, getting paid good sums to lecture and do research. What none of them knew was that Merck was going to play by different rules. Normally, experts and opinion leaders merely have an unspoken arrangement with drug companies to do their bidding. But Merck was also making up a "neutralization" list to target any doctor who did not agree with the company. People on this list would be offered additional incentives to support Vioxx, but most strikingly and altogether unprecedented, major opinion leaders, including at least two who attended this meeting, Drs. Michelle Petri and Lee Simon, would be threatened with loss of career opportunity, intimidated, or be smeared by Merck. In addition, the company would send out a senior medical executive to personally bully medical school leaders and others who refused to support Merck in the Vioxx campaign.[6]

Another unusual outcome of the meeting was that the term "super aspirin" became enshrined not only in the news media, but within the scientific literature itself. A noted pharmacologist in attendance, Dr. David DeWitt, wrote an article for *Molecular Pharmacology* entitled "Cox-2 Selective Inhibitors—The New Super Aspirins." It is one thing for a popular magazine like *The New Yorker* to use the term, but it was unheard of for a prominent medical journal.

The significance of this would not be lost on either drug executives or doctors. Aspirin has been the most popular drug in world history. It has been sold continuously for more than a hundred years and its benefits are unquestioned. Its drawback is its potential harm to the stomach. The remuneration for a company that could come up with a significant but benign advance over this pill would be incalculable, for in many ways aspirin was the drug that established the astronomical value of the chemical-based modern pharmaceutical industry.

The future appeared unlimited for super aspirin, the new holy grail of medicine.

CHAPTER 4

The Pharmaceutical Miracle

Medicine is for the people. It is not for the profits.
—George Wilhelm Merck, 1954[1]

It is not a coincidence that pain control medications like Vioxx and Celebrex became part of one of the largest drug scandals in world history. Treating pain has been a primary goal of healers throughout time and substances to reduce or eliminate it have always been among the world's most valuable commodities. Anti-pain compounds were often associated with divine origins, and finding new ones or the substances comprising them has determined the fate of empires and the evolution of civilizations. Major armed conflicts have literally been fought over pain medicine. The British and Chinese battled in the 1800s Opium Wars for the trading and merchandising rights for that precious narcotic.[2]

Ironically, pain is one of the most important senses of the human body, without which life could not exist. Pain warns us of danger to our body and prevents us from damaging the fragile structures comprising our biological systems. For instance, when we come in contact with a hot substance, we immediately withdraw, preserving our essential organs. As succinctly put by Dr. James Fries, a professor of medicine at Stanford University and a world expert on arthritis: "Pain keeps us alive."[3]

Equally necessary is pain medication, for analgesia—relief from pain—is necessary to keep armies in the field, return the wounded to battle, and aid in the emotional and physical health of the citizenry. Quelling pain is an elemental longing that allows our bodies to rest and heal, and our minds to find relief.

The cox-2 inhibitors were but the latest of miracle interventions for pain, whose history stretches back thousands of years. The first known written reference to the poppy appears in a Sumerian text dated around 4,000 B.C. The flower was known as *hul gil*, plant of joy, and cultivated in places now known as Greece, Egypt, Turkey, and Iraq. It was from poppy seedpods that the ancient world made a medicine that could provide potent relief from pain: opium.

Pictures of the Greek god of sleep, Hypnos, show him wearing or carrying poppies. Another god was associated with opium: Thanatos, the god of death.

History's first drug salespeople were known as the Marsi, who lived in central Italy in about 400 B.C. The Marsi were known for their ability to handle snakes and remove the venom, which was used in potions that protected against poison. The Marsi could best be described as semicivilized. The Romans thought of them as "fearsome" warriors, and it took a number of bloody encounters to defeat them. Eventually the Marsi were incorporated into the Roman legions.

Dr. Vivian Nutton, a medical historian with the Wellcome Institute in England, writes that the Marsi "had a store of knowledge about poisons and venoms and were considered to have magical powers to sing snakes to sleep." Their reputation was such that their tribal name, *marsus*, became the regular Latin equivalent of "snake charmer," and even of "poisoner." The Marsi were "marginal men, in more than one sense, halfway between civilization and savagery, between expert and quack, between bringer of health and minister of death," Dr. Nutton continues.[4]

The Marsi eventually came down from their wild habitat and became traveling salesmen or *circulatores*. They were best known for the daring shows they put on in the local markets, which served to attract huge crowds of the curious. In fact, they were known as crowd pullers, as Nutton describes them: "One must imagine the marsus standing in the market place, brandishing his wooden box of snakes, talking twenty to the dozen, screaming out his wares at the top of his voice."

Galen, one of the world's most famous doctors and pharmacologists, and physician to the Roman emperor and poet Marcus Aurelius, was impressed by the Marsi and commended their remedies, one in particular made from the fruit of the sphondylium and catmint, pounded and mixed together in wine. This potion was guaranteed to protect against the bites of both snakes and insects.

Drug sales were also made by perfume manufacturers, who had access to the fragrant and very expensive herbs and spices from Arabia and India. These artisans were sought out by the Roman nobility to make special potions to rub on their bodies. The perfume makers had a good knowledge of the chemistry used to distill aromatic lotions and they used these same skills to formulate elaborate drugs, often using the same exotic substances.

A truly elegant drug could be sold at a price as much as $5,000 a dose. The drug market was thus segmented into high- and low-end products, the low end serviced by the Marsi and other herb gatherers, the high end by the elite chemists who could provide rare and complex mixtures. Sometimes drugs were sold by merchants from containers, whose origin was not easily known. Roman philosophers warned that "using an already pre-made potion or relying on the word of a drug seller" was an act of suicide. Better to purchase directly from the perfume chemist.

No evidence exists of anything remotely approaching the Food and Drug Administration in ancient Rome.[5] The sellers of drugs, whether they were from the dense forests or perfume makers or merchants peddling bottles of potions, could make any claim they wanted about their wares. This was not altogether different from the early pioneers of modern drug advertising who roamed America with potions and sold them in their Wild West shows. As far as Roman legal rights went, edicts did permit lawsuits against the Marsi in the event that one of their snakes injured a member of the crowd. No United States Supreme Court existed to confer immunity on any drug peddler.

The Romans also made use of opium, or "poppy juice." Galen invented an opium-based compound known as theriac, which remained in existence until the nineteenth century. Its use was limited, however, because of its complexity, unreliability, and very high price. Theriac evolved into a drug that could cure everything—a *panacea*. Marcus Aurelius still remains known as a philosopher and warrior who battled Germanic tribes along the Main river near a shallow crossing that became known as Frankfurt am Main. The emperor died in a Roman encampment that later gained great fame for its ideas of the mind, Vienna. The manufacture of theriac provided an early laboratory for the modern pharmaceutical industry. The compound was created in elaborate public ceremonies, almost like festivals, so that everyone could personally see what went into it. The drug was then sealed and shipped to new shops known as apothecaries. (Galen locked precious ingredients in a Roman storage area known as the *apothecarium*.)

Astonishingly, among Galen's greatest contributions to medicine is a theory that two thousand years later would contribute to the downfall of Vioxx. Galen believed that disease was caused by an imbalance of the elements, known as humors, of which he thought the body was composed. He believed it was critical that the body maintain a balanced state—and if not in balance, to bring it back to harmony by such methods as bloodletting and purgation. These therapies proved either disastrous or useless (although both were used until modern times) and the concept of humeral balance disappeared . . . only to be resurrected in the twentieth century in a different form: We now understand that the body does indeed have an ingenious balancing system, known as homeostasis. (Garret FitzGerald was one of the scientists who worried that Vioxx could upset the delicate balance that maintains cardiovascular health and discovered in 1996 that that was indeed the case.)

Poppy juice spread quickly, but its price remained extremely high. The Italian city-state Venice grew up in the twelfth century with a navy powerful enough to enforce a monopoly of the spice trade with the mysterious lands to the east generally known as the Indies. Venice became a city of enormous wealth and European monarchs were determined to break its power (theriac became known as Venetian treacle).[6] Fortunately, European royalty found their champion in a man from a rival Italian state to Venice, Genoa. Sponsored by Spain, Christopher Columbus set out to break the Venice drug cartel and eventually found what Europeans called the New World, or West Indies.

The new center of commerce and heir to Rome was by now the Holy Roman Empire, whose capital was the burgeoning center of commerce, Frankfurt am Main. Around this city, new shops known as apothecaries grew as more precious goods, such as opium, flowed into Europe.

In the 1600s, a physician named Dr. Thomas Sydenham, known as "The English Hippocrates," invented a drug cocktail that came to be known as Sydenham's laudanum. "Take one pint of sherry wine, two ounces of good quality Turkish or Egyptian opium, one ounce of saffron, a cinnamon stick and a clove, both powdered. Mix and simmer over a vapour bath for two or three days until the tincture has the proper slightly viscid but still easily poured liquid consistence, easy and pleasant to administer."[7]

Others copied him and drug marketing took a great leap forward. The new compounds, such as Dover's Powder, could be manufactured and sold in distinctive, colorful containers, not merely formulated in apothecary shops. Drugs could now be easily distributed and laws grew up protecting not the ingredients, but the *packaging* or "trademarks." Dover's Powder survived at least until 1936 when it was still recommended by noted medical experts and texts such as the *Merck Manual*.

The history of pain medication changed overnight in 1805 when a German pharmacist isolated the active ingredient in opium: morphine. A few years later, in the 1820s, Emanuel Merck revitalized his ancestors' pharmacy in a town just south of Frankfurt am Main called Darmstadt and set out to expand it. Merck decided to take advantage of advances in both chemistry and pharmacology and create a new kind of company, one that would combine the older practices of the apothecary (brewing and mixing of compounds to create remedies), with the newer methods of chemical manufacturing.

In so doing, Merck expanded the apothecary to include both a research center where the active ingredients of previously known substances called alkaloids could be studied and isolated, and a manufacturing unit where new substances could be made with uniformity and purity. In 1826, Merck published a famous essay with the simple title "On the Preparation of Morphine," and by 1832 Merck was manufacturing 150 pounds of the substance. By 1842, Merck was producing 1,688 pounds of morphine. The E. Merck Laboratory in Darmstadt became the world's first modern center for pharmaceutical research and development. A new industry was born.

In 1851, Emanuel Merck promised customers that he would legally guarantee the purity of any of his drugs. This was no idle claim at a time when medicine containing any ingredient, in any form or dose the owner wished to dispense, was common. (Other German chemists also took the opportunity to create "pure ingredients." One of these scientists emigrated to the United States and set up his own company at the same time as Merck. This was Charles Pfizer and he built his pharmaceutical company in Brooklyn, New York, bearing his name and guaranteeing "Pfizer Quality.")

The drug that brought Merck even more riches came from its experimentation with another "divine compound"—the active ingredient in coca leaves. The leaves remained a curiosity until once again German chemists isolated its active ingredient: cocaine. By 1862, Merck was manufacturing half a pound of the substance. Its first rival was the American pharmaceutical company Parke-Davis.

In 1883, a Viennese ophthalmologist discovered that cocaine's anesthetic properties made it ideal for eye and other forms of localized surgery. At almost the same time, a German physician found that cocaine administration enhanced the endurance of soldiers in the Bavarian army. The stage was set to launch the greatest scientific painkiller in history. What Merck needed was a medical authority who had superb writing skills, wide influence, and a gift for inspirational thinking. In short, the company needed a man like Dr. Jerome Groopman, a world-renowned scientist with a talent for self-promotion who could not only write authoritatively about the miracle compound but who was in desperate need of it himself.

The doctor turned out to be a physician from Vienna who suffered both from mental distress and an unsettled love life. In 1883, Dr. Sigmund Freud, intrigued by the many possibilities of purified cocaine, made a request to the Merck pharmaceutical company for a small amount of the substance to conduct experiments. Freud had not only read the reports about positive results on German soldiers, but American reports from *The Detroit Therapeutic Gazette*, hailing the drug as a cure for depression (and nearly everything else). Such substances were known derogatorily as panaceas.

The *Therapeutic Gazette* was actually a medical journal created by Parke-Davis for distribution to doctors—and whether Freud knew he was reading a subtle form of advertising is not known. This was one of the first instances of a pharmaceutical company blending advertising techniques with publishing, and it would not have been familiar to many in the German scientific world. Merck and Pfizer later used similar means to promote Vioxx and Celebrex.

In any case, Freud, who himself was suffering from depression, as badly as Groopman was suffering from inflamed joints, tried cocaine and clearly indicated it was a breakthrough for pain and suffering. In 1884, Freud wrote to his American fiancée, Martha Bernays, "Woe to you, my Princess, when I come. I will kiss you quite red and feed you till you are plump. And if you are forward you shall see who is stronger, a gentle little girl who doesn't eat enough or a big wild man who has cocaine in his body. In my last severe depression I took coca again and a small dose lifted me to the heights in a wonderful fashion. I am just now busy collecting the literature for a song of praise to this magical substance."[8]

In July 1884, Freud published his findings in the *Centralblatt für die gesammte Therapie,* a prestigious German medical journal, and both a blockbuster painkiller and a marketing war resulted.

The increase in the amount of cocaine production was astonishing. Before 1884, Merck had produced about three quarters of a pound of cocaine. A year later, after Freud's article, production jumped to 3,179 pounds. By 1886, Merck was producing 152,352 pounds of cocaine.

Ironically, the world's first bitter drug marketing battle was between the Merck company and Parke-Davis, which is now part of Pfizer. And a real war it nearly became. According to innovative research by Paul Gootenberg from the State University of New York at Stony Brook, the U.S. Navy and consuls in the Andes "worked to identify and secure coca supply routes and aided Peruvians to upgrade their shipping and leaf-drying process."[9] Thus, we have the United States armed forces to thank for our cocaine supply routes.

The wide availability of both cocaine and opium sparked a unique American institution for selling drugs: the medicine show. Medicine shows traveled from town to town, bringing with them any outrageous act the drug peddler could find to draw in the locals and even town doctors and pharmacists. The peddlers could sell just about anything, from snake oil to magnetic boxes, that allegedly had the power to remedy diseases, from cancer to overactive livers. Cocaine cures were particularly popular for treating "neurasthenia" (the nervous disease), and were promoted in the medicine shows by Indians dressed in elaborate native costumes, beating tom-toms and performing war dances by torchlight (a good show is always an effective selling technique whether in the 1900s America or 2000 Maui). A doctor in topcoat and tails interpreted the "Indians"; he then exhorted the crowd and related how the native compound cured all manner of ills. According to Dr. James Harvey Young in his book *The Toadstool Millionaires*, the most famous nineteenth-century remedy was Kickapoo Indian Sagwa—its ingredients were: "Soda Bicarbonate, Gentian Root, Mandrake Root, Cubebs, Rhubarb Root, Senna Leaves, Aniseed, Red Cinchona Bark, Yellow Dock Root, Dandelion Root, Burdock Root, Sacred Bark, Licorice Root, Aloes, Alcohol Glycerine, and Water." The original recipe was reputedly aloes and stale beer.[10]

By 1905, Merck, in combination with other firms, tightened their grip on the cocaine trade by contracting with the German government to protect what was now a booming world commodity.

Sigmund Freud renounced the use of cocaine by 1890 and the deleterious effects of the miracle pain-control drug started showing up in a few medical journals that either were not controlled or owned by pharmaceutical companies. Unlike his endorsement of cocaine, Freud's denunciation of the substance had no effect on Merck sales, nor did doctors seem to take much notice of the drug's potential lethality. Although Freud had first experimented with cocaine for its miraculous effect on the heart and mind, widely regarded and trusted medical publications sounded warnings:

> Because cocaine's effects may last only about 30 minutes, the user takes repeated doses. Cocaine also increases blood pressure and heart rate and narrows (constricts) blood vessels. These effects can cause a heart attack, even in healthy young athletes. Other effects include constipation; intestinal damage; extreme nervousness; the feeling that something is moving under the skin (cocaine bugs), which is a sign of

possible nerve damage; seizures; hallucinations; insomnia; paranoid delusions; and violent behavior. Long-term users may damage the tissue separating the two halves of the nose (septum), causing sores (ulcerations) that may require surgery.[11]

These side effects, noted in the 2005 *Merck Manual*, apparently went unnoticed by the pharmaceutical company for decades, for cocaine remained the largest selling product in Merck's nineteenth and early-twentieth century inventories. Pope Leo XIII, whose papacy was in the late 1800s, said that he relaxed with a cocaine drink, Vin Mariana, and "carried a hip flask to fortify him in time of need."[12] The Pope awarded a gold medal to Angelo Mariana, the world's first international cocaine peddler, and the aged Holy Father died peacefully in his sleep, none the worse for his daily nip. Religious belief and morals declined no known measure.

Thus by the beginning of the twentieth century, the basic principles of creating the blockbuster drug were in place and a modern pharmaceutical industry had evolved, a fact lost to many who have written daring exposés about the evils of drug companies.

Dr. Marcia Angell, former editor of *The New England Journal of Medicine*, wrote in her book *The Truth About the Drug Companies: How They Deceive Us and What to Do About It* that the pharmaceutical industry "has strayed from [its] original mission of discovering and manufacturing useful drugs and instead has become a vast marketing machine with unprecedented control over its own fortunes."[13]

Not exactly.

The largest pill factory in nineteenth-century America was located in the New York town then known as Sing Sing (now Ossining). Founded by a physician who had emigrated from Liverpool, England, Dr. Benjamin Brandreth, the plant churned out hundreds of thousands of "Vegetable Universal Pills." The manufacturing facility had a motto emblazoned over the front door: *Cavando Tutos*—"Tested and Not Found Wanting." The pills were touted as "perfectly safe" all-vegetable substances and were guaranteed to remedy indigestion as well as purge and purify the body. Their principal ingredient was sarsaparilla, a plant first brought to the attention of Europeans by Christopher Columbus.

Brandreth recognized several principles of a blockbuster pill. It should have a simple theme and a plausible explanation that can be easily advertised: "This is the whole subject in a nut-shell, *Whatever makes bad digestion breeds disease; whatever makes good digestion cures disease.*"

It should also have impeccable medical sources. Brandreth distributed much scientific literature to back up his product, ranging from cheap pamphlets to the impressive leather-bound tome *The Doctrine of Purgation, Curiosities from Ancient and Modern Literature, from Hippocrates and Other Medical Writers—Some Two Thousand Hundred Sages Cited—Covering a Period of Over Two Thousand Years.*

Finally, a blockbuster pill needs the backing (whether accurate or not) of impeccable world experts. Brandreth cited the best-known scientists of his era, who were both celebrities and researchers: William Harvey (who theorized that the heart was a pump, forcing blood to circulate through the body) and Benjamin Franklin (who was nearly electrocuted by flying a kite in Philadelphia).

It is also paramount to have some sort of health epidemic, real or imagined, that is putting the populace at risk and creating untold misery that the blockbuster pill can quickly relieve—in Brandreth's case: poor digestion contaminating the body and causing general "debilitation and suffering." Brandreth was also aware that during an epidemic, no one asks too many questions about how—or even if—a pill works, so long as there is promise and hope.

Even during the time of the plague in fourteenth-century Europe, which killed at least a quarter of the population, some survived, and if they were taking a certain therapy, why not consider *it* the cure?

Marcia Angell is not the only one who has problems with how the modern drug industry has strayed from its noble beginnings. A fellow editor of *The New England Journal of Medicine*, Jerome Kassirer, complains in his book *On the Take: How Medicine's Complicity with Big Business Can Endanger Your Health* that the fault of the pharmaceutical companies lies with the fact that "sums of money for health care have transformed medicine from a sleepy mom-and-pop operation to one of the most successful businesses in an otherwise dormant economy."

Interestingly, Dr. Brandreth did start his business quite literally in 1835 with his wife and three children. While the doctor mixed the ingredients for the pills, his wife pasted labels on the boxes, and his eldest son finished the packaging.

The Brandreth family fortune grew rapidly along with the establishment of the penny press—sensational newspapers that could be churned out rapidly in the thousands—and were supported with lavish ads from drug companies—particularly Brandreth's. So lucrative was drug promotion in the nineteenth century that medical advertising agencies themselves invented pills and created whole journals as vehicles to peddle them.

From 1859 to 1904, medical sales grew from $3.5 million to $74.5 million. The mom-and-pop apothecary gave way to huge drugstore chains in the twentieth century as pills became a mass-produced item. By 1913, Bayer, which had developed two very famous products, aspirin and heroin, employed more than ten thousand people worldwide. Legal charges were made of collusion among the druggists, physicians, and pill makers. Such accusations were not new, of course.

In fourteenth-century England an astute poet and friend of Chaucer's wrote: "The physician and the crooked apothecary really know how to scratch each other's backs: one empties your stomach as often as he can, and the other is an expert at cleaning out your purse. . . . One writes out the prescription and the other makes it up, yet it costs a florin to buy what's not worth a button."[14]

In the twentieth century, the road to a super pill and a super company to market it was well established. Only the traveling medical shows vanished, although these too reappeared, sometimes in venues as far away as Hawaii.

PART II

CHAPTER 5

The Evolution of Ethics in Modern Medicine: How a Dye Changed History

Ethics are part of our core values. We live them and breathe them every day.

—Merck Corporation[1]

To understand how a major pharmaceutical company could have so long allowed a poison pill like Vioxx to remain on the market, it is necessary to delve further into the origins of the pharmaceutical industry. Some of the worst ideas in science developed from an ideal of helping humanity, not destroying it.

Certainly, the creation of super aspirin never began as an effort to increase heart problems and potentially cause more deaths among those with Alzheimer's disease. However, Merck's constant denial and evasions of its own research, combined with the company's financial ambition, contributed to the slide from concern for patients to the preservation of a corporate elite and the corruption of medical goals.

In order for Merck to compete in the nineteenth century, when giant chemical cartels became its fiercest competitors, the company had to adapt the same principles to survive. Survival of the fittest was the philosophy that dominated the era, and the ethics it spawned had dramatic consequences in the twentieth century. How the modern chemical, pharmaceutical era started is a highly improbable story.

In the 1850s, the art of silk and cotton dyeing was both elaborate and complicated. It required mixing natural pigments, some of which had to be imported from the Indies (India or Asia), then applying them in such a way as to adhere the dye to the material without it running. It was a time-consuming and expensive process and not within the financial reach of the average consumer. This changed in 1853 when a precocious eighteen-year-old British chemist, William Henry Perkin, working in a home laboratory, discovered that coal tar, used in heating boilers to make steel, could be chemically treated to make a dye with an intense purple color. Perkin wasn't looking to find either a colorant or start a major industry; he was trying to make a chemical version of quinine, commonly used to treat fevers and malaria.

The relationship between dyes and medicine had been previously studied, particularly in Germany and France. Doctors and chemists had learned to "stain," or color, a laboratory slide to make the objects under study more visible. One of the key scientific findings of the nineteenth century was that different parts of the cells composing the human body react differently to various dyes. This phenomenon could be observed under a microscope, and it gave rise to the hope that dyes, or substances involved in their manufacture and composition, might be able to be used as drugs. Many doubted this idea for the simple reason that most dyes are poisons.

Until Perkin's discovery, research moved slowly because of manufacturing limitations. Dyes were in limited supply and expensive. But Perkin was smart enough to exploit his new finding and explore its commercial potential. He sent the substance he had synthesized from coal tar to be tested and found that it could easily be applied to silk without being affected by either washing or sunlight. It was colorfast.[2]

The economic potential was fantastic. Coal tar was a cheap, plentiful chemical waste product, and transferring it into an invaluable product for clothes and fashion could prove highly lucrative. Perkin probably never realized that it had the potential to place the chemical industry at the forefront of modern science and transform the world.

Within a few years of Perkin's discovery, new drugs, derived not from botanicals, but from tar, coal waste, and other scrap material, would start being processed and investigated both in laboratories and new factories known as chemical plants. One of the most popular synthetic products derived from these chemical dye companies was a pill that could control pain—and its discovery quickly led to the creation and development of a unique drug that acted against pain, inflammation, and fever: aspirin.

In 1863, two German entrepreneurs, silk merchant Friedrich Bayer and textile designer Johann Friedrich Weskott, founded Friedr. Bayer & Co, a new corporation to capitalize on the dye and chemical revolution sweeping Germany. Along with colorants, the companies were discovering medicinal properties for the new chemicals and were developing more and ingenious ways of marketing them.

Doctors in the 1880s had a great fear of body fever, which they believed was not only a symptom of disease, but disease in and of itself that actually "burned" critical organs. Through a chemical fluke, Bayer discovered a medicine that could swiftly reduce fever, based on laboratory work on a coal tar derivative. The resulting medicine, known as phenacetin, "a fever reducer," or "antipyretic," became an extremely popular and profitable medicine and generated further interest in chemical drugmaking.

Other companies, such as Hoechst, began making similar synthetic pain and fever reducers and more German companies rapidly followed. The chemical companies also changed the face of agriculture with the invention of pesticides that rid cultivated fields of insects and allowed for a huge surge in agricultural development. These pesticides, and other similar toxic chemicals, would unfortunately provide the underlying model for the deadly agents used in chemical warfare.

The step from eliminating animal pests to human ones was not foreseen during the 1880s, but nonetheless happened. After the start of World War I, the Bayer company began producing an explosive known as TNT. Other military chemicals soon followed, including chlorine, phosgene, and mustard gases for use in chemical weapons. By the end of the war, Bayer was Germany's foremost munitions maker. The manufacturing of health and the manufacturing of death were now inexorably bound.

The fact that a new medical science was developing that promised the ability to effectively cure people had raised the question of *who* should be treated. In 1853, a French count proposed a theory that racial purity was an important factor in determining the evolution of the human species. He coined the term "Aryans" as those having superior intelligence.

In 1859, the biologist Charles Darwin revolutionized science with the publication of his book, inaccurately abbreviated as *On the Origin of Species by Means of Natural Selection*. The full title leaves out these key words: *The Preservation of Favoured Races in the Struggle for Life*. Darwin wrote, in a later book on the descent of man and selection in relation to sex, "Our medical men exert their utmost skill to save the life of everyone to the last moment. . . . Thus the weak members of civilized societies propagate their kind. No one who has attended to the breeding of domestic animals will doubt that this must be highly injurious to the race of man."[3]

Natural selection spawned a group known as social Darwinists who attempted to apply the new principles to medicine in order to address such problems as "moral decadence, crime, mental disability, alcoholism, venereal disease, and tuberculosis" as symptoms of "hereditary degeneration."[4] Researchers developed the "science" of eugenics to devise methods of strengthening the human race and began advocating the elimination of "social diseases" by determining who would and would not be allowed to reproduce.

As eugenics gained favor, the new industry of dyes and chemicals began to take a dominant role in the development and financing of medicine. However, few of the new entrepreneurs were doctors, who at least proclaimed to follow the medical ethics of Hippocrates, immortalized by his dictum: "First, do no harm." Galen and his disciples through the centuries may have created much human misery with such therapies as bloodletting, but there is no evidence that the "physicians' physician" deliberately set out to harm humanity. Galen also warned physicians to be men of "humble means" and not allow greed to interfere with their care of patients.

The new masters of German medicine were manufacturers, not apothecaries or physicians, and they abided by the ethics of mercantilists, not doctors. The German chemical conglomerates viewed drugs as but one division of their enterprises, sometimes the most profitable one.

Scientists in other countries took notice of Germany's late-nineteenth-century evolution. An early-twentieth-century commentator stated: "Drug production took place in an industrial setting. Drugs were commodities similar in most respects to any other commodity: they were manufactured for profit."[5]

During the same period, letters began to appear in the British journal *The Lancet*. Commented a certain Dr. Pope of the Leicester Infirmary: "Every week, almost every day, brings its new drug, each in turn praised as being the greatest discovery of modern therapeutics. . . . There is a growing tendency among German medical men to convert the 'Republic of Science' into a commercial oligarchy for the benefit of plutocrats at the expense of suffering humanity."[6]

In a turn-of-the-nineteenth-century medical lecture, the tone of one doctor sounds eerily familiar to that of FDA whistle-blower Dr. David Graham at the Vioxx Senate Finance Committee investigation:

In an address on the progress of medicine in the nineteenth century, Dr. F. Roberts confessed, "Out of the enormous number of medicinal agents brought under our notice by puffing advertisements in the press, medical as well as lay, by pamphlets or even large books delivered by post, or by actual 'specimens for trial' [drug samples] which are nowadays so liberally delivered at our residences, comparatively few hold their ground, or stand a fair and candid criticism and investigation of their vaunted merits."[7]

There is a much more cynical explanation of physician concern. The German chemical industry was threatening the power and profits of doctors and pharmacists. Before the measured chemical remedies pouring out of Germany, a sick patient had to rely on the advice of the local practitioner or apothecary to obtain a cure amidst obscure vials filled with potions and herbs. As chemical manufacturers began to bottle and brand their products, any person could simply walk into a drugstore and purchase ready-made cures for a comparatively small price. For centuries medicine depended on secrecy and the semimystical realm of the physicians and apothecaries. Companies like Merck and Bayer altered this role, eventually making some in these health professions feel like mere pill dispensers under the control of industry.

But it was not only in Germany that this new science, eugenics, took root. In the United States there were drug trials such as the Tuskegee Experiment, which began in the 1930s, that were designed *not* to give medicine to certain patients, in this case African-Americans with syphilis, in order to test the safety and efficacy of current therapy. The Tuskegee Experiment was not terminated until 1972.

Not only racial minorities were at risk. Eugenics was particularly detrimental to those deemed "mentally unfit," who were denied treatment or mandatorily sterilized, a practice held legal by the U.S. Supreme Court. As historian Nancy Schaefer writes, "Justice Oliver Wendell Holmes, Jr.'s, famous majority opinion in the 1927 case *Buck v. Bell* upheld a forced sterilization law in Virginia. Holmes famously concluded that Carrie Buck, who was deemed the 'feebleminded' product of a mother who was not of very hearty stock, could be sterilized along with her daughter. As the opinion famously declared, 'three generations of imbeciles are enough.' "[8] Present-day justices should ponder this opinion. Law and medicine seldom mix without poisonous side effects.

Many American physicians eagerly took to this evolving science of genetic purity. In 1931, an editorial in *The New England Journal of Medicine* stated: "The burden on society resulting from this increase in feeblemindedness is tremendous. For one thing, persons with subnormal intelligence are always potential criminals. . . . The financial loss to the country is appalling. . . . We should recognize this danger that threatens to replace our population with a race of feeble-minded. . . . If we wait too long, this viper that we have nourished may prove our undoing."[9]

Eugenics eventually lost favor in the United States, although it continued with disastrous results in Germany. After World War II, a series of tribunals known as the Nuremberg Trials put German scientists and doctors on trial for their actions in concentration camps. One result of these trials was the Nuremberg Code, limiting medical experimentation. This was adapted by a more formalized ethical framework known as the Helsinki Agreement, which guaranteed every citizen the right of "informed consent"—that is, to know of any harmful side effect of a drug before they enter a medical experiment. These codes became part of American law and are the bedrock of our current medical principles.

The question now is whether Merck abided by them.

Did Merck and Pfizer inform all the patients on whom Celebrex and Vioxx was tested of their potential heart risk problems? And did the companies give sufficient warnings to the medical community and public? In Merck's own clinical trial consent form, from December 4, 1998,[10] the "side effects considered possibly associated with the use of MK-0966 [Vioxx] may include, but are not limited to headache, dry mouth, mouth sores, heartburn, loose stools, abdominal discomfort, nausea, acid reflux, vomiting, drowsiness, dizziness, blood in stool, shortness of breath, abnormal liver function, temporary stroke-like symptoms that go away, fluid retention with swelling, hypertension [high blood pressure], itching, upper respiratory infection, and virus-like symptoms," but despite the fact that the company was aware of FitzGerald's warnings[11] and had been cautioned by Dr. Thomas Musliner,[12] nowhere on this otherwise extensive list is there mentioned any possibility of increased risk of a heart attack.

An article in the British *Sunday Times*, detailing a special investigation on Vioxx by reporter Brian Deer, reports ethical abuses similar to what occurred in the United States. The newspaper said that although the possibility of Vioxx causing heart attacks was noted in official documents discussed by the British equivalent of the FDA (Committee on Safety of Medicines), volunteers for a major Vioxx study, known as VICTOR, were never told the key side effects.

One of the subjects who died of a heart attack in the study, a retired laboratory technician named Kenneth Wood, was not informed in the study consent form that he signed of the "possibly fatal side-effects long reported" with Vioxx. Wood's widow only learned about this "oversight" by the London *Times* reporter conducting the investigation.

The same ethics apply to all patients (not in just those human trials), for the Food and Drug Administration has strict rules about providing patients with clear warnings about drug side effects and a careful balance between benefit and harm.

Carol Ernst framed the issue perfectly when she said that everyone deserved the right to know what a pill could do to them—good and bad. Her husband never would have taken Vioxx *if he had known* of the potential lethal effect on his heart.

CHAPTER 6

The Advertising Miracle

Twentieth century advertising may be said to be the art of awakening in the public a demand for things which otherwise, it might not even know about, and for which it certainly has no craving.[1]

—Arthur J. Cramp, M.D., 1920

The most important scientific advance for pain control in the early twentieth century came from a curious observation made almost thirty years after the invention of aspirin by two astute doctors at the Mayo Clinic in Minnesota. Drs. Philip Hench and Edward Kendall noted that a woman with arthritis experienced symptom relief when she was pregnant. Hench did not know what caused the effect but he reasoned that it had to be a chemical or hormone produced in the body during pregnancy. The more Hench studied the mysterious chemical, the more he was impressed by its effect, and he speculated that "substance X" could not only relieve arthritis symptoms but actually *reverse* the disease.

But what was this substance—and how was it produced? The Mayo team suspected that a chemical from an organ in the human body known as the adrenal gland might be responsible for producing it, but the problem was that not enough of it could be made to find out if it had any therapeutic value. The problem was solved by a chemist at Merck & Co. The company was now run by George Wilhelm Merck (son of the senior George Merck, who started the U.S. division of the German company in 1890). Merck chemists also worked on "substance X" and by the late 1940s had identified it as cortisone and made it in pure enough form to test in humans.

The Merck company decided to share a small amount of the newly synthesized compound with some of the drug's original inventors and researchers at the Mayo Clinic, who quickly put it to use. The results were revolutionary from two perspectives, medical *and* marketing. The Mayo Clinic set up cameras and filmed a bona fide medical miracle that electrified doctors and patients worldwide. First a woman was shown in a wheelchair. Next she was shown getting a cortisone shot. Finally the camera depicted her literally rising from the chair and *dancing*. This was a woman who for years had been unable even to walk.

This was the first time that "reality" filmmaking had been used on a patient and drug—and its impact was immediate. Dr. Howard Polley at the Mayo Clinic was present when the first cortisone injection was given to the woman with crippling arthritis. "Within 24 hours, we knew we had a hot item," Polley related to *The New York Times*. "It was like night and day." Cortisone miraculously "cured" thirteen additional arthritis sufferers, all of whom were able to go from near paralyzed to perfectly normal, though not all began to dance.

The new steroid became a hot item, indeed. The *Times* continued: "The world promptly embraced cortisone as a miracle and it was tried to extend its use to such disorders as rheumatic fever, schizophrenia, depression, burns, tuberculosis, eczema and morning sickness. Researchers also speculated on its potential role against heart disease, cancer and various degenerative diseases."[2]

Marketing executives also took notice. No one disputed the power of radio, the primary means of broadcast news in the 1940s, but it had nowhere near the impact of an actual moving picture. Coincidentally, the radio networks were just putting into use another medium called television, which would further revolutionize how information was conveyed. True, the Pope had endorsed opium drinks and Enrico Caruso, the world-famous opera singer of an earlier era, had extolled aspirin for his headaches, but what if an entire nation could watch and experience what a small audience had seen at the Mayo Clinic? Advertisers must have dreamed of a "miracle commercial." What if one of the world's most famous athletes could be watched rising from a state of near-paralysis and shown in gorgeous color and sound, skating ethereally on a sea of ice, like a water nymph skirting over water? Imagine the impact!

In 1950, both Kendall and Hench won the Nobel Prize for medicine. In his acceptance speech, Kendall speculated about the future role of cortisone in medicine. "There is no doubt that the use of this hormone of the adrenal cortex will continue to increase. Its effect is unique in rheumatoid arthritis, rheumatic fever, asthma and hay fever, and other allergic conditions." Kendall also mentioned promising results in both skin and eye diseases.[3]

But almost before the Nobel Prize–winning scientist had finished speaking in Stockholm, doctors noticed that the miracle drug had a dark side.

And the dark side blackened. Cortisone caused severe mental effects including psychotic behavior and insomnia. It delayed wound healing, caused ulcers, weakened the muscles, and made infection more likely. When patients stopped taking the drug, their disease, instead of reversing, sometimes worsened. They experienced withdrawal symptoms: fatigue, weakness, dizziness, difficulty breathing, and sometimes death. Doctors who had embraced the drug now recommended it only for emergencies.

The original formulation for cortisone was modified and eventually took a place in modern medicine. Cortisone and its derivatives that comprise a class of drugs known as "steroids" did become agents to effectively treat asthma—and athletes still get cortisone shots to control tennis elbow and many other inflammatory conditions. However, the shots are painful and can only be used a very limited number of times. Cortisone and the related steroids never again were thought of as harmless miracle drugs.

In stark contrast, the use of moving pictures to convey the power of a drug's benefits had a lasting impact. No one forgot how just a few minutes of celluloid had created a worldwide sensation overnight. The Mayo Clinic cortisone film was a prototype: A desperate woman, virtually unable to function, had gone from despair to elation as if by a miracle.

Despite the disappointment with cortisone, drug manufacturers continued the race for a super aspirin. Scientists focused on drugs that were neither steroids or related to narcotics, and invented the new formulations called non-steroidal anti-inflammatory drugs, or NSAIDs. Ironically, the pharmaceutical industry used this term to reassure physicians that the drugs were *not* like cortisone. They further boasted that the pills were not like morphine, codeine, or any other habit-forming formulation.

Many NSAIDs were subsequently invented: Motrin, Advil, and Aleve are among the best known. Each was originally available only by prescription, but by the 1980s could be bought by anyone in a drugstore or supermarket. Because the drugs were over-the-counter, OTC, they were no longer "ethical"—prescription-only—and the pills could be marketed directly to the public. Advertisers already knew the power of radio and television to sell what had once been proprietary products, but were now available as OTC drugs.

With television advertising, serious painkillers that had once been available only by prescription became enormous sellers. The next logical question became: If advertising formerly ethical drugs was effective, why couldn't the same be done for drugs that were *still* prescription-only?

This presented a startling dilemma for the major pharmaceutical companies. Wasn't the entire business founded on promoting ethical drugs only to health care professionals? Wasn't the mission of the American Medical Association to divide the therapeutic world into "ethical" and "unethical" or bogus products that would be sold by completely different rules?

Certainly the world had changed since 1847. At that time it had been necessary to separate out the quacks selling their nostrums from the back of wagons from the newly emerging pharmaceutical and chemical companies who supplied clearly labeled, pure, and carefully prepared agents.

Now both types of products were being manufactured and sold by the exact same companies. Most important, the ethical companies like Merck would never stoop to the circus stunts and phony and deceptive promotional practices of the medicine show. Unlike in the 1800s, the drug industry was scrupulously regulated and the Food and Drug Administration would never allow the industry to deceive the public.

A debate raged throughout the pharmaceutical industry in the 1980s. True, things had changed in the last 150 years, but the ethical companies still saw their primary customers as physicians and health care professionals. Advertising to the public might very well jeopardize the centuries-old relationship that the pharmaceutical industry and medical profession had forged.

Lawyers fretted about the possibility of lawsuits if drugs were identified by the public with a specific pharmaceutical company. And many doctors and scientists, perhaps remembering the lesson of cortisone, worried that advertising would expand the market for a drug too quickly. The last thing drug companies wanted was *too many* people using a pill before doctors became familiar with how to prescribe it and to whom.

The FDA had its own issues. They had seen how marketers had taken advantage of radio and knew that policing television advertising would be daunting if not impossible. Also, promotional laws required that the entire label of a product had to be shown in a television advertisement. That alone would use up minutes of precious airtime.

Nonetheless, in the 1970s and 1980s, major pharmaceutical companies, advertising agencies, and the government began to form task forces to investigate whether television advertising of prescription drugs was possible.

Nobody could have imagined the Pandora's box that was opened in 1997 once the FDA officially allowed direct-to-consumer advertising of prescription drugs. Ironically, the company that was to produce the most popular, direct-to-consumer advertisement of all time was the company that set the standard for ethical drugs. It was the company that had literally written the book that forbade the mention of drugs sold directly to the public. It was the company that scorned gimmicks like medicine shows and the Pope endorsing cocaine, preferring the weight of scientific evidence. Merck.

In 2001, Merck & Co. began producing advertisements featuring a world-class Olympic female athlete who would spring back to life after taking a single tiny pill called Vioxx. Pfizer fought back with ads featuring joyous arthritis patients, singing "Celebrex, Celebrex, and Dance to the Music!" Everyone was happy.

CHAPTER 7

Super Aspirin Is Born

But then we did the T-shirt experiment. You know like when you're with your kid and you get a stenciled T-shirt, so you wear it across your chest. It's to see through, to the very end. And you want to wear it on your chest like "Save the Whales" to announce to the world how committed you are.[1]

—Dr. Philip Needleman

Who actually invented Celebrex and Vioxx? Scientific credit for any pill is difficult to assign, and drugs that control pain seem to arouse particular controversy. Perhaps the most bitter scientific dispute over the inventor of a therapy concerns anesthesia, a painkiller necessary for surgery.

In the first place, what *is* successful anesthesia? Alcohol, opium, cannabis (marijuana)? Defining the term is hard enough. The generally accepted meaning is a substance, or combination of substances, that can safely render patients temporarily unconscious, keep them safely in this state, then be withdrawn and have the patients regain consciousness with a minimum of side effects.

One of the first anesthetics was the opium sponge. As early as the twelfth century, an opium solution was placed under the nose of a patient until he was sedated. The surgeon proceeded with his work and removed the sponge at completion. Although this procedure was used in Italy, it was later abandoned, perhaps because the results were unpredictable; perhaps because too many patients simply never awakened.

The battle for credit for modern anesthesia has been captured by Dr. Thomas Dormandy in *The Worst of Evils: The Fight Against Pain.* The book documents the world-class fight for recognition of the discovery among two dentists and one doctor: Horace Wells, Thomas Morton, and Charles Jackson. Each claimed in the 1840s to have invented a gas under which surgery could successfully be performed.

Dr. Horace Wells used nitrous oxide in a famously botched operation in Massachusetts General Hospital (where a patient suddenly sprang to consciousness during his procedure howling at the top of his lungs). Not long after, Dr. Thomas Morton, using a different gas, ether, used the same medical facility to perform a successful procedure. He was quickly hailed by the medical establishment as the "inventor of anesthesia."

But Dr. Charles Jackson, with whom Morton had allegedly consulted, claimed that *he* had conceived the idea of using ether, and that Morton had stolen the concept from him.

Meanwhile, Horace Wells continued to claim that nitrous oxide was effective and demonstrated successes to independent observers in his native town of Hartford, Connecticut. However, perhaps as a result of stress or too much exposure to the gas, Wells committed suicide by slashing his wrists while incarcerated for insanity in New York's infamous Tombs prison in 1848. Undeterred, his widow carried on the fight for recognition of her husband's invention.

Morton and Jackson were far from giving up the battle, also. Both had wealthy backers and, according to Dr. Dormandy, "their battle went on for years, characterized by: Congressional hearings, lawsuits, judgments, overturned appeals and supplementary actions for slander, libel and infringement of patents."[2]

Like Horace Wells, Thomas Morton eventually went insane, racing from a buggy in New York's Central Park and nearly drowning. He died shortly thereafter in St. Luke's Hospital of Columbia University. Thomas Jackson, the sole survivor of the trio by this point, continued his lone crusade to be considered the anesthesia inventor—however, like his competitors, his health and mental functioning worsened and he died in an insane asylum in August 1880, after a "terminal decline."

Matters have not turned out as badly for the discoverers and developers of super aspirin (as of yet). But thus far there have been at least four lawsuits—*University of Rochester vs. Pfizer; Brigham Young University vs. Searle; Merck vs. Pfizer;* and *Pfizer vs. Merck.*

Another suit claims that nobody discovered super aspirin—that it was a product of a scientific accident and observation, hence no patent protects it and any drug company can manufacture its own version. A generic pharmaceutical maker is suing Merck and Pfizer by making this claim.[3] The most interesting contention in this suit is that there is no super aspirin to begin with—and that the whole science of cox-2 inhibition is simply a marketing ploy and thus there is nothing to patent.

The story of how super aspirin originated and was tested has the eerie ring of the anesthesia battle, complete with lawsuits, patent hearings, appeals, suppressed data, intimidation, and the dissemination of misleading findings.

As with aspirin, there is a more or less standard story of super aspirin's invention. Several alternative versions also exist that probably will never be completely proved or disproved—but at least give an interesting glimpse into how a miracle drug is born.

In 1971, a group of British pharmacologists led by Sir John Vane was attempting to uncover how aspirin and acetaminophen (Tylenol) worked. While both drugs had existed for decades, no one understood their method of action.

Acetaminophen was discovered before Bayer aspirin, in the era of German drug discoveries of the 1880s. However, its therapeutic potential wasn't realized at the time. That promise finally occurred in the 1940s, when a group of New York scientists demonstrated the toxicity of a similar compound, acetanilide. The researchers also uncovered the fact that a related drug, acetaminophen, was not only relatively nontoxic, but effective in reducing fever and pain. (Although acetaminophen, later branded as Tylenol in North America, is not an anti-inflammatory like aspirin, it does safely reduce pain and fever.) Acetaminophen could not be patented because its chemical structure had been previously discovered years before; however, it could be ingeniously marketed.

Unbelievable as it might seem, a small Pennsylvania drug maker, Mc-Neill, came across a large stash of toy red fire trucks cheaply available for sale. The company came up with the idea of filling the trucks with aceta-minophen and selling them as a pain reliever for children. The trucks and their contents became a huge success, and McNeill was purchased by the pharmaceutical giant Johnson & Johnson. J&J gave the remedy the brand name Tylenol, mounted an enormous marketing and advertising cam-paign, and created a product that eventually sold as well as aspirin. Tylenol was later designated the "front-line," or first-choice, treatment for those suffering from arthritis by the American College of Rheumatology, the leading professional association for arthritis specialists.[4]

Vane's group had discovered that when an injury takes place in the body, chemicals known as prostaglandins rush to the wound site to deal with the swelling, heat, and pain. Prostaglandins have important functions for hu-man well-being. They play a part in ovulation, protect the stomach from acids, and ensure that blood clots normally. This latter effect explains why aspirin reduces heart disease. It prevents clumps of blood from forming that can potentially block an artery. Prostaglandins actually make nerve endings more sensitive to pain. NSAIDs reduce the production of prostaglandin and thereby relieve the pain associated with swelling and soreness. Unfortu-nately, in the process of doing so they irritate the stomach.

Sometime after Vane's discovery, scientists found that a substance called cyclooxygenase, or cox, was produced as part of the mobilization of prostaglandin, and was the enzyme that actually controlled pain and in-flammation.

Later, there was a *conjecture* that cox might have an additional part and that this second substance might be responsible for stomach irritation—but this remained a theory and was of little interest to the pharmaceutical industry. Drug companies could not directly use this idea to develop pills, even if it were true, because no one had actually isolated (or even proved the existence) of this second cox and thus there was no way of testing it. Nonetheless, drugmakers continued to hunt for NSAIDs that were easier on the stomach.

This changed rapidly after a scientific conference in Montreal in July 1992, when several groups announced that they had identified and even produced two different versions of cyclooxygenase—cox-1 and cox-2. This discovery fit with the speculation that the second enzyme, cox-2, was involved with the harmful side effects of the NSAIDs because it seemed to appear only when pain was present. Cox-1 was thought to be the "good" chemical that protected the stomach.

Thus, if a pill could be found that blocked only cox-2 (a cox-2 inhibitor), that pill would be aspirin without the side effects: *it would be super aspirin*. Equally as important, researchers described a new test, so that drug companies could actually examine the content of cox-1 or cox-2 in their compounds.

How the discovery was made, as usual, is controversial.

The official version, still cited today, is from Dr. Philip Needleman, who ran an important laboratory at Washington University in St. Louis in the 1980s. At the "Cox in Paradise" meeting, and at conferences years thereafter, the Pfizer story was that Needleman was the visionary of the cox-2 phenomenon and, in particular, Celebrex. Dr. Needleman tracks his claim back to the *conjecture* made in 1985 about noticing "certain properties" about the workings of cox in the body. He never claimed that either he or his group discovered cox-2, just that he had "predicted" its existence, based on his laboratory observations. In astronomy, this would be like claiming discovery of a tenth planet, but never actually seeing it.

In his groundbreaking *New Yorker* article Dr. Groopman quotes Needleman: "So I'm cranking along, you know, studying inflammation in rabbits and this rabbit's kidney was exploding with prostaglandins. Where I asked myself where was this explosion coming from." Needleman "cheerfully" credits the discovery of his billion-dollar molecule to the rabbit's kidney he was studying years ago when he was the chairman of the Pharmacology Department at Washington University.

"But then we did the T-shirt experiment," Needleman says.

"You know like when you're with your kid and you get a stenciled T-shirt, so you wear it across your chest. It's to see through, to the very end. And you want to wear it on your chest like 'Save the Whales' to announce to the world how committed you are."[5]

Needleman had bathed tissue from the inflamed rabbit kidney in a chemical that eliminated the source of ordinary prostaglandin manufacture. And yet prostaglandins were still being pumped out. What if inflamed cells had a way of manufacturing prostaglandin that was completely different from the way healthy ones did? At this point it was merely a conjecture, but Needleman felt so confident of it that he was ready to wear it on his chest.

The more research Needleman did, the more he became convinced that there were two kinds of cox enzymes. Late in 1990, at an international conference in Florence, Needleman gave an address predicting that two such forms of cox would be found, and that blocking cox-2 would selectively control inflammation without disturbing our stomachs.

It was a fairly safe prediction. Cox-2 had already been discovered.

CHAPTER 8

Discovery

I have seen the things that others have only dreamed they have seen.
—Arthur Rimbaud

Dr. Kerry O'Banion, assistant professor of neurology at the University of Rochester, saw something puzzling show up in an experiment he was performing in 1989. He had no idea that a substance he was examining would influence a trillion-dollar industry or shake the world of medicine. All he recalls is a faint band that appeared on his measuring instruments.

"We were examining the process of inflammation," O'Banion explains. "I was working in the laboratory of my professor and collaborator, Dr. Donald Young, who is a world expert on inflammation. . . . Eventually we isolated a substance that looked like cox, but didn't act the same way."[1]

After many more experiments, the Rochester scientists concluded that what they found was later to be known as cox-2. Professor Young had a number of special pieces of electronic equipment capable of detecting and visualizing these tiny chemical substances. Just as important, the Rochester scientists discovered a way to actually manufacture cox-2. They then tested it and made the key observation that this mysterious chemical was released by the body in the presence of inflamed or damaged tissues.

Once this was proven, Young and O'Banion were quick to realize the implications. If cox-2 was the enzyme responsible for pain and inflammation, they had helped unravel one of the biggest mysteries about pain control. Young called the university's lawyers, who were assigned to see if they could patent the discovery.[2]

"There was tremendous excitement when we all realized what this discovery could mean for science and the royalties it could provide the lab," said a public relations representative from Rochester.

At about the same time, two other research groups were performing similar experiments on cox-like substances: one group led by Dr. Harvey Hirschman at UCLA, and a second group led by Dr. Daniel Simmons at Brigham Young University in Utah.

Each academic group contests exactly who made the very first discovery. The courts granted the University of Rochester a patent after eight years of investigation. The patent included a claim that Dr. Young and his colleagues were the first to link cox-2 with inflammation and create a method by which to screen other compounds for the presence of this enzyme.

After the patent award, Rochester sued Searle, but eventually lost, not because the court disagreed that they had made the cox-2 discovery, but because the discovery itself was deemed not enough to justify the right to claim ownership of super aspirin.

Dr. Hirschman of UCLA simply states that the Rochester group filed for a patent, but that his group never did. According to a Brigham Young spokesperson, that university did not file for a patent either, but "Daniel L. Simmons is credited by numerous scientists as the discoverer of cox-2."[3] He did not say how numerous.

According to court papers, Simmons entered into an agreement with Monsanto/Searle to help develop a drug based on the cox-2 discovery. Donald Young's team eventually worked out a patent agreement with Merck that covered portions of the discovery.

Anesthesia, aspirin, super aspirin. Who really invented them? Often the answer turns on very tiny differences in interpretation of very sophisticated scientific knowledge. Does credit go to a group or person who first "conceives" an idea? To a group or person who first makes an imperfect version of a substance that later turns into a successful product? Or to the group or person that perfects a pill for use in human beings? It is a question for endless scientific and legal debate.

What most experts agree on is that, yes, Pfizer/Searle's Needleman at least theorized the possibility of two "variations" of the cox enzyme but was never able to make them either himself or in his lab.

In any case, while Needleman was doing the T-shirt test keeping up the belief that cox-2 would be discovered, the Rochester group was analyzing how it worked.

They made their work public along with the other teams investigating cox-2s at the Montreal scientific meeting in 1992. "The drug companies pounced," Young says. "It started an international competition."[4]

Needleman had the largest bullhorn. He used his power as president of Searle Research to position the company as both the inventor and developer of the super aspirins. In Jerome Groopman's *New Yorker* article, the dispute over its discovery is summarized in one sentence: shortly after Needleman stated his hypothesis in Florence in late 1990, "Other scientists confirmed his hypothesis and isolated the second enzyme."[5]

Dr. Young is philosophical. "When I was a young student at Cambridge, there was a famous scientist, Sir Joseph Needham. And he was one of the big luminaries in the world of biochemistry. And Sir Joseph gave lectures and he gave all the different possibilities that might exist in the world of science, and explained that he had discovered them all."[6]

CHAPTER 9

The Epidemic Blossoms

Vegetable Universal Pills will finally cure the epidemic of purgation.
—Benjamin Brandreth[1]

Soon the pharmaceutical industry had developed a story that was very easy to understand. Cyclooxygenase, cox, is the chemical responsible for blocking pain and swelling, as well as causing harmful side effects, such as ulcers. But cyclooxygenase is actually two different chemicals. Cox-1 is the "good" cox (the enzyme wearing the white hat), responsible for all the helpful things NSAIDs do: relieving pain, fever, and swollen joints—even protecting the lining of the stomach to prevent ulcers. But there is also cox-2, a "bad" cox (wearing the black hat), responsible for causing stomach erosions.

If a drug could be developed that would block cox-2, while still allowing cox-1 to do its job—that would be *aspirin without the bad part*. Such a drug would be called a "cox-2 selective inhibitor," coxib for short—or super aspirin in common parlance.

The pharmaceutical industry now set out to create a new miracle pain drug in the marketing tradition of Bayer with aspirin, Brandreth with vegetable pills, Merck with cocaine, and Galen with theriac.

To create a blockbuster drug or wonder pill, drugmakers need a short, easy, and logical answer for how the pill works. A blockbuster remedy, whether theriac or cocaine, should also have prestigious medical backing. For Vioxx and Celebrex, Merck and Pfizer both paid homage to Sir John Vane, who unraveled the mystery of how NSAIDs worked and won a Nobel Prize in medicine for his discovery.

The fact that the cox story was quick and simple (at least in the condensed version) met another timeless objective of a pharmaceutical breakthrough: cox-2 took little time to explain. Physicians did not have to pore through complex texts to understand the cox revolution. Nor was the sales literature, which sometimes is as short as a flash card, difficult to understand.

Drug company executives are critically aware that physicians are flooded with paper, especially mail. British doctors writing in a December 1983 issue of the *British Medical Journal* made suggestions either for its use or how to get rid of it. Dr. Tony Chapman recommended that all the mail from drug companies be returned to the sender marked "Doctor in Prison." Dr. Chapman imagined that "because drug companies never take no for an answer" their mailings would circulate between prisons marked, Not here, try Sing Sing.[2] Another doctor suggested that drug company mail be used as scrap paper for taking notes; and that brochures with "pretty pictures be passed to the occupational therapy departments of psychiatric hospitals" or sent to grade school children.[3]

Knowing both physician skepticism and time constraints, drug salespeople learn to impart their entire message in three minutes or often much less. It only takes a few seconds to say, "cox-1 is good, cox-2 causes ulcers. Our pill just has the good part."

It also provides a good lead-in: "Doctor, do your patients have stomachaches with their pain meds?" (Of course they do. Many medications irritate the stomach.)

"Yes."

"We have pills that don't cause this problem. Here's a sample."

The transaction is completed in thirty seconds . . . about the time of a television commercial. Like physicians, the viewing audience does not have the time or expertise to understand the intricacies of prostaglandin production, but they can understand that a pill has been scientifically developed to do away with the harmful stomachaches caused by aspirin. Even at medical conferences, the super aspirin story had a nice ring.

"Starting with groundbreaking experiments uncovering how the wonder drug aspirin worked by the Nobel Prize–winning team of Sir John Vane, scientists have taken another huge step forward by actually uncovering the basic cause of pain—cyclooxygenase—or cox. Meticulous research shows that cox has two parts. . . ."

The presenter flashes cute, colorful slides showing cox-1 (GOOD) and cox-2 (BAD). The next slide highlights a "COX-2 INHIBITOR TABLET." The lecturer concludes with a reminder that the medical profession now has aspirin without the side effects.

A super pill is born—almost.

In order to have a bestselling drug, you need a reason to sell it. There must be a demand for a miracle pill. And if there is no demand, it must be created. In sum, the drug seller needs an epidemic (whether it involves bowel toxins, a corroding liver, or a plague of foul-smelling mouth germs), and he or she must convince people that if the wonder drug isn't taken, anyone listening will risk becoming *part* of the epidemic.

Thus it came about that aspirin, Motrin, Aleve, and all the other NSAIDs became . . . poisons.

In the early scientific papers reporting on the discovery of super aspirin in 1994 and 1995, the use of NSAID drugs was simply described as *potentially* causing sores in the stomach, increased bleeding, and kidney problems. In one of its first press releases on Vioxx, in 1996, Merck suggested that its super aspirin is expected to have fewer gastrointestinal side effects than existing NSAIDs.[4] That release went out on July 7, 1996.

But on July 8, one day later, Searle raised the ante in *its* press release. Speaking about its own super aspirin, Celebrex, Dr. Philip Needleman, reporting on early drug tests in humans, said the results "indicate that Celebrex may be a medication that can relieve pain and inflammation without putting the patient at risk for gastrointestinal damage. . . . Toxicity from NSAIDs—resulting in *life-threatening* [emphasis added] GI [gastointestinal] ulcers, bleeds and perforations—is a serious concern when physicians prescribe these drugs. If it lives up to its promise, Celebrex could represent a significant advance in the treatment of arthritis and related painful conditions."[5] Now taking Motrin and Aleve don't just cause stomach sores, *but they threaten your life.*

In the same press release, Searle stated that cox-2 is now responsible for "wreaking havoc in the joints."[6] Fortunately, Searle continues:

"Dr. Needleman and other researchers pointed the way toward a potential solution when they discovered two forms of cyclooxygenase."

By the end of 1996, only six months after the first Searle super aspirin press release, the company issued another, in conjunction with a meeting of the American College of Rheumatology. The press release headline read modestly: "Experts Are Optimistic About Breakthroughs in Arthritis; End of Decade Could Signal Beginning of New Medical Era."

An important milestone had been reached for super aspirin. Now outside experts recognized its potential, not merely drug company executives.

The Searle press release explained that Dr. Steven Abramson, spokesperson for the American College of Rheumatology, believed that doctors had been limited in their treatment of arthritis because medications caused a host of side effects. "However, scientific research was now moving at a rapid pace and was resulting in several exciting new agents." Which new agents? Searle and Merck representatives, along with paid physicians, informed every doctor present about Vioxx and Celebrex, just in case they had not heard about them by this time.

As for the conclusion of the press release, it left no doubt about the health crisis overtaking America. Motrin and Aleve had the potential to cause platelet dysfunction [impaired ability of the blood to clot] that could be "life-threatening." *So the once mildly irritating pain pills not only destroy your stomach, but cause you to bleed to death.* Dr. Lee Simon noted that patients and physicians *desperately* needed new solutions.

Simon and Abramson both played pivotal roles in the approval of the super aspirins. Simon remained as an FDA advisor, led the drug trials for Searle, and later joined the FDA. Abramson became the chairman of the Arthritis Advisory Committee, which was assigned to objectively assess super aspirin.

But even by the end of 1996, cox inhibitors had not yet attained the status of wonder drugs. That would take a headline from a cancer publication, which stated in 1997 that a new class of pills known as *super aspirin* "could help prevent and even treat bowel [colon] cancer."[7]

"We are very excited by the possibility of using aspirin-like drugs because they could pave the way for better ways to prevent and perhaps one day even treat bowel cancer," Dr. Chris Paraskeva, a professor at Bristol University,

England, was quoted. Some scientists believed that super aspirin was fifty times more effective at killing cancer cells than ordinary aspirin![8]

By June of 1998, Jerome Groopman struck with his tale of a desperate need for a super aspirin. According to Dr. Groopman, he was suffering terrible side effects from the usual pain therapies such as aspirin, Motrin, and Aleve. In despair, Dr. Groopman underwent back surgery, which proved to be disastrous. When he awakened from the anesthesia he could not move his legs because of the severe pain. In addition, his spinal nerves were surrounded by blood. Groopman believed the terrible medical issue was caused by NSAIDs because they kept his blood from clotting.

Dr. Groopman was given a powerful narcotic, which caused him to lose mental focus and made him nauseous. He ended up worse than before the operation, and had to cope with the usual pain relievers, which he found grossly inadequate.

How widespread is the NSAID epidemic? Groopman claims that "eighty thousand people are hospitalized and some eight thousand die." By the end of 2001, the number of deaths had doubled. Merck claimed that roughly 16,000 people died with over 100,000 hospitalizations in the United States alone. But that is just from stomach complications.

Groopman also added Alzheimer's disease and more kinds of cancer to the long list of maladies that super aspirin could treat and possibly cure.[9]

Merck took a final crack at epidemic scare tactics when its public relations department published a report in 2001 indicating that arthritis is: more common in most developed countries than heart disease, cancer, or diabetes and is one of the world's most crippling diseases. More than 40 million people in the United States and at least an equal number in Europe currently have the disease. The number of sufferers is poised for rapid growth as the world's population ages.

There was nothing new about this fact. Arthritis has plagued humanity for millennia. The Roman doctor Galen attributed the disease, like many of his more ancient predecessors, to the influence of "rheums"—bad humors or elements that infiltrate the joints of the body. This infestation of foul influences became known as "rheumatism." The rheums throw the body out of balance—the good humors overwhelmed by the bad. The trick is to expel the bad elements without disrupting the good.

Treating arthritis has never been easy, for rheums tend to be resistant—even hostile—to outside influence. The toll of arthritis comes not only from the disease itself, but from the drugs used to relieve it. Modern medications, NSAIDs, may cause gastrointestinal side effects—sometimes serious ones—perforations, ulcers, and bleeding. Or at least they might have done that at first. But according to Dr. James Fries, whose database was used to calculate the catastrophe, the deleterious effects of NSAIDs were vastly exaggerated. No matter.

The only people who did not yet understand the growing Aleve menace by the late 1990s were financial analysts. Two months after Groopman's article and one month after members of Merck, Searle, the FDA, and the FDA advisory committee panelists and other "independent" experts met in Hawaii, the Food and Drug Administration announced on August 25, 1998, that the federal government was "giving an expedited review of Celebrex." This meant that the pill was now a top priority, and could be approved within six months. The news sent Monsanto (which owned Searle at the time) shares soaring and caused one analyst to paraphrase George Gershwin, saying that "the company could not ask for anything more."

Merck raced out with its own press releases touting Vioxx and pointing out that Merck was the pioneer in pain relief—beginning with the discovery of cortisone in 1941 and one of the first NSAIDs, indomethacin, in 1964. (No mention was made of either morphine or cocaine.)

Now that the FDA, financial analysts, university experts, and journalists were scared, it was time to get the ordinary doctor terrified. The utter horror of Motrin and Aleve needed to be brought dramatically to life. And so it was, on September 8, 1998, in a news article in the *Toronto Globe and Mail*: "There are more deaths from NSAIDs than multi-vehicle accidents, fires and gun shots . . . what's worse is that with NSAIDs often there are no symptoms until the side effects are severe."[10]

The story of Bill Benson, a Canadian doctor, is told in vivid detail:

Whenever Dr. Benson rounds up a group of arthritis patients to try out a new pain-relieving drug the phone usually rings off the hook.

They call about the nausea, the diarrhea, the possible side effects. Some get fed up and drop out. Others just stop taking the drug altogether.

But not this time. This time Dr. Benson's group took their cox-2 inhibitor pills, went home, and never called once. "I started to worry," he said.

This time it was Dr. Benson who picked up the phone. He called patients to make sure they were all right. "We had 150 people on these drugs for 18 months and we had no problems.

"People were joyful getting on with their lives. Their pain was under control and they were feeling good." When the trial ended, patients hit the roof.

"There was just rage," he said. "They were living life and then . . . it's over. They are furious."

Dr. Benson understandably concluded: "We have never been this excited about a brand-new drug and the potential for what it can do." Benson was unable to keep the exuberance from his voice. He believed there would be a use for super aspirin "in every field of medicine where there is concern about inflammation."[11]

Since inflammation occurs with nearly every known malady with which humans are afflicted, the FDA certainly felt compelled to act with all deliberate speed, for only the super aspirins could quell the raging epidemic caused by aspirin and its chemical cousins—a situation that Merck believed was getting worse as the world's population aged.

Thus on the eve of the FDA advisory committee hearings to assess cox-2s, the medical situation had degenerated into furious patients, general rage, and a crippling disease made worse by its own customary remedies.

The once modest side effects of NSAIDs had evolved into a menace to society. Fortunately, there was a pill that could not only prevent the menace, but cure just about everything else. By 1998, Merck and Pfizer/Searle/Monsanto had convinced people that, with their present medicines, they were at risk of severe bleeding and deadly ulcers, as well as depression, debilitation, memory loss, and cancer.

Nonetheless, the ultimate message was hopeful. A new pill was at hand. It was like the expression of wonder by Columbus in the New World when he beheld the lush vegetation stretching far and wide that heralded miracle drugs for Spain.

It is no mystery why Celebrex and Vioxx became some of the fastest selling pills in pharmaceutical history before advertising for them had even started.

Dr. Phil Needleman went from university scientist to savior. His inflamed rabbit kidney story entered folklore. Needleman nearly single-handedly discovered the chemical that was leading to, as one expert put it, "a new era in the treatment of disease." The Searle research chief savored every second of the limelight. Celebrex was the chance of a lifetime.

But Merck was ready with a counterattack. It had hundreds of years of science and innovation on its side. It was the best pharmaceutical research company in the United States, maybe the world, and it was ready to prove the superiority of Vioxx at any price.

Interestingly, as often happens, Merck believed its own publicity about the link between the NSAIDs and the threat to public health. This helps explain why not even the possibility of its pill causing heart disease halted Merck's Vioxx development, launch, and vehement defense. The company's tablet was addressing a dire public health issue. Vioxx could prevent thousands of deaths.

The worse a medical problem, the more the health care system tolerates the risk of a new pill. A patient suffering from serious cancer, for example, is much more likely to be given a poisonous drug than a person with a mild headache. All medicine is a question of risk versus reward.

Given all the potentially life-threatening dangers now associated with NSAIDs, perhaps the slight increased risk of heart disease might be justified. No one at Merck said this precisely, but that assumption underlay many of the company's statements.

In the midst of an epidemic, no one asks too many questions about the cure—or the hope of one.

PART III

CHAPTER 10

The War Begins

Competition is. In every business, no matter how small or how large, someone is just around the corner forever trying to steal your ideas.[1]

—Alice Foote MacDougall

The chief scientist of Merck & Co., Dr. Edward Scolnick, was livid when he learned that Celebrex had beaten Vioxx to an FDA advisory committee hearing by three months—and his rage percolated down through the entire ranks of the giant Merck company. He fired off an angry e-mail to senior executives threatening to quit: "MERCK marketing for once has to compete and win. If you do not beat PFIZER 2/1, MERCK should throw in the towel and just give up and hand the company over to someone else. IF YOU lose, I will leave, because I will not be able to have any respect for this company."[2]

Scolnick was angry for many reasons. He believed some of his colleagues had been raising unreasonable objections about the completion of his research. The research head had wanted to do a huge and very expensive clinical trial in humans to show that Vioxx caused fewer serious ulcers than competing drugs. But the study had been killed by others in senior management, who were afraid that the results might more clearly illustrate the negative cardiovascular side effects of Vioxx.

However, Pfizer was going forward with such a study, and if successful, it would give Merck's archrival a huge advantage. Once again, the stakes were high. Scolnick thought from the start that Vioxx was a once-in-a-lifetime opportunity.

Both Merck's own business analysts and outside financial experts predicted that the cox-2 inhibitor that got to market first would have a significant advantage in taking the market lead—an advantage estimated in the hundreds of millions of dollars and perhaps the number one position in the pharmaceutical industry.

The battle between the two drug giants, Merck and Pfizer, was symbolized by the growing rivalry between Scolnick and Phil Needleman. Scolnick is a tall, imposing man with razor-sharp medical sensibilities, an encyclopedic knowledge of the pharmaceutical industry, and a Boston Brahmin air of sophistication. Unlike the flashier Needleman, whose brash behavior and heavy New York accent charmed some audiences and alienated others, Scolnick was a far more subdued presence who generally shunned the public eye.

Like many at Merck, Scolnick was a graduate of Harvard Medical School and a researcher at the National Institutes for Health who prided himself on his academic and government contacts. He was responsible for some of Merck's greatest drug successes of the 1980s, often risking his job to support medicine about which the marketing department had doubts.

These remedies—for lowering cholesterol, treating AIDS, asthma, and glaucoma—had all shown problems during their development, but Scolnick had tenaciously backed them and pushed them through the bureaucracies of both his own company and the FDA. This was one reason that Merck was named *Fortune* magazine's most admired company, one year after another.

Scolnick was known behind the scenes to have a sharp temper, to be difficult to work with, to have an autocratic, almost dismissive personality, and to be a fighter who simply never surrendered. Even the top echelon of the FDA did not like going up against Scolnick when the Merck scientist was determined to get his way. Some at the company believed that compromise was not a word in Scolnick's vocabulary.

Merck had started off the super aspirin race at a disadvantage. Needleman had used both his academic background, his larger-than-life personality, and his reputation as a leader in the field of anti-inflammatories to galvanize his colleagues at Searle, Monsanto, and Pfizer.

As Celebrex went through development from a theoretical molecule to a blockbuster drug, Needleman evolved from university scientist, to drug company research chief, to pharmaceutical savior—the person who had predicted and developed the revolutionary drug that was going to profoundly alter medical therapy.

He also had the backing of the most aggressive and ambitious drug company in the world: Pfizer. Merck was feeling the pressure. Scolnick's e-mail threatening to quit was just one of many indications of the Merck–Pfizer marketing battle and how competitive the company's troops had become. Sometimes it was difficult to believe that the venerable Merck pharmaceutical company lived with the credo of "putting patients first."

The war to develop cox-2 inhibitors began in 1992, although it does not appear that way from reading official accounts of the super aspirin discovery. The standard histories by Merck and Pfizer portray the development of super aspirin as the result of years of basic research on the molecular structure of the human body, followed by additional years of tedious and exacting drug development and human testing.

However, at the 1992 inflammation conference in Montreal, when university scientists announced the discovery of cox-2, researchers from both Searle and Merck realized that at least two cox-2 inhibitors *had already been invented.* Scientists made presentations on these compounds, one from DuPont Pharmaceuticals, DuP-697, the other from a Japanese company, Taisho, known as NS-398.

Both Merck and Searle obtained molecular drawings of the pills and started developing versions of their own. Few people know that the cox-2 inhibitor that would be the precursor to the innovative miracle drugs, Vioxx and Celebrex, had already been invented by serendipity.

At Searle, Phil Needleman assigned an army of molecular chemists at Monsanto to work on the project. Soon after, Merck Frosst, Canada, did virtually the same. Edward Scolnick authorized a huge team to start research and development on a cox-2 pill at Merck Frosst—with support from Merck laboratories in New Jersey and Pennsylvania.

In 1992, the most powerful pharmaceutical executive in the world was Dr. Roy Vagelos, chairman and chief executive officer of Merck and Co.

Merck was still located in the same old brick headquarters in Rahway, New Jersey, it had occupied since the discovery of cortisone in the 1930s.

Vagelos was famous throughout the drug business for a number of reasons. He was a hometown boy, born and raised in Rahway. He had modernized Merck and succeeded in maintaining its legendary tradition of drug discovery. He had expanded upon George Wilhelm Merck's concept of centralized drug development, and enlarged the Rahway facility to resemble a huge campus where scientists, marketers, and executives could interact. In short, he had maintained the tradition created by Emanuel Merck in the 1820s when the young German chemist personally set out to merge the tradition of the apothecary with modern chemical research, development, and manufacturing. Also like Emanuel Merck, Vagelos was a brilliant scientist who was comfortable not only personally assessing, but guiding, research.[3]

In his latter years at the company, Vagelos had acquired a managed care company called Medco, which would be responsible for supplying drugs to insurers, hospitals, governments, and other large buyers that were starting to take a bigger role in the drug selling system.

Pfizer took the opposite approach, increasing its own sales force to directly reach more doctors by making alliances and acquisitions.

Vagelos's purchase turned out to be a costly mistake. Many of Merck's loyal and promising executives departed, and Merck was left without a firm succession plan. As the mandatory retirement of Vagelos rapidly approached, the Merck board of directors decided to seek a more business-oriented executive to lead the company.

They may also have sought an outsider who would not interfere with research chief Dr. Edward Scolnick. Without the approval of Dr. Vagelos, the Merck board replaced him with a man who neither was a local boy, M.D., nor even a member of the pharmaceutical industry. Raymond Gilmartin was a Harvard MBA and electrical engineer who had been head of Becton, Dickinson and Company, a medical-device maker.

Instead of moving into the famed aging research facility in Rahway, Gilmartin entered a newly built mahogany palace in Whitehouse Station, New Jersey, known in the drug industry as "the mountaintop" or "temple."

Gilmartin envisioned Merck as a modern-day formal corporation, rather than a research campus. The new CEO focused his energy on creating "business units," rather than personally reviewing scientific data. Gilmartin appointed a lifetime Merck employee from Australia who rose through the business side of the company to head marketing, as President, Human Health: David Anstice.

Anstice had worked his way up through the Merck ranks for thirty years, heading various divisions around the world. He was usually soft-spoken, articulate, and clever. But Anstice easily shed his polished executive image to roll up his sleeves and give stemwinder speeches that would whip up a pharmaceutical sales force into a cheering crowd.

Anstice saw marketing as leading the way to the future and wasn't afraid to flout the conservative Merck "ethical pharmaceutical" traditions to push advertising and sales to the absolute limit. More than once, under Gilmartin, Anstice bumped up against Merck Research Laboratories president Scolnick, the company's top scientist. While one man was a marketer, and the other a scientist, both had a fanatical desire to be first and *win*.

Even so, Scolnick would no longer have the kind of power he once had under Dr. Vagelos to control the medical side of the company and plan and execute his own drug development. Power subtly moved from basic research to marketing.

One other thing happened. The most admired company in America from 1987 to 1993 never again got that distinction after Roy Vagelos retired. In fact, the next pharmaceutical company to be so honored was the New York City–based company Pfizer Pharmaceuticals.

Canadian work on Vioxx proceeded at a frantic pace. The Merck Frosst team was led by Tony Ford-Hutchinson and Dr. Peppi Prasit, the young scientist who had taken notice of NS-398. The first job was to create a new molecule that did not infringe on the Taisho patent and to make it a more specific inhibitor of cox-2. Both tasks were completed by 1993 with a series of compounds that were put through early tests for strength and toxicity.

By 1994, the company decided on a molecule named L-748,731 as their lead compound and began testing it in animals. The results seemed almost too good to be true. It appeared to be safe, powerful, and cause no irritations in the linings of rat stomachs—even at doses that were higher than aspirin. Excitement that the cox-2 hypothesis worked—and that a blockbuster drug was at hand—started to run high.

In October 1994, the Merck super aspirin was first tested in humans and by early 1995, L-748,731 was given the Merck code name MK-0966. The brand name would later be Vioxx. Young Dr. Peppi Prasit could not believe that he and his team had accomplished what could only be described as a once-in-a-lifetime opportunity.

Philip Needleman and his Searle/Monsanto team were chemically modifying the same pills as Merck Frosst. At almost the same time that Merck created the Vioxx code, MK-0966, Searle designated its lead compound SC-58635, and put it into early testing.[4]

The Searle drug was first tested in a human being in March 1995, only five months after Merck had started testing Vioxx in humans. Much to Dr. Needleman's dismay, Searle was behind.

The next step for both Merck and Searle was to test the effect of the coxibs on the human stomach. Once again, both super aspirins seemed remarkable. At much higher than usual doses, neither Vioxx nor Celebrex was reported as having any stomach irritation. Doctors at both Searle and Merck now began dreaming the impossible. Super aspirin was moving from theory to reality.

Bill Steere, Pfizer's CEO, began taking note of Searle's research, and almost overnight what started as a skirmish between a handful of universities turned into a battle between Searle and Merck Frosst—then became a war between Pfizer and Merck. The two giant drug companies were about to enter the longest, most expensive, bitter, and ultimately destructive competition in pharmaceutical history. The prize was a simple, safe way to control pain.

"It was like watching a heavyweight boxing match between the undisputed champ and the scrappy challenger," one pharmaceutical financial analyst said. "It was brutal."

Both companies knew that super aspirin was worth billions in revenue, scientific prestige, and perhaps a Nobel Prize in medicine. Each company began to believe that it had the *superior* super aspirin and was willing to do just about anything to prove it. Moreover, the companies were already developing second-generation super aspirins that would be more effective than the first—and thus provide decades of profit.

In 1998, Dr. Jerome Groopman made this point in *The New Yorker* about the gleaming future of super aspirins. He wrote: "Monsanto's computer analysis . . . has already yielded a 'son of Celebra'" that held out untold promise.[5] The drug, which later did become known as "son of Celebrex," was named Bextra.

As he concluded his article, Groopman talked of having developed an elbow inflammation that required a painful cortisone shot. Groopman knew that cortisone was at best a temporary and perhaps risky fix for his problem. But his friend, colleague, and personal physician who was giving the injection, Dr. Lee Simon, reassured him. "If our luck holds, in less than two years, I won't have to do this to you."

The 1948 dream of cortisone with its patient leaping up from a wheelchair and dancing was on the horizon. Fifty years after that miracle, in 2001, Bextra was approved by the FDA.

Groopman did caution against the euphoria he felt about the super aspirins. But he concluded his 1998 *New Yorker* piece by writing about his personal expectations for the future: "So far all the signs are good—and for people like me they are more than good. I imagine myself, in the year 2000, popping a pill, comfortably bending down to tighten the laces of my sneakers, and beginning the twenty-six miles from Hopkinton to Boston."

That same year, Dorothy Hamill's arthritis was making it impossible for her to skate. She too was dreaming of a cure. It seemed to everyone involved that a miracle was at hand.

CHAPTER 11

Bursting the Bubble

The tragedy of science is a beautiful hypothesis slain by an ugly fact.
—Thomas Huxley

Dr. John Wallace, professor of pharmacology and therapeutics, University of Calgary, Canada, had never been frightened before a scientific meeting, but now he felt his muscles tense and breath shorten as he walked down the corridor to the podium where he was about to give his talk.

Wallace is considered one of the world's experts on anti-inflammatory drugs, and he had been conducting research on cox-2 compounds for more than a decade. He first started to doubt the data put out by Searle and Merck in 1994, and from that time on, the hostility between Wallace and the two drug giants grew steadily.

At a scientific meeting in Thailand in 1999 just after giving a talk on super aspirin, Dr. Wallace found himself alone in an elevator with an "average-looking man" who appeared to be reading lecture notes. The man looked at Wallace and complimented him on his presentation. "But if I were you, professor, I'd get myself a bodyguard."[1] Before Wallace could reply, the elevator door opened and the man stepped out. Wallace assumed it was just a joke.

A few months later, he was at another international conference on the cox-2 inhibitors in Florence, Italy. Sales of both Celebrex and Vioxx were exploding and the tension between Merck, Pfizer, and other companies selling pain pills was palpable.

Wallace's publications questioning the safety of Vioxx for the heart, kidneys, and stomach were being carefully scrutinized in the pharmaceutical establishment.

"I gave my talk and typically what I did was not to come out and say the cox-2 drugs were horrible or anything. I would just say, here's the theory and let's look at the basis of the theory," Wallace explains. "Then I would urge the audience to reevaluate some of its basic assumptions about how cox-2 works and its safety."[2]

Then Wallace presented the data he'd gotten from his laboratory. What began happening was that after his presentations people from Merck would jam the aisles where the microphones were located for asking questions.

"As soon as my talk ended," Wallace says, "I saw these two people run to the microphone and I recognized both. They were scientists from Merck. One at one microphone and one at the other. And basically what they did was to use up the entire question period."

The Merck scientists actually used their time to give speeches in praise of super aspirin and reaffirm that it did not have the side effects Wallace was talking about.

"They would always assure both me and the audience that they had thoroughly studied whatever problem about the drug I raised and that it simply didn't exist. My work was not accurate. And they just went back and forth, so that no one else could ask a question." Eventually, the discussion period would end with only Merck getting in its points.

"I got down from the podium and I realized, gosh, they've just undone everything I said, because I came across looking like a loose cannon who had done sloppy science."

The Merck people made a point that their research operations were both sizable and state-of-the-art—and that the drug company had access to far more information and testing materials than a humble university laboratory in the western provinces of Canada.

But being put on the spot and actually being threatened are two different matters—and at the international conference in Florence, Wallace felt that things were downright spooky.

Wallace is a meticulous scientist, and before each talk he and his researchers would thoroughly review the data on the super aspirins. It was clear that they could potentially damage the vessels leading to the heart. His team had replicated the research many times. There was also no

doubt that super aspirin could potentially damage the kidneys and interfere with healing in the stomach and the colon.

That was not the message that Merck and Pfizer were spending hundreds of millions of dollars to tell. And if Wallace was right, the beautifully constructed, easy-to-understand, deeply scientific story of cox-1 and
cox-2 would be destroyed. If cox-2 played an important, constructive role
in the body, why would anyone want to block it? And if the story about
how these two enzymes interacted was complex, super aspirin would be
a tough sell.

"So things really got bad in Florence," Wallace said. "I saw one of the
people from Pfizer who had written a lot of the papers about Celebrex.
And I've met her several times. Very pleasant lady. You always have nice
chats with her and whatnot. Strict scientist type.

"So it was about ten minutes before my talk and I was just standing
there and she and some others came up to me and I remember it caught
me off guard, because they walked up very quickly and stopped very close
to me. You know the kind of situation where you want to take a step back.
And I said 'hi' and she said, 'John, we just want you to know that we are
here.' And then they walked away.

"And I . . . You know. What the hell was that? Because it left me baf-
fled."

The drug company scientists sat in three very different places in the audience. Wallace thought they were going to use the usual gimmick of mo-
nopolizing the microphones. The companies also used the trick of fanning
out, so that it would look like criticism was coming from every part of the
audience.

"But then the next thing that happens is Phil Needleman was there
and he sat right in front of the podium. And it was a room where the
podium was quite close to the audience, and he sat down smack right in
front of me.

"And because of what had happened a few minutes earlier, I thought,
okay, it's all supposed to intimidate me or whatever.

"So anyway I gave my talk and referred to the harmful effects of the
cox-2s on the stomach and colon, increased high blood pressure, and the
possibility of adverse effects on the heart, this kind of thing.

"And when I got to the end of my talk, Needleman—he never got out of his chair—he just snapped his fingers and the women with the microphones . . . just snapped and waved them over. She—the woman had to wade through the audience to come and hand him the microphone.

"And he was sitting back with his arm across the chairs next to him like he was on a La-Z-Boy kind of thing, and he just spoke for ten minutes solid. And it was like, you know, we've done this work before. We've done it in a much better way. We didn't see any hint of side effects.

"The data you showed on high blood pressure were just in animals. We know that only happens in—

"And so I interrupted. I was tired of these people taking all my time and—I mean—I'm not a shrinking violet . . . so I just kept interrupting him and saying, excuse me, doctor, but I showed human data, as well as rat data."

Wallace explains that once the scientists from Merck or Pfizer are confronted by human data, they try to blame the side effects on the other company's drug. "So if you are talking about Vioxx, the scientist will say it only happens in Celebrex, or if it's Celebrex that it only happens in Vioxx.

"It's always the other guy's drug. And so I just kept interrupting, saying, no, no, no. So I showed data on both drugs, Vioxx and Celebrex. You know, because I wasn't going to let Needleman destroy the message.

"After the meeting it just amazed me that I had to battle these two drug companies and that they were so concerned that anyone would say something that didn't fit in with their story."

"Quite a bit of what we see [in our lab] is contradicting current dogma," says Scott Morham, an American Cancer Society postdoctoral fellow.[3] In the June 1996 issue of *Environmental Health Perspectives* Morham was one of a number of independent scientists working with Dr. Robert Langenbach at the National Institutes of Health (Environmental Science). An expert on anti-inflammatories, Dr. Langenbach stated, "The cox story just didn't make sense. It was just too simplistic." Ironically, the NIH article appeared just as Merck scientists were beginning to worry about the cardiovascular toxicity of Vioxx and Pfizer scientists were hammering home the simplistic cox-2 miracle story.

Langenbach explains it this way. The cox enzyme is really one entity, despite the fact that it has two parts. And if it's really the same entity, why should it work in such different ways? "Both cox-1 and cox-2 make similar products so how could one be totally bad and one totally good? You know this good guy/bad guy. And that's when our laboratory really started investigating."[4]

Throughout this period, the drug companies continually dismissed Wallace, Langenbach, and a handful of other researchers by claiming that their findings relied solely on animal data. But the cox-2 hypothesis had been formally proposed by Needleman and his team in the journal *Proceedings of the National Academy of Sciences* in April 1994 based on the "rat air pouch model." The paper concluded that "potent anti-inflammatory agents [can be made] which do not produce the typical side effects (e.g., gastric ulcers) associated with the non-selective, Cox-1 directed anti-inflammatory drugs."[5] From this, Searle scientists jumped to the far-reaching hypothesis that inhibitors of cox-2 may be efficacious anti-inflammatory drugs devoid of the side effects associated with the inhibition of cox-1 and thus provide a *significant improvement to current therapy*.[6] Jumping from a good result in the rat air pouch model to a potential wonder drug is quite a leap.

Based on additional animal experiments, Searle and Merck took the cox theory further. Cox-1 exists everywhere in the body simply performing normal functions. It also serves to protect the stomach from acids. By contrast, cox-2 is only produced in response to inflammation.

Langenbach decided to actually see if the theory was true. He and his team developed an extremely elegant scientific model. They developed two sets of mice. In one set they were able to eliminate or "knock out" cox-1, and in the other mice they were able to knock out cox-2. (Not surprisingly these test animals are called "knockout mice" and they are frequently used in research to test the effect of a drug on various body systems.)

The cox-2 knockout mouse was essentially a test animal that resembled a subject who had swallowed a cox-2 inhibitor like Vioxx or Celebrex. (Because the cox-2 inhibitor "knocked out" cox-2.) The mice with no cox-1 functioned more like a mouse given simple Aleve or Motrin.

"What we expected," Langenbach relates, "is that the mice without cox-1 would be in terrible shape. Cox-1 is supposed to perform the body's normal functions and protect the stomach. But what we found was that the mice lacking cox-1 did not develop ulcers. And the most surprising thing was that the mice without cox-1 were really quite healthy animals. *When these same mice were given a standard drug like Motrin, we found them more resistant to developing ulcers."*[7]

So what about the other set of mice? This set of mice was the equivalent of mice that had been given super aspirin and therefore had no cox-2. "They were born with kidney problems," Langenbach explains. And they certainly developed pain and inflammation. Quite a bit that the NIH group found contradicted the stories released by Merck and Searle about super aspirin.

"We really found the reverse of what was supposed to be happening," Langenbach says. "Without cox-1, we only disrupted a few bodily functions. And it was definitely involved in inflammation. So it had a good guy/bad guy role on its own." With super aspirin, which knocks out the "bad guy," "We found we disrupted a number of normal functions . . . development of the kidney, fertility in females. . . .

"They [cox-1 and cox-2] both were essential for some things and could contribute to diseases in other ways. So they both had a good guy/bad guy personality."

The NIH lab also showed that cox-2 was necessary for ulcer healing, wound healing, and tissue regrowth after an injury.

Langenbach contends that the cox-2 hypothesis was widely believed because when the enzyme was first discovered in 1990, it was assumed there was only one form of cox (cox-1) and that it was responsible for ulcer formation. While he says the early mice experiments in 1994 and later human experiments showing low levels of ulcer formation with super aspirin are valid, the many detrimental effects of the drug were ignored. "And Merck paid a terrific price for doing that."[8]

Like John Wallace, Dr. Robert Langenbach started finding his life and scientific work becoming more and more difficult. The drug companies were aware of the NIH data because they would often exchange information or listen to talks at scientific meetings.

"So finally I went to Searle/Pfizer and presented a seminar in 1995 on cox-1 and cox-2 to the whole group and they were pretty much in a state of shock over the data from these animals in which we knocked out cox-1 and cox-2.

"They were in a state of shock because they had an almost biblical belief about these enzymes before there was any data to support it. I mean it was taken on faith, I guess.

"The hypothesis for cox-1 being the good guy and cox-2 being the bad guy was just there and people had already assumed they knew what their roles were before the data showed how."[9]

Unlike the Merck and Pfizer stories, which were being picked up by financial analysts, being presented in special, drug-company-sponsored seminars, and written up in *The Wall Street Journal,* the work of Langenbach was sparsely published in esoteric journals. No major public relations firm was on hand to set up interviews, Langenbach recalls with a laugh. "I had similar meetings with Merck and even the Food and Drug Administration to talk about the experiments with these drugs."

Like Wallace, Langenbach had battles every time he presented his work at scientific meetings. "There was a campaign to argue with me about everything I did."[10]

John Wallace definitely agrees, and adds, "You know," he says, "the really strange thing about super aspirin is that it just seemed to come out of thin air."[11]

Like so much in the history of medicine, the super aspirin story seemed both reasonable and scientifically sound. Furthermore, as with so many other remedies, from Galen's bloodletting to leeches, actual experimentation disproved what had been taken on faith. Why shouldn't bloodletting be used for pain, as recommended by the *Merck Manual* until 1936? The reason is that no one in 1,500 years ever tested it to find out whether it worked. As Thomas Dormandy writes, for centuries a medical argument could end with the simple words: "Galen said so."

Wallace had been researching pain drugs in the 1980s. "At that time," Wallace says, "none of the pharmaceutical companies had any interest in cox-1 or cox-2. As always, they were looking for new pills, but whether or not they blocked cox-2 was completely irrelevant."

John Wallace is in one of the best positions to know, because he was working for DuPont on their super aspirin—DuP-697—before anyone had discovered cox-2.

"So it was certainly not a drug development plan to find a cox-2 inhibitor because we didn't know or care about cox-2. DuPont was looking for a new anti-inflammatory [pain pill], just like all the other companies. What happens is you discover a drug just by trying chemical combinations." (In the same way that German dye companies in the 1880s created new remedies.)

"It doesn't matter why a pill works—look at aspirin—no one had a clue for almost seventy years, but it didn't hurt sales."[12]

However, the drug companies can't simply come out with a new pain compound and tell people they don't have a clue about its mechanism. The marketing departments want to promote a pill along with a "brilliant new concept" of what the method of action is.

When Wallace's boss at DuPont heard about the link between cox-2 and inflammation he immediately wanted to find out if DuP-697 worked the way the University of Rochester scientists had speculated. Much to everyone's surprise, it did.

"It wasn't part of some grand new program at all," Wallace says. "And I was familiar with what was going on at Merck and Searle—and they weren't doing anything like that either."

In fact, years after Vioxx was discovered, Wallace was asked to be a judge for a chemical and drug innovation prize in Canada called the Manning Award. One of the entries was for Vioxx. Wallace relates what he found: "I read this huge, great dossier. I read through it and then what surprised me was I assumed that they'd started from scratch to build a molecule."

That process is called rational drug design. It is a term that refers to a drug that has been developed because of a basic scientific discovery. For example, a company might find that certain bacteria cause a disease, so they design a pill to kill the germ.

"But in fact what Merck did was to take the Japanese drug NS-398 and change it ever so slightly . . . that's it."[13]

What both concerned and surprised Wallace and many other scientists was that the super aspirins were heavily marketed before anyone had done significant human testing on them. One of the problems researchers outside a drug company have with assessing a new compound is that it remains in the sole possession of the pharmaceutical manufacturer that owns the patent. Independent laboratories cannot either confirm or deny the data or claims. The reason that Wallace was one of the very few people in the world who could threaten the drug companies was that his laboratory still had access to DuP-697, a cox-2 inhibitor not much different from Vioxx or Celebrex. Therefore, he could objectively test super aspirin and the claims made about it. Wallace had good reason to be worried.

Both Merck and Pfizer very early on stated that the super aspirins would not cause an ulcer at all. "They were pushing these drugs as GI *safe*—not GI *safer*," Wallace says. "They were very much pushing the story that these drugs will not produce an ulcer at all. And that's dangerous, because I'm a pharmacologist and every drug has side effects. It's all a question of how high the dose to become toxic."[14]

For example, a report broadcast on CNN on November 6, 1998, showed an interview with a leading physician about the cox-2 drugs: "To call them a super aspirin is probably not correct, in the sense they're not stronger than the aspirins we have," said Dr. Thomas Schnitzer of Northwestern University. "But what they are certainly super about is they're super safe."[15] Super Safe. It was like a mantra.

The problem of making a safety claim is particularly acute with pain medication. A patient who is prescribed antibiotics will generally follow the directions of the physician or pharmacist. If he or she is told to take one pill a day, that is what the person is likely to do. (Certain type A personalities might take two pills, hoping the illness will go away more quickly, but this behavior is rare.) For patients in pain, the exact opposite is the case.

A patient instructed to take one pill a day for pain will often ignore that advice and take as many pills as necessary to eradicate the pain. This is one of the many reasons that pain medications can be so dangerous. An actual clinical name exists for this condition: "dosage creep."

For this reason, drug regulators prefer to approve very low doses of pain pills. They know the patient will almost automatically increase the amount he or she takes. In fact, with Celebrex, this happened 70 percent of the time, according to Dr. John Wallace.

According to a study conducted at Vanderbilt University by Marie Griffith, M.D., professor of preventive medicine, Vioxx was also used by patients in "high" doses.

As Wallace says, "It's very dangerous if you start pushing a drug, telling people that it's completely safe. Because if the drug doesn't work as well as the patient hoped, they're going to take two of the pills, three of the pills, four of the pills and you're eventually going to get into side effect problems."

That's exactly what happened in the early human testing of Vioxx.

Drug development proceeds in a highly systematic way. First drugs are tested in the laboratory in test tubes (toxicology). Next they are given to various animals—mice, rats, dogs, sometimes chimpanzees, depending on the drug, in what is called pre-clinical development.

The next step is known as Phase I. In this step, the pill is given to healthy volunteers, usually young men between the ages of eighteen and twenty-four. (Phase I testing is sometimes accelerated with critical diseases such as AIDS and certain forms of cancer.)

Phase II testing involves the introduction of the drug into small groups of people who have active disease. It usually involves a series of tests known as dose ranging. In dose ranging trials, the test groups are divided up and given various strengths of a drug, for example: 20 milligrams, 40 milligrams, and so on. During this period (in fact during all phases of drug testing), laboratory work and animal work may still continue, depending on what scientists observe in humans.

It was in the Phase II dose ranging trials of Vioxx that Merck first got signs of trouble. A high-level research evaluation committee got the bad news at the October 1996 meeting in the village of Blue Bell. Blue Bell is a quaint town in Pennsylvania, not far from the Merck research laboratories at West Point, Pennsylvania. The firm has an unpretentious facility where executives and scientists can meet in relative privacy.

The clinicians were looking at "protocol 017," a Phase II study in rheumatoid arthritis in which patients were given different doses of Vioxx. One of the groups initially took 175 milligrams of Vioxx, then a lower amount, 125 milligrams. As previously noted, dangerous side effects such as heart attack, chest pain, blood problems, and high blood pressure became evident."[16]

Worrisome side effects indeed, and *extremely dangerous* with a pain pill. The dose for "acute pain" for Vioxx would eventually be 50 milligrams, limited to a period of five days. However, people in excruciating pain such as that caused by arthritis can suffer for far more than five days, and as John Wallace points out, may take "two of the pills, three of the pills, four of the pills . . ."[17] It is not very hard to jump from 50 mg to 100 mg and more. Furthermore, most people have no idea what dose of a drug they are taking.

Even among the most knowledgeable there is confusion. In the debate broadcast on CNBC that followed the trial involving Carol Ernst, leading pharmaceutical expert lawyer Richard Epstein identified the Vioxx doses used in research as "800 milligrams." A lethal amount. (He may have been confusing Vioxx with Celebrex, the high dose of which is 800 mg.) Bob Ernst was taking 25 mg of Vioxx (lethal enough). Ernst's lawyer, Mark Lanier, said this was the Vioxx study dose.[18] Actually, it was double that, 50 mg. If two such experts could get confused, imagine what might happen to the average Vioxx patient, especially one who is elderly and in terrible pain with less tolerance for a pain drug in the first place.

The problem faced by Merck at this point, therefore, was how low they could make a "safe" dose of Vioxx and still have an effective pill. And why were these dangerous side effects on the heart showing up in the first place?

The answer came, ironically, from a study sponsored by Merck itself. This study was never intended to discover the link between super aspirin and heart disease, but it did. Fortunately for the drug company, the scientists who performed the work at the University of Pennsylvania were contractually forbidden from speaking or publishing the results without Merck's consent.

In 1996, Dr. Garret FitzGerald and Dr. Francesca Catella-Lawson were contracted by Merck to study the effect of both Vioxx and a standard NSAID in the kidneys. They were concerned by the fact that the cox-2 inhibitors seemed to disrupt homeostasis, the theory related to the ancient notion developed by the Roman physician Galen concerning balance in the human body. By this time, of course, the theory was vastly more detailed, but surprisingly its basic hypothesis seemed to have remained correct—and it had intrigued FitzGerald for years.

One very important substance that protects the heart is called prostacyclin. This chemical widens the blood vessels so that blood can flow more freely. Think of the blood vessels as pipes. The body is carefully designed so that the width of these pipes can comfortably allow blood to circulate. The heart is the motor that pumps the blood through these vessels; prostacyclin ensures that the heart will not have to work too hard by widening the pipes. However, another crucial function of blood is to form small clumps or clots. If we bleed, the blood hardens so that a wound is naturally "patched." This patch is created by air hitting the blood, causing it to harden and eventually seal off the injury.

But if the blood clots *within* the body, it can get trapped in one of the small vessels leading to the heart and block the flow of blood, potentially causing disruption to the heart. Prostacyclin, by keeping the blood flowing freely, stops the clumps from forming.

However, there is another chemical in the body called thromboxane that does just the opposite of prostacyclin. Instead of widening the heart vessels, making it easier for the blood to flow freely and the blood less likely to clot, thromboxane *narrows* the blood vessels and *promotes* blood clots. Why? Because without a chemical to promote clots, we would bleed to death with a cut. Therefore these two chemicals—one that keeps the blood moving freely, and one that encourages it to clot—need to be kept in balance.

When super aspirin enters the body, it prevents thromboxane from being eliminated through the kidneys and into the urine. (Remember that in Robert Langenbach's animal experiments, animal systems affected with super aspirin developed kidney problems.) So when the body has too much thromboxane, it ends up with too much of the chemical that causes clotting. The arteries get clogged and a stroke or heart attack can occur.

FitzGerald and Catella-Lawson may have for the first time actually proven what Galen had memorialized. The legendary physician stated that the body humors, one of which was blood, had to stay in balance to thwart illness. When this harmony was disrupted, disease occurred. A few thousand years later, FitzGerald and Catella-Lawson found the same thing.

Super aspirin interferes with that balance. Therefore, when Vioxx enters the blood, a chemical chain reaction is set off that increases the risk of cardiovascular disease and causes deadly heart rhythm problems (arrhythmia). Eric Ding and colleagues confirmed the link in their article for *The Journal of the American Medical Association (JAMA)* eight years later. It was too late for Robert Ernst and his widow, Carol.

Merck could criticize both Langenbach and Wallace for their conclusions because of "sloppy research," and the use of animals. But FitzGerald and Catella-Lawson were working on experiments approved by Merck itself, and the scientists made their findings based on thirty-six healthy *human* volunteers.

The University of Pennsylvania researchers tested super aspirin against the common NSAID indomethacin. They found that the patients given indomethacin *did not* experience the imbalance in the blood that could lead to heart attacks.

Merck could not very well deny the careful research of its own investigators and consultants. So the company chose to do the next best thing. Merck's executives argued endlessly about what the research meant, did not allow the researchers to discuss it, made the results look confusing, and delayed publication for years. "This paper has been held up in ways that are unprecedented in my experience and it is time for it to go,"[19] Dr. FitzGerald angrily wrote to Merck.

To give Merck the absolute benefit of the doubt, drug companies almost always find inexplicable and sometimes potentially dangerous biochemical reactions in the blood. And maybe FitzGerald and Catella-Lawson's discovery might have meant nothing in and of itself.

But by 1997, two years before Vioxx was approved, Merck had numerous human warning signals: Study 017 (Phase II dose ranging study)— "high" doses of Vioxx were causing kidney damage and an excess of heart-related disorders in a study of humans—and Study 023 (FitzGerald–

Catella-Lawson). A chemical imbalance that could lead to heart attacks had been found in humans.

Now add in the animal work. Robert Langenbach linked animals showing kidney damage with super aspirin. This finding not only coincided with the FitzGerald–Catella-Lawson data, it indicated that super aspirin could dangerously raise blood pressure. (Damage to the kidneys can raise blood pressure.) Two smaller studies in humans, coded 069 and 091, also raised red flags.

These observations were strengthened as early as mid-2000 by one of the world's leading cardiologists, Eugene Braunwald, former chief of cardiology at Harvard Medical School. Drs. Roberto Bolli and Ken Shinmura at the Cardiology Department of the University of Louisville wrote that cox-2 is a cardioprotective protein[20] that helps to prevent heart attacks. Eliminate cox-2 and the protection disappears. (Their work was submitted to the *Proceedings of the National Academy of Sciences* by Dr. Braunwald.) By 2001, a Harvard group was consulting with Merck, helping the company plan a large human study named VALOR to "definitively" learn whether Vioxx was a danger to the heart. Mysteriously, the study was suddenly canceled just after Merck was required to put an ambiguous message about possible Vioxx-related damage to the heart in the "Precautions" section of the label. This cancellation and FDA's action are all the more odd, because FDA's own internal consultant, Dr. Shari Targum, wrote that the heart warning should be placed unambiguously in the "Warning" section. At almost the same time, FDA's Office of Drug Safety, a different division of the agency from the one responsible for approvals, was beginning a study to more definitively determine the Vioxx heart-toxicity issue.

Drug companies have huge research departments that track even the most minute scientific communication about a drug under development. Not paying attention to Dr. Braunwald would have been inconceivable.

Almost none of FitzGerald's 1996 data was initially made public, nor did Merck do anything to publicize it. The company states that its scientists did not learn of FitzGerald's conclusions until October 1997. Considering the small size of the study and the fact that it was easy to accomplish, this delay makes little sense. Such a study would be very carefully monitored by Merck (the University of Pennsylvania is a short distance from Merck Laboratories and the two institutions collaborate frequently). Certainly neither FitzGerald nor Catella-Lawson had reason to hide their findings. In fact, FitzGerald pleaded with Merck to conduct additional experiments to either confirm or disprove the hypothesis. Merck declined. This was documented in the "Martin Report," a special study commissioned by Merck, in which John S. Martin, Jr., investigated Vioxx marketing and development for twenty months, resulting in a public report of over 1,400 pages. The Merck investigation reveals that Edward Scolnick, Merck's president of research, and other senior executives "discussed the various study proposals but decided not to undertake them."[21]

FitzGerald's experimental data was presented to an outside panel of Merck advisors in May 1998, by now more than two years after the University of Pennsylvania scientists had started. In the written notes of the meeting, the board made its conclusions. These conclusions were in keeping with the bogus notion (according to Dr. James Fries) of a raging epidemic that was tearing at the health of the United States: The Merck notes state: "Approval of Vioxx should not be held up because the gain in safety achieved by the elimination of serious and fatal gastrointestinal toxicity will free patients from one of the most serious adverse effects in current drug therapy [taking Motrin or Aleve]. Thus, there is a strong mandate for introduction of Vioxx into medical practice as soon as is feasible."[22]

But wait, was there as yet any *proof* that Vioxx reduced the number of ulcer deaths or serious complications as compared to dreaded drugs like "non-super" aspirin and Aleve?

No. Why not? Because the scientists at Merck already realized the bind they were in. Researchers knew that real proof of the superiority of Vioxx over NSAIDs required them to do an outcomes trial—in other words, a trial in humans comparing Vioxx with an NSAID, to find out whether in a real-life situation super aspirin lowered the risk of serious ulcer complications.

The problem was that Merck knew there was enough evidence that Vioxx had the potential to cause more heart disease than standard

NSAIDs; if they performed an outcomes trial it might show a lowering of the ulcer rate, but also an increase in heart disease. "A trial with that design could kill [the] drug," a Merck scientist wrote.[23]

A possible answer was to include aspirin in both groups to help protect the heart. The problem of course was that by adding aspirin to Vioxx, it might eliminate any benefit super aspirin might have to prevent stomach injury. An outcomes trial seemed like a no-win proposition.

"I sure don't want to be the one to show those results to senior management," commented Dr. Alise Reicin, a senior director at Merck Research Laboratories, who was eventually given the task of designing and carrying out such a study.[24]

In the meantime, what happened to the FitzGerald and Catella-Lawson protocol 023? It was included in Merck's application to the Food and Drug Administration in such a way as to confuse even the most astute drug reviewer. The theory that the human study could cause more heart attacks was not emphasized. However, the company did add that the points raised by 023 might require more study.

This is an excellent example of how a company can seem to follow federal requirements to submit all of its data to the FDA, yet not show the agency anything significant.

Nor did the FDA ever get the studies that FitzGerald and Catella-Lawson proposed—because the research was never done. Further, the two scientists clashed with Merck about how, where, and to whom to present the data.

There were lengthy discussions, Dr. Briggs Morrison, a Merck executive, concedes. He and his colleagues at Merck wanted to focus on the kidneys; FitzGerald wanted to focus on heart disease. The correspondence between Dr. FitzGerald and Merck became very heated and difficult. On March 25, 1999, Dr. FitzGerald sent an e-mail to Merck that stated, "I am getting very concerned about the delays with this manuscript. As you know, we have made multiple changes to accommodate the suggestions from Merck. I have sincerely tried to phrase the manuscript in a way that is sensitive to your interests, but is still honest to the data. However, I have the uncomfortable feeling . . . that this process is being strung out indefinitely for a variety of purposes."[25] As well they should have been. FitzGerald could have scuttled the Vioxx ship.[26]

Interestingly, Catella-Lawson did get a chance to "leave slides" of a talk that she gave at the Cox in Paradise meeting in Hawaii. It was presented during day two of the meeting, on July 29, 1998. The experiment was related in Session 6, "Cox-2 and Kidney Function." The title of the talk was "Renal and Extra Renal Biosynthesis of Prostacyclin During Long-term Cox-2 Inhibition."[27] The abstract of the talk was not made public.

The FitzGerald and Catella-Lawson article was finally published in May 1999 in the *Journal of Pharmacology and Therapeutics*. The timing was excellent for Merck. Vioxx was approved by the FDA on May 20, 1999, approximately three years after FitzGerald and Catella-Lawson began their study and *after* the FDA had made its label-warning decisions.

FitzGerald and Catella-Lawson conducted a similar study with Celebrex that was published in January 1999—in the *Proceedings of the National Academy of Sciences* within weeks *after* that drug's approval.

The headline from the University of Pennsylvania press release on the research was different from the title of the talk in Hawaii. It read: "How Super Are the Super Aspirins? New Cox-2 Inhibitors May Elevate Cardiovascular Risk."[28] Had this been the title of Catella-Lawson's talk in Hawaii, it certainly would have garnered considerable attention. FitzGerald stated ominously that the trials submitted to the FDA were too small to find heart attack damage. Will such damage develop over time as more patients use Vioxx? "The question hangs out there," FitzGerald wrote.[29]

The article adds some very good advice: "Many older people, including some who may want to take super aspirin for their arthritis, could be among those at risk for such [heart-attack-related] events."[30] What is particularly astonishing is that Merck's legal team would use this precise reasoning to win their legal battles. As the company's attorneys put it: "We know there are many risk factors that will make it difficult to prove Vioxx is responsible for heart attacks." In some respects, the reasoning is unassailable. You might as well not put in the FitzGerald warning because people will have heart attacks anyway. Merck lawyers endlessly pounded in the multiple risk factors of heart disease—so why not add another?

Dr. Eric Topol pointed out a good answer in his *NEJM* article, "Failing the Public Health—Rofecoxib [Vioxx], Merck, and the FDA": "Even a fraction of a percent excess in the rate of serious cardiovascular events would translate into thousands of affected people . . . there may be tens of thousands of patients who have had major adverse events attributable to rofecoxib [Vioxx]."

All of Merck's analysis of the "true meaning" of the FitzGerald hypothesis is, of course, well and good and part of science. But an easy way to tell how frightened Merck was of its implications was the delay between the start of the trial in 1996 and publication of the results in 1999, three years later. Had the experiment shown that Vioxx *helped* the heart, the company would have informed scientific advisors before FitzGerald had time to rinse his test tubes. A huge research team would have followed up every facet of the FitzGerald and Catella-Lawson trial and eagerly presented the findings at every opportunity. Articles would have been prepared for immediate publication, press releases written, and major lectures scheduled.

Later, Merck boasted that it only took three months to analyze one of the most complicated trials ever designed, the Vioxx outcomes study (VIGOR), which used over eight thousand patients. And yet it took Merck three years to analyze the FitzGerald and Catella-Lawson study, which used only thirty-six patients.

Months after the study was published in 1999, Dr. FitzGerald remained at his lab in Philadelphia. Dr. Francesca Catella-Lawson accepted a senior research position at Merck.

CHAPTER 12

The Vioxx Mystique and Hypnotized Water: The Development of Modern Drug Testing

A large part of the history . . . of medical science has been a progressive weaning away from the superficial seductiveness of individual stories . . . the human mind is a wanton storyteller and even more a profligate seeker after pattern. We see faces in clouds and tortillas, fortunes in tea leaves and planetary movements.

—**Richard Dawkins**

D r. Benjamin Franklin is best known as a scientist for attempting to discover electricity by running through a Philadelphia field, flying a kite in a lightning storm. He succeeded. Indeed, it seems there are few things Franklin did not either discover, invent, or improve—from the printing press, the post office, the Constitution of the United States, or—most important for this book—how to know if a drug actually works.

It was Franklin's work, and the work of a few other pioneering scientists, that later influenced the stinging debates over whether Vioxx and Celebrex were effective compounds—or whether, as Dr. John Wallace suspected, they were nothing more than the product of smoke and mirrors, invented by modern-day conjurers.[1]

Dr. Franklin was one of the world's first parapsychologists—a person who studied what effect perception had on the human mind. His conclusions were nothing short of inventing key elements of scientific medical trials that tested whether treatment worked or only *seemed* to work.

The approval of the cox-2 inhibitors by the FDA in 1998 and 1999, and the subsequent controversies surrounding them, can be traced directly back to an experiment commissioned by the King of France, Louis XVI, in the 1700s to test a therapy then sweeping Paris known as "animal magnetism."

As a parapsychologist, Franklin was keenly aware of observational bias. What this means is that people see and conclude whatever they believe or are persuaded to believe. For example, doctors continuously informed by myriad sales representatives that Vioxx is a miracle compound will generally find that their patients vastly improve after taking it.

A team of scientists who have spent $100 million and four years studying the wondrous effects of Vioxx are likely to find that the pill does extremely well to alleviate pain. When Merck researchers analyzed the FitzGerald hypothesis, they were clearly influenced by their observational bias, which experts in parapsychology know will make the conclusions of the Merck researchers invalid.

The Food and Drug Administration has the responsibility to approve a drug's safety and effectiveness based on studies *without any bias.* This is no easy task, given that drug approval trials are conducted by the very companies who have the largest stake in their outcome.

Because of this, the FDA helps design trials that eliminate bias by means of the randomized, prospective, placebo-controlled, double-blind clinical trial, or RCT, for short.

Many people have probably heard these terms in reference to medical studies but do not know either what they mean, why they need to be included for drug approval, or the history of medication studies that led scientists to conclude they are critical. For centuries, the efficacy of a therapy depended on the authorities who endorsed it (such as Greek and Roman doctors), not by experimental testing. Belief in dogma was far more important than the scientific method.

This medical notion changed very slowly, and still plays a part in the promotion and selling of even the most sophisticated new drugs such as Vioxx. To see how this belief system changed, it is critical to return to the basics of the randomized, controlled trial and the terms that comprise it.

Start with the term "blinding." Blinding refers to the concept that the participants in a clinical trial are not permitted to know which type of therapy they are receiving. Thus, even if they believe a certain treatment works, it won't make a difference because the subjects do not know what they are taking. A "double-blind" trial refers to further efforts to eliminate bias. In these trials, the doctors who administer the drugs are also unaware of which therapy they are administering.

Blinding began with Dr. Franklin's experiment to assess the miraculous magnetism therapy sweeping Europe in 1784. Franklin was joined by the most prominent scientists of his day, including Joseph-Ignace Guillotin, inventor of the very effective device for removing people's heads that bears his name—and Antoine Lavoisier, the "father of chemistry," who explained much about oxygen, but who unfortunately was executed by Guillotin's invention.

These testers were probably aware of an important British experiment carried out by a naval surgeon named James Lind in 1747. Lind set out to find a means of preventing scurvy, a serious disease that plagued British seamen. The scientist took twelve sailors with the disease who were about equally ill, and divided them into pairs. While this sounds like a simple enough procedure, Lind actually accomplished two important tasks.

Because the sailors all had about the same degree of illness, Lind had "matched" the subjects. No one could say that one sailor was sicker than any other before the experiment was begun, so any benefit or harm would not have been due to the initial condition of the subjects.

Next, he divided the group up randomly, thus eliminating another form of bias known as allocation bias. When a drug trial is started, it is important that no one person be deliberately chosen (allocated) to be in one group or another. (This also prevents doctors and researchers from determining whether a given subject is in one set or the other.)

Therefore, the patients are assigned to different test groups at random: by the flip of a coin, or by drawing lots, to be in one or another of the test sections. (Today, randomization is performed by a computer.)

Lind randomized the sailors to four test groups: one was given a quart of cider; one sulfuric acid; one six spoons of vinegar, sea water, and nutmeg—and the final participants were given two oranges and a lemon.

Lind wrote: "The consequence was, that the most sudden and visible good effects were perceived from the use of the oranges and lemons; one of those who had taken them being at the end of six days fit for duty . . .

the other [in the group fed fruit] was the best recovered of any in his condition and being now deemed pretty well was appointed nurse to the rest of the sick."[2]

Lind's trial eliminated allocation bias and illustrated the principle of random choices for therapy experiments. Lind also indirectly proved another critical idea. Therapy does not depend on understanding a disease or even how or why a remedy works. It was centuries later that researchers discovered that Vitamin C, contained in fruit, prevented scurvy.

Dr. Franklin faced a more daunting challenge than Lind. He not only had to assess a therapy viewed as miraculous, he had to do so by challenging one of the wiliest and most popular healers in Europe. The dramatic confrontation between the greatest scientist of his era and its greatest charlatan would forever alter medicine.

The name of the charlatan was Franz Anton Mesmer, a "fabulously charismatic" doctor so famous that he is immortalized by the technique he practiced: mesmerism. Mesmer knew a number of venerable medical principles. One is that a physician must have a strong, unshakable belief that his therapy works and must constantly and insistently advocate it, without hesitation or doubt.

The second principle is that the physician must elaborate a rationale for why the drug works. Perhaps it is the phase of the moon, or the motion of the planets, or an invisible enzyme called cox-2—it doesn't matter. What matters is that the principle sounds plausible, is new and inventive, and uses elaborate and scientifically advanced terms to explain its efficacy.

Mesmer recognized one other important principle. The scientific theory should be very difficult to either prove or disprove. The Vioxx cox-2 hypothesis fit all these principles perfectly. Doctors could not go into their exam rooms and investigate the effect of cox-2 on the stomach or the heart. They had to rely on experts, with varying points of view and, of course, distinctly opposing biases to render their opinions and provide data for them.

Mesmer's basic observation was that people placed into a relaxed state often gained a sense of well-being. That was nothing new, but Mesmer developed an elaborate system of "animal spiritualism" and "universal fluids"—often using magnets—to turn his simple observation into a modern miracle cure.

As it happened, Europe was undergoing a terrible epidemic known as "anxiety syndrome" or "disease of the nerves," which primarily affected women, but also enveloped many noted celebrities such as composer Wolfgang Amadeus Mozart. Mesmer first practiced his craft in Vienna, once the Roman settlement where Emperor Marcus Aurelius died, and now the influential capital of the Holy Roman Empire, known for its culture and cuisine.

Mesmer began curing the populace with his "special" magnetized soaking tubs. The doctor's looming presence as he presided over the therapy was an undeniable part of both its effectiveness and allure. Not a few women were known to swoon in Mesmer's presence and rumors flew through Vienna of notorious and highly clandestine love affairs.

Mesmer was despised by the medical authorities. It would be charitable to think that local physicians were particularly disturbed by Mesmer's lack of scientific evidence. More likely they were far more worried that patients were deserting them in droves, resulting in an intolerable loss of revenue.

Mesmer was eventually driven from Vienna and set up shop in Paris, where he was an immediate success. The French medical authorities became every bit as enraged as their Viennese counterparts—but they faced a dangerous dilemma. How could they disprove a celebrity doctor who seemed to cure everyone who entered his presence, including the Queen of France, Marie Antoinette?

The dyspeptic Louis XVI ordered a special panel of scientists to investigate Mesmer, but it failed in its first attempts to cast doubt on the mesmeric doctor's therapy. Dr. Franklin, now eighty and ill, the designated head of the French commission, studied the problem and came up with a brilliant new method of scientific assessment.

Mesmer claimed he could "magnetize" trees to effect his cure and was willing to travel to Franklin's estate to demonstrate.

Franklin had designed a careful experiment using two revolutionary methods that have since become the basis of modern drug research: the use of blinding and placebo. Mesmer magnetized four trees and was allowed to choose a patient to cure. A blindfold was placed over the eyes of the subject. (Yes, blinded trials really began with a blindfold.)

Then Franklin chose a fifth tree, which Mesmer was not allowed to magnetize. All agreed that this completely untreated tree, chosen at random, had no particular hypnotic powers whatsoever. This tree was known as the "placebo" or "control." It was the object against which the magnetized trees would be tested. To the outside observer, all the trees appeared similar.

The "blinded" patient was unaware of the proceedings and had no way of knowing which tree was magnetized (the active experimental group) and which tree was not (the placebo). The patient was also "blinded" from seeing the influential Mesmer himself.

The result of the experiment was that the patient or subject had the exact same reaction to the placebo tree as to those that were magnetized. Franklin proved that Mesmer's trees held no special therapeutic power. The commission used several other blinded trials and came up with the same result. They deduced that Mesmer's technique worked because of the doctor's power of persuasion and the belief by patients in the doctor's magnetized tubs. Franklin, and his fellow scientists, wrote up the experiment and Mesmer was put out of business.

Thus, by the end of the eighteenth century, much of the knowledge of the modern medical clinical trial had been established. Patients should be randomized to matching groups; be tested using both the active therapy and a control, or placebo; should not know which group they are in, nor be aware of whether they are getting an active drug or placebo. They must be blinded from the doctor who might influence the treatment.

Lind's and Franklin's experiments should have opened up an entirely new era in the evaluation of therapy. Unfortunately, neither trial did. It was not until almost 170 years later that the modern clinical trial was first established in England. And not until the 1970s and 1980s that the principle became accepted by most physicians—although controversy still remains.

In the nineteenth century, medicine took a great leap backward and useless and even dangerous pills continued to be dispensed. The question is why?

The scientific world made two very interesting conclusions about Franklin's experiments that were universally circulated with the impressive title "Report of Dr. Benjamin Franklin and Other Commissioners. Charged by the King of France, with the Examination of Animal Magnetism."[3]

The first conclusion was that Mesmer had not been entirely wrong. He had proved something very valuable—the power of the mind and a charismatic doctor to influence healing. This particular belief took hold where Mesmer first practiced, in Vienna. There, a young Sigmund Freud took up some of Mesmer's principles to develop a theory of how the mind and body interacted, how mental problems could be cured, and what role medication played in psychological illness.

Freud and other physicians and philosophers were fascinated by Mesmer's therapeutic results. Magnetized water may not have held any special medicinal therapies, but why were so many people "cured" by a remedy that had no inherent value? Clearly, the mind played an enormous part in determining health and general well-being. What if that power could be constructively harnessed in legitimate medical treatment?

Mesmerism and hypnotism moved from the realm of the charlatan to the research laboratory and physician's office.

Another by-product of Mesmer's work and the evolution of German chemistry was what effect new compounds could have on the mind and in healing mental illness. If a bogus remedy could cure nervous afflictions, surely one of the modern pharmaceutical remedies should have the same effect.

Freud developed a relationship with the company that he felt related to this concept: Merck of Darmstadt. Freud grasped the extraordinary influence on both mind and body of a new miracle pain medication known as cocaine. Surely the two were connected.

Because the "anxiety epidemic" worsened in the latter part of the nineteenth century, in part from the pressures of the industrial revolution, Merck sought to take the lead in developing additional pills to alleviate this condition. Cocaine brought in huge sums of money for the company, and at the outset of the twentieth century, Merck sought to expand its line of pain compounds to "own the market."

Merck succeeded. It developed a class of drugs known as barbiturates, or "hypnotics," the first of which, barbital, was released by Merck in association with the Bayer Company in the early 1900s. Barbital was the world's first synthetic psychiatric drug, and its ability to calm the agitated was remarkable. It also became the first drug effective for the treatment of epilepsy.

The Merck company was well on its way to leading the world in mind-altering substances, an expertise that would lead to a fantastic future little more than forty-five years into the new century. The "barbiturates" became one of the most widely sold compounds of the twentieth century and even found their way into the bourgeoning science of eugenics.

Between 1941 and 1945, because of its gentle, soothing action, phenobarbital and similar drugs were used in German psychiatric hospitals to kill five thousand children who were deemed of insufficient quality to survive in the new world of the Master Race.[4]

Benjamin Franklin's report caused the medical profession, and later drug concerns, to make another unexpected conclusion. They recognized that if they had to prove that a pill actually was effective in a controlled trial, then all of medicine might well be eliminated. Suppose every new compound that was being peddled in the eighteenth, nineteenth, and twentieth centuries had to go through the rigors of double-blind, placebo-controlled, randomized trials? The thought was frightening to quack and regular practitioner alike. The *Merck Manual* in 1899 contained mostly bogus remedies.[5] Included in the manual were such remedies as True Unicorn and tobacco, which were recommended to treat asthma and nymphomania (so as to cause nausea; effectual but depressing). In whose benefit would it have been to test them as they developed through the hundred years after Franklin's report? Certainly not the nostrum peddlers, who relied on advertisements and medicine shows. Nor the regular medical practioners, who used bloodletting, leeches, and arsenic.

In addition, if scientific clinical trials were demanded, the power of the doctor and the medical societies would vanish, their authority displaced.

In the early 1900s both *The Journal of the American Medical Association* and *The Lancet* developed laboratories to evaluate new drugs. But neither used randomized, controlled trials to evaluate remedies, and much of the reporting was grounded on the age-old system of relying on "medical authorities."

The greatest of these at the time was Dr. William Osler, one of the founders of the Johns Hopkins Hospital in Baltimore and a doctor known as the "physicians' physician." Osler held professorships at no fewer than three universities: Hopkins, McGill in Montreal, and Oxford. One would think that by the 1920s, the principles evolved from Benjamin Franklin would have been well accepted. They weren't. In fact, by 1916, Osler and his colleagues had lost faith in many of the "medical miracles" that had poured out of Germany.

A. D. Blackader, M.D., professor of pharmacology and therapeutics, McGill University, wrote in July 1916, "Years ago [drugs] were deemed to be of the first importance; without them there was no therapy. To-day, with the exception of the few which have a definite specific action on some of the discovered causes of disease, drugs in general have been relegated to a distinctly secondary place. For the cure of disease the physician to-day places more confidence in fresh air; on rest . . . or a carefully arranged diet . . . and on a rational application of the principles of hydrotherapy."[6]

In other words, fresh air, good food, and a warm bath.

No wonder. In his famous medical textbook, Dr. Osler laid down his leading choices for the treatment of diabetes: opium and arsenic. It certainly would not have been a wise choice to be a diabetic in the early twentieth century seeking treatment at world-famous Johns Hopkins. A female patient would not have fared much better, although at least she would have lived. Osler is quoted in the authoritative 1936 version of the *Merck Manual* as recommending Dover's Powder for menstrual cramps. "However if the congestion is due to masturbation or unhygienic sex life, these conditions need to be taken care of."[7] The *Manual* does not say how.

Besides which, doctors were considered "artists," not scientists in a laboratory, as "chemists" were perceived. They had no problem with the notion that like Mesmer they healed because of their own charismatic (some might say divine) powers. Statistics and clinical trials were for mathematicians, not those who practiced by the "bedside." Numbers and dots ignored the fact that all patients are different and need "individual" treatments to heal them. Only a great man could determine whether a therapy worked, not a statistician.

In some ways, therefore, Mesmer won out. It was more important to develop an elaborate theory about a pill and someone to endorse it than to design a careful clinical trial to objectively make sure it worked. And it was certainly more important for doctors to take on the role of mesmeric and caring healers than to become enmeshed in the minutiae of randomized experiments. Later, motion pictures and television created a genre of healers who by their very nature seemed to radiate cure. Drs. Kildare and Marcus Welby relied more on the techniques of Anton Mesmer than the therapies of the pharmaceutical industry.

The year 1962 was a momentous one in the history of medicine. President John F. Kennedy signed into law the Kefauver-Harris Amendments, introduced in Congress by Tennessee senator Estes Kefauver and Arkansas representative Oren Harris. For the first time, any new drug that was approved in the United States had to prove, not only that it was safe, but *that it actually worked*. And for the first time, anybody who entered an experiment to test a new drug had to be given "informed consent." In other words, patients had to know the exact risks and benefits of a drug before it could be tested on them.

The enforcement powers were given to the Food and Drug Administration, which had been established in 1906 and already had the authority, although severely limited, to regulate drug advertising.

The Kefauver-Harris Drug Control Act seemed to finally bring medicine into a new scientific era. Doctors would now have precise, scientifically verified information about how well a drug worked *before* either prescribing or recommending it.

So it is all the more curious that the American Medical Association, which was founded on the principle of separating "ethical" from "unethical" drugs, sharply opposed the idea. Dr. Hugh H. Hussey, dean of Georgetown University's School of Medicine and chairman of the AMA's board of trustees, put the organization's position eloquently: "efficacy" is beyond the FDA's power to judge because it is a misleading term: "A drug that works for one patient may be useless for another with what appears to be the same illness, and only the individual physician treating the individual patient can determine efficacy in each case. . . . The marketing of a relatively useless drug is infinitely less serious than would be arbitrary exclusion from the market of a drug that might have been lifesaving for many persons."[8]

This opinion was shared by many other physicians and would have been heartily endorsed by Dr. Benjamin Brandreth. He had hundreds of testimonials from both physicians and patients that said his Vegetable Universal Pills worked.

Most thrilled of all by the AMA's position would have been the manufacturers of Kickapoo Indian Sagwa—a relatively useless drug if ever there was one, but lifesaving for anyone with addled blood.

Dr. Philip Needleman and Pfizer would never have agreed with either Ben Franklin or Estes Kefauver.

Needleman and his counterpart at Merck, Edward Scolnick, may have been scientists, but both were surrounded by a system of belief—the bias that made it obvious that Celebrex and Vioxx worked. In order to sell their products, Pfizer and Merck created a mystique around their drugs. If Dorothy Hamill could resume a championship ice-skating career after taking Vioxx, just how important was the randomized, placebo-controlled, double-blind trial? The word many people and doctors used to describe the Vioxx commercials that played night and day for years was "*mesmerizing.*"

The AMA and other medical groups lost the battle not to have a government agency assess whether or not a pill worked. The Kefauver-Harris Amendments became the law of the land. However, many questions remained. How effective does a drug have to be? How long does it take to prove a drug is effective? Most complicated of all, how does a company go about proving whether a drug *is* effective?

Ben Franklin established that hypnotized trees did not help a soul. But he did not chart a method to find out if something *did* work. The answer to that question is one of the most challenging in medicine—and one that both Merck and Pfizer feverishly addressed in order to win the battle of the superiority of their drugs.

CHAPTER 13

Is Super Aspirin Safe and Effective?

Facts do not accumulate on the blank slates of researchers' minds and data simply do not speak for themselves.[1]

By 1998, *everyone* knew that a miracle drug for pain was at hand. Dr. Jerome Groopman said so. Dr. Lee Simon said so. Many of the faculties of the world's leading universities said so. The financial analysts said so. Dr. Philip Needleman of Pfizer/Searle said so. Dr. Edward Scolnick of Merck said so. Prestigious medical organizations said so. The media said so.

About the only authorities who didn't say so were Ben Franklin and Galen. But they were long dead.

On March 24, 1998, the Food and Drug Administration held an advisory committee meeting to determine: "NSAID Cox-2 Safety Issues." The meeting was public—meaning anyone, expert or not—could attend and comment on the issue.

Advisory committees are composed of independent, nongovernment medical experts who specialize in a drug or issue on which the FDA wishes advice. The most important role of an advisor is to supply unbiased opinions. In other words, just as clinical trials must be designed to eliminate bias, so must be the FDA advisors who *interpret* data. Everyone grasps the fact that in order to prove whether a drug is safe and effective, the tests of the drug must be carefully and scientifically designed and carried out. Less appreciated, and even ignored, is the fact that *interpretation* of data is just as important. Without totally unbiased and objective analysis, the best medical trials in the world are completely useless. Interpretation can produce sound judgments or systematic error.[2]

Because of that, the FDA is required to determine the biases of any member of the committee and determine whether they would influence the advisor's conclusions. To that end, the secretary of the committee must read off the "conflict of interest" statement to all the members involved in the meeting. The March 24 disclosure is one of the strangest in FDA history, especially considering the multibillion-dollar potential of Vioxx, Celebrex, and other cox-2 inhibiting agents.

The secretary stated: "This is a conflict of interest statement. . . . The following announcement addresses the issue of conflict of interest with regard to this meeting and is made a part of the record to preclude *even the appearance* [emphasis added] of such at this meeting. . . . In accordance with 18 United States Code 208, general matters waivers have been granted to *all* Committee participants who have interests in companies or organizations which could be affected by the Committee's discussions of NSAID COX-2 agents."[3]

In plain language, to avoid even the *appearance* of a conflict of interest, any member of the panel, no matter what his or her arrangement with the drug companies (who were in a multibillion-dollar race to get approval of cox-2 agents) would be permitted to give the FDA, the public, and the media any opinion they wished without having to say a word about their motives.

This was certainly a good idea. Three months after the committee met, four of the participants would be jetting off to Hawaii for further discussions and receive Cox in Paradise T-shirts: Dr. Michelle Petri, committee chairman, Dr. Steven Abramson (designated to succeed Petri), Dr. Lee Simon (who was conducting clinical trials for Searle and Celebrex), and Dr. James Witter, a pivotal player in the FDA's oversight of super aspirin.

Stranger still was the avowed purpose of the committee. It was to give drug companies "guidance" on how to construct its clinical trials and what criteria would be used to judge the safety and effectiveness of the drugs.

Drug development for Vioxx and Celebrex had started in 1993–94. It was now 1998, four to five years after the companies had begun testing their drugs. Searle was about to submit its final data in three months.

Why would the FDA hold a meeting four years after a drug started to be tested to determine what tests would be necessary to determine its approval? And why would Dr. Lee Simon, who had already completed the final trial, be called upon at this point to tell Pfizer/Searle how to conduct one?

About the only thing either Pfizer or Merck could do at this point to change the years of experiments they had already conducted was to make typographical or subtle changes in their submission documents. As it turned out, this was not far from the truth. The companies could now easily tailor their slides and presentations to comply with the committee's recommendations. Merck and Pfizer resorted to considerable deceit. In Merck's case, one of its Vioxx papers published in *The New England Journal of Medicine* (*NEJM*) was brought into severe disrepute because of exclusions, deletions, and rearrangement of data. These alterations spelled huge profits.[4] Certain of Merck's conclusions on a second paper were also questioned.

This was the APPROVe study, the clinical trial for colon cancer that Merck claimed caused it to withdraw Vioxx. The company's statistician made an unfortunate "mathematical error" that caused the *NEJM* to demand a correction. In the case of the VIGOR study, another important trial, Merck deleted three heart attacks in the Vioxx group, greatly improving the outcome, the *NEJM* editors stated.

The March advisory committee took place as planned. The FDA cared so much about digging out the truth that they brought in a "special advisor" in gastroenterology, Dr. Loren Laine, who turned out to be a leading spokesperson for Vioxx and principal author of the study known as VIGOR that was used to prove whether Vioxx caused more serious ulcers than older NSAIDs. The study was published in the *NEJM* but was one of the two Vioxx studies later questioned.

The entire March FDA committee proceeding took place about forty-five years after the Kefauver-Harris Act, demanding safety and efficacy for any new prescription drug. And occurred several centuries after Benjamin Franklin established the importance of eliminating bias.

Could Merck and Searle pass this critical examination by people granted waivers if they worked for the companies? The suspense in the advisory committee room was . . . not exactly overwhelming.

There were two essential questions. The first one was very simple. Could super aspirin solve the initial medical "crisis" at hand: that is to say could it reduce the number of hospital admissions and deaths being caused by standard NSAIDs? The second question was what level of proof would be required in order to establish this?

Unfortunately, not a shred of evidence existed that answered the first question. Neither Merck nor Pfizer had performed a study demonstrating that so much as one less person would present to the emergency room (or die of a bleeding ulcer) by taking Vioxx or Celebrex rather than Aleve.

The reason such a study had never been done was that they were very expensive, very complicated, very lengthy, and very risky. Risky because neither company could be sure of the answer. If no fewer people could be proven to enter the hospital or die with super aspirin, the pharmaceutical companies would each lose years of research and billions of dollars of actual and potential revenue.

An outcomes study with super aspirin would return us to the question James Lind and Benjamin Franklin first addressed. It would have to take a medical hypothesis: Take the number of people admitted to the hospital with complicated ulcers, that is, very serious ulcers, and compare the results in two different groups of patients.

In other words, Merck and Pfizer would have to perform a placebo-controlled, randomized, double-blind trial comparing Aleve, Motrin, or a similar drug against super aspirin (an outcomes trial), with the objective of finding out how many people died of ulcers in each group and how often they were admitted to an emergency room. Conducting such trials could further delay the drugs' approvals, and both Merck and Pfizer were under intense pressure to get their compounds on the market.

So both companies tried to get their drugs approved by the world's regulatory agencies by conducting what are known as endoscopy studies. An endoscope is a very narrow tube that is inserted down a patient's throat and into the stomach cavity. A specialist can see the lining of the stomach and examine it for sores and erosions. Pictures of the stomach may also be taken for further analysis.

Thus what Merck and Pfizer did was to give both animals and humans various NSAIDs, including Vioxx and Celebrex, and compare the number of stomach sores. The fact that much fewer (or none as Lee Simon famously stated) occurred with super aspirin seemed proof of the remarkable safety of cox-2 inhibitors, *without* performing an outcomes trial.

The FDA advisory committee engaged in a lively debate as to whether sores found in the stomach had anything to do with dying in a hospital of a complicated ulcer.

The most immediate problem was simple. There was no evidence that the number of sores, or even their size, led to hospital admissions or even whether there was a correlation between the sores and the development of ulcers. The problem went beyond that. Hospital admissions and death are caused by very serious ulcers that promote stomach bleeding or holes (perforation).

So the issue was more complex than just the relation of stomach sores to ulcers. The question was if the correlation between the sores and ulcers was serious enough to cause hospital admission and death. At first there was a debate about the meaning of both the size and depth of the sores. But a number of experts pointed out this was extremely difficult to measure.

Another problem is that stomach sores come and go. In other words, when a person has an endoscopy, a sore might show up, but the sore might go away as a natural part of the body's healing process. Then there was the matter of observation bias or "greed": as Merck advisor Dr. Loren Laine put it: "We have to remember that when you're talking about these studies, there's an economic incentive [for] the investigator to find an ulcer, because if he finds an ulcer he enters the patient [into a study] and he or she gets lots of money for that endoscopy."[5] In other words, good health does not pay. This point was immediately seized on by Dr. Lee Simon: "To take your comments before, Loren, to its obvious conclusion and the sake of argument, why in the world would we do endoscopy trials at all, if in fact they're not predictive, if in fact we can't know what the real outcome will be, other than the costs associated with supporting the field of gastroenterology?"[6]

"Which is not unimportant," Laine replied, undoubtedly trying to be witty.

Laine finally admitted there's no particular reason to do an endoscopy trial in the first place, "if you're worried about clinical outcome." Yet no clinical outcomes trial had ever been done.

Wasn't the whole purpose of developing super aspirin to prevent death and emergency room admissions, not to mention any other clinical outcome such as milder ulcers or even stomachaches?

The committee's doctors haggled for several more hours, their tone and demeanor sounding more and more like a debate from the thirteenth-century Medical School in Paris, where students and faculty argued over the precise meaning of Galen's thousand-year-old text, without ever performing an experiment to test its validity.

Finally, a breath of fresh air blew in from an FDA committee member who represented the patients and had no M.D. or Ph.D.: Leona Malone. She said: "There should be a way in medical training that the doctor has to get the ailment—that they can somehow give you the ailment for a week—and you have to live through everything that the patient has to go through, and I think you would be a lot more understanding." (In other words, Ms. Malone was saying none of the doctors in the room knew what they were talking about because none of them had ever experienced the ailment being studied.)

Ms. Malone continued: "This [debate] is very confusing because all I've heard is that with the endoscopy, the results don't mean anything anyhow. So why are we haggling over this? I mean obviously there must have been some thought as to why to do the endoscopy, that it must be proving *something*."

Dr. Michelle Petri: "Well, I think the bottom line is that ulcers are not good."

Malone: "Which we knew from the start."[7]

Dr. Petri and Ms. Malone both agreed that if the FDA recommended super aspirin for prevention of severe stomach ulcers, then it should actually back up the assertion with clear scientific evidence. "You have to be very definite," both agreed.

The advisory committee finally decided that in order to get super aspirin approved, endoscopy studies would be all that was needed, but that an outcomes study would be mandated in the future. Four months later, Dr. Jerome Groopman would publish the incredible story of super aspirin in *The New Yorker* and not a word of what Leona Malone said would ever be mentioned.

Why was everyone so excited on the basis of endoscopy studies that proved nothing? And if that was the case, what was the FDA going to do: Say a drug was effective but that no study actually proved it?

It didn't matter. Merck and Pfizer designed and interpreted their own trials with their own statisticians and scientists. Hence the outcome was only of doubt to the medical doctors who published the results.

CHAPTER 14

The Cool Blonde

It was a blonde. A blonde to make a bishop kick a hole in a stained-glass window.

—**Raymond Chandler,** *Farewell, My Lovely*

In addition to Merck's chief counsel, Kenneth Frazier, Merck had another brilliant and charismatic executive to carry forward the Vioxx development plan. Dr. Alise Reicin, a graduate of Harvard Medical School, had comparatively little experience in the pharmaceutical industry before joining Merck, but her ambition, poise, and manner quickly impressed nearly all with whom she came in contact.

Some have described her as a "Hitchcock blonde": beautiful, brainy, immaculately dressed, and highly articulate—with an alluring aura that drew people to her (like moths to a flame). Although brilliant and insightful, she put on no showy pretense. An easygoing, friendly manner overlay an intense and dedicated scientist who could work days at a stretch to come up with a solution, yet show not the slightest sense of strain.

Dr. Reicin was a team player who could get along with executives at the highest level, as well as the most humble research assistants. She could galvanize support and incisively, authoritatively, and lucidly make her points. And no one doubted her toughness. She could deal with the most ego-driven academic investigators and leave no question about what Merck wanted, or in some cases, *demanded*.

But, as it would turn out, perhaps her greatest asset was her ability to explain science, ethics, and the complex issues of a clinical trial with warmth and sincerity.

At one Vioxx court trial, Reicin was asked by a juror about the fate of the animals involved in the Merck rodent studies. Faced with this question, many investigators would probably have stifled a laugh and explained that rats and mice by the hundreds are killed and dissected (sacrificed) in order to learn the workings of a drug. Blood and animal parts are common sights in drug company labs and are hardly given a second thought.

But Reicin took a different tack. She smiled warmly at the juror and suddenly her face took on a look of concern. Reicin explained, her voice gentle and understanding, that Merck had no choice in some cases but to sacrifice the animals, quickly and humanely, in order to better protect patients.

The juror seemed extremely pleased by the answer.

Merck eventually won the case. It is unlikely that this single answer by itself influenced the trial outcome, but as any lawyer will explain, jurors in complex cases often base their verdicts more on their impressions of the witnesses than the facts. Dr. Reicin was superb in both areas.

A few weeks after the March Arthritis Advisory Committee meeting, Merck found itself in a serious bind. Not only had the committee, with the agreement of the FDA, mandated an outcomes trial, but Pfizer/Searle had already started a study known as CLASS. Pfizer may have been impressed by Dr. Needleman's assurance that Celebrex worked because he had seen the results of patient recovery with his own eyes, but the company did have to come up with some scientific proof to support the assertion.

The dynamics of the bitter cox war now changed again. If Pfizer succeeded in demonstrating their drug safer in an outcomes trial, and Merck had no comparative data, Pfizer was assured a huge victory in the super aspirin competition.[1]

Merck had struggled since the early days of testing Vioxx to design a trial to determine if Vioxx prevented serious ulcers and death, but eventually canceled it. Many believed that the reason was the risk that the study would show more cardiovascular events in the Vioxx arm than the group given other NSAIDs. Merck had hoped to get its approval and win the race to get Vioxx to market on the basis of endoscopic studies and small-scale human trials—not a full-blown outcomes study that could result in a negative conclusion. Another controversy about conducting such a trial concerns whether to allow the use of aspirin in conjunction with Vioxx.

As related earlier, there was another problem, which very few people worried about. What if combining aspirin with Vioxx actually made patients worse? Until two drugs are actually studied together, no one can safely predict an outcome, and such a clinical trial had not been done with this combination in any large study. It seemed a no-win situation for the company.

In fact, so great had been the concern during the planning of the first outcomes study that a senior Merck scientist wrote a confidential memo saying that such a clinical trial could "kill [the] drug."[2] Dr. Alise Reicin was highly skeptical. "I just can't wait to be the one to present those results to senior management," she wrote in a confidential e-mail.[3]

Another huge problem hung over an outcomes trial. If the company had doubts about the danger of heart attacks, or either the inclusion or exclusion of aspirin, how should the informed consent forms read?

In order to do a huge human trial of this kind, many hospitals would have to be involved. Hospital ethics committees known as institutional review boards would have to sign off on these forms. Clearly, the company was concerned about the cardiovascular risks of Vioxx because of the FitzGerald studies and other human tests, but how much of that concern should be shared with doctors and patients?

Informed patient consent is one of the most important parts of the 1973 FDA reform acts. Any violation of this agreement would be an extremely serious breach of medical ethics.

In spite of all these serious problems, by 1998, Merck could no longer dodge the outcomes trial issue. The FDA would never allow Merck to make the safety claims about Vioxx it needed to win in the marketplace without such a study—and there was a distinct possibility that if Pfizer's trial was successful, Vioxx would be crushed.

Both Merck's marketing and Merck's science departments were for once in exact agreement. Merck *had* to move forward. In fact, while the company tried to maintain a calm demeanor in presentations to the press and financial community, inside the corporation the pressure and intensity caused by the Vioxx competition was creating unbearable stress. One possible solution to making the trial look better for Vioxx was to try to exclude patients at risk of heart disease. A secret Merck memo by Alise

Reicin suggested an approach out of a Hitchcock film: "What about the idea of excluding high risk CV [heart disease] patients, i.e. those that have already had an MI [heart attack], CABG [bypass surgery], or PTCA [procedure to widen artery]? This may decrease the CV event rate so that a difference between the two groups would not be evident. The only problem would be: Would we be able to recruit any patients?"[4]

"We're going to be putting Prozac in the cafeteria water soon," Merck employees joked. Scientists and regulators were burning out trying to complete the Vioxx FDA submission—and the marketing and finance departments were working and reworking profit figures to calculate just how much they were going to lose by coming in *second* to Celebrex. The figures were in the hundreds of millions of dollars.

"This is not a company that comes in second," was the refrain from senior management. But Searle *was* ahead, and Pfizer management seemed to be taking a particularly spiteful pride in beating the industry's then number one company. Merck marketing chief David Anstice put out the word to pull out all the stops to prepare for battle, a sentiment echoed by science head Dr. Edward Scolnick.

None of this was lost on Dr. Alise Reicin, who, despite her doubts, was designated the "clinical monitor" of the Vioxx Gastrointestinal Outcomes Research trial or VIGOR. As such she was the point person for all medical aspects of the trial, including the design, administration, analysis, and interpretation of the resulting data.

Why exactly Dr. Reicin was chosen for perhaps the most important clinical trial in modern Merck history will never be exactly known. It is possible that sensing the trial might end in disaster, no one more senior would take the job.

It is also possible that senior executives were already planning a legal defense strategy, should the outcome prove that Vioxx was toxic to the heart.

Most likely, though, was that Dr. Reicin had the commitment, energy, and drive to perform the task, and she was brilliant in court. A *Philadelphia Inquirer* reporter described her thusly: "Reicin, appearing polished and confident, has engaged in a tense back-and-forth with attorney David Buchanan, who has tried to show Merck knew about certain risks but did not disclose them fully or promptly. Sitting near the jurors, Reicin would answer Buchanan curtly, then almost always turn to smile and stare at jurors, seemingly trying to make eye contact with each one."[5] When Reicin was pressed about her loyalties to Vioxx, she snapped back at Buchanan and said, "Whether it was good for sales or bad for sales didn't matter to me. . . . I wanted to do what was right for patients taking Vioxx."[6]

True to the worries expressed earlier by Merck scientists and outside consultants, VIGOR would indeed turn out to be one of the most controversial medical trials ever conducted. Its results were eventually published in *The New England Journal of Medicine*—and then repudiated by the editors after discoveries of "improprieties." Reicin became involved in disputes, accusations, and Vioxx litigations. The VIGOR results are still debated and all the issues may never be resolved.

But in August 1998, Dr. Reicin plunged in. Using many of the great resources available to Merck, the physician set out to design a trial that would once and for all prove that Vioxx was not only super aspirin, but the *best* super aspirin. It was a high-stakes gamble on which many thought the future of Merck—and to some degree, the future reputation of organized medicine—rested.

By the late twentieth century, the design of medical trials had moved far beyond those designed by Ben Franklin, but they might not have ever taken hold had it not been for a brilliant experiment performed shortly after the end of World War II. The study involved one of the most important drugs ever developed, the application of statistics to medicine, a pharmaceutical company on its way to a Nobel Prize, and one of the world's most famous writers. The principles established by the trial would determine how the pharmaceutical industry developed and how the VIGOR trial came to be so controversial.

In one of medical history's oddest coincidences, the plight of the world-famous British writer George Orwell, who wrote the novel *1984*, illustrates the remarkable set of circumstances that gave scientists the ability to plan the world's first modern, large-scale, randomized clinical trial. This study involved testing the medicine streptomycin, a true miracle drug developed during World War II in the 1940s. The drug showed promise in eliminating one of the world's most deadly and debilitating diseases, tuberculosis. It would have been debatably unethical to deny this drug to sufferers, but British investigators had a unique, if grim opportunity. There simply was not enough of the compound to put into general use. Hence a study was allowed by ethics committees that allowed some patients to get streptomycin and others to be given the best alternative care available. To be absolutely fair, patients who received streptomycin had to be chosen completely "at random." By being forced to make this macabre decision, modern medicine was born.

George Orwell hated armed conflict. He had fought against Nazi-backed troops during the Spanish Civil War in 1937 and was nearly killed when a bullet struck his neck. Friends commented that he was a very lucky man. Orwell replied that he would have been "much luckier" if he had never been struck at all.

Orwell also hated dictatorship. After World War II, Orwell's feeling about this form of government became all the more evident as Allied troops poured into the remnants of Hitler's Germany, sifting through the rubble of enforced labor and extermination camps. The air was filled with the stench of decaying corpses. Even more horrifying from a medical point of view was that the German pharmaceutical industry had used these camps to conduct medical experiments on unwilling prisoners of war. The German Merck company, which since the end of World War I was separate from the American Merck, was one of the first to use slave labor. (In 1918, the German Merck company was stripped of its patents in the United States. The United States Merck subsidiary, founded by the first George Merck in 1890, was put up for sale. In a brilliant financial maneuver, Merck repurchased all of the stock and kept the name of the company. From that time on there have been two Merck companies, one headquartered in Darmstadt, Germany, and one headquartered in New Jersey. Today, the companies remain separate.)

George Orwell had already gained fame by writing *Animal Farm*. But the revulsion of the war inspired him to write another book—a book about the ultimate totalitarian state that would be capable of committing the horrors of World War II on a routine basis. This state would be run by Big Brother and would be set in the far-off time of 1984.

Orwell went to Scotland to write the book, but the work was hard-going. By 1947, he was dying of infectious tuberculosis. Word spread quickly in England that a pharmaceutical company in the United States had succeeded in finally coming up with a cure for this illness. This cure, streptomycin, had ironically been developed by the cousin of the German Merck, Merck America.

The leader of the American Merck in 1947 was George Wilhelm (W.) Emanuel Merck, son of the founder George Merck. George W. Merck was in the process of establishing the company as the world's leading pharmaceutical corporation, inventing and manufacturing truly scientific drugs that would alter the treatment of disease.

In America, streptomycin was rapidly combating tuberculosis, then the world's most prevalent and dangerous infectious disease. But England did not have either the financial currency or the resources to purchase or manufacture the drug. The country only had a tiny supply, and how and to whom it should be provided became a major postwar dilemma, perhaps no better illustrated than by George Orwell's plight.

In order to solve the problem, England turned to its best scientists for an answer. The solution came from a brilliant British medical epidemiologist named Dr. Austin Bradford Hill. Hill had written a series of pioneering articles about how to conduct clinical trials in *The Lancet* that culminated in a book, *Principles of Medical Statistics,* in 1937.[7] The articles, book, and lectures became the basis of drug evaluation in the twentieth and twenty-first centuries.[8]

Hill's goal was in some ways unthinkable and abhorrent to the medical profession, for it would eventually remove the medical assessment of pills from the opinions of doctors and place it under the more objective control of mathematicians. Hill was in part building on Franklin's assumption 150 years earlier that various biases have to be removed from the drug testing process. Franklin and others had already shown the need to blind the patient and create a control or placebo group. But Franklin's study, and those that succeeded it, were fairly small and did not involve analyzing large groups.

Furthermore, Hill used not only advances in mathematical theory, but those from psychology. The importance and understanding of human bias was derived in part from the work of Sigmund Freud (who, as previously noted, had a brief relationship with the Merck pharmaceutical company). Freud theorized that humans acted on the basis of unconscious motivations and desires. This meant that doctors might add bias to a drug trial even if they were unaware they were doing so. Hill's *Principles of Medical Statistics* made frequent mention of unconscious bias.

Another problem that Hill had to contend with was that in a placebo-controlled trial, one group was getting treatment, while the other was not. Was this ethical, even though the treatment was unproven? After all, researchers must have seen *something* that made streptomycin seem therapeutic. How then could they justify not giving ill people this substance?

Hill's answer was that the RCT was not justified "if the drug showed dramatic results." But he argued that this was seldom the case. Later drug designers overcame this obstacle by using the data and safety monitoring board (DSMB), the only group of people who would have access to the results of the ongoing study. However, the DSMB itself is blinded as to which group is receiving the experimental drug, and which group is taking placebo. If the DSMB is biased in any way, the trial is considered "contaminated," hence useless.

Hill's greatest contribution was explaining the notion of randomization. For a drug trial to be fair, each group being tested had to be equal. In other words, any factor favoring the outcome of the experiment had to be the same in each group. For example, if scientists were testing a new drug for arthritis, each group would need to have the same number of men and women, they would need to be close in age and weight, and they would need to have an equal severity of disease.

These factors are easy to match in each set of patients. But Hill reasoned, correctly, that patients might have many other factors that could affect the outcome that would not be apparent to researchers. How then could the experiment be made fair? Hill explained that once the obvious matches were made, patients without any obvious differences would be placed *at random* into each trial set.

Therefore, the characteristics comprising each group would turn out to be the same, because the computer generating the codes that would assign people into one group or another would make its choices with no bias whatsoever, unlike doctors, who might make unconscious decisions.

The Medical Research Council of England (MRC), the government group responsible for public health, had secured a small amount of streptomycin from the Merck company and was given the job of testing its effectiveness. (Merck had started such tests in the United States, but the early results proved so successful that studies were abandoned and the drug made available to anyone with tuberculosis. This was good in the sense that many were cured, but bad because many issues of how best to use the drug and its side effects remained. The Medical Research Council needed to resolve the issues, the most important of which was who benefited most from the rare drug.)

The MRC and other groups in the United States had performed drug trials similar to the one Hill designed. Like each advance in science, a number of people could be considered "first." Hill is generally given credit for a number of reasons. He had "written the book" on RCTs and lectured on many of its principles. Even more important, the publication of this particular trial captivated scientists both because of its precision and undoubtedly because it resolved the question of cure for the most common deadly disease affecting the human race.

Hill and the MRC proceeded by giving one group of patients the best nondrug cure known at the time. This consisted of being placed in a special hospital where they were exposed to fresh air, excellent diets, warm baths, and rest. The other group received the same care, with the addition of streptomycin.

The characteristics of a successful outcome were proposed in advance (lessening of symptoms such as coughing, and general, overall health improvement). Thus, the study was "prospective." Who got placed in the active and placebo groups was purely by chance: randomized. Patients did not know whether they were participating in the experiment.

The modern drug trial was now in place: prospective, blinded, randomized trials—RCTs.

Ironically, Orwell's hospital in Scotland was not chosen by the MRC and the writer did not initially get the drug. His publisher managed to make a special arrangement with the United States government to obtain a small amount for him. It seemed to work at first, but the author developed an allergy to it and could not continue treatments. As he was dying, Orwell attempted to finish the novel he called *1984,* but was dissatisfied that he did not have time to make corrections.[9] He died in 1948, at almost the same time the Medical Research Council published its pioneering work on streptomycin in the *British Medical Journal.*

The study caused a medical sensation and Hill was invited to both write and speak in the United States, where his methods began to be both debated and adapted.

Hill was a brilliant and entertaining speaker who argued for simplicity in medical statistics, pleading his own ignorance of certain realms of mathematics. He told audiences: "When I got to the subject of statistical tests of significance, I started by stating that these were based on the laws of probability over which statisticians quarreled violently. I was entirely ignorant of them but I knew more than the lady who congratulated her friend on the birth of triplets. 'It is remarkable,' said the mother, 'Getting pregnant with triplets happens only one in 8,000 times.' 'Good gracious,' said the friend, 'However did you find time for the housework?' "[10]

But Hill's most important statement and one that Dr. Alise Reicin of Merck must have pondered in trying to design the impossible VIGOR trial was this: "You can prove anything by statistics," and "you can prove nothing by statistics. You can 'prove' anything by the misuse of statistics, and politicians, advertisers do just that, and unless you know something about them you will be misled. In the strict sense of the word 'proven' you can 'prove' nothing, but you can make one interpretation of the data more probable than any other."[11]

And that explains more than anything else why the VIGOR outcomes study was so "successful." Whereas Hill founded the principle of eliminating bias, Merck introduced bias from the start. Because of the danger that there would be more heart attacks in the Vioxx group, VIGOR investigators sought to reduce the number of people who would be at risk of heart attack and stroke. And, according to Merck's own Martin Report, to ensure that Vioxx was shown to be less harmful to the stomach than standard NSAIDs, investigators chose naproxen (Aleve), an NSAID known to be more harsh on the stomach than others at the given dose.

Over and over, Merck repeated the pattern that Hill had warned about, trying to make their outcome study, VIGOR, a success by the misuse of statistics as well as the inclusion of bias.

But in a war, both sides eventually use the same weapons. Pfizer fired back with its own data, and soon both doctors and patients were seeing "carefully designed clinical studies" that *proved* Vioxx was safer and more effective than Celebrex, and Celebrex was safer and more effective than Vioxx.

In the end, the new world of medical objectivity that Austin Bradford Hill had spent so many decades developing became no more helpful than the magnets used by Anton Mesmer to cure his patients. The trials of Vioxx and Celebrex might as well have been based on the astrological signs that governed when and how bloodletting should be administered.

Eventually the data would have to be submitted to both the FDA and a very high-quality medical journal. Clearly, Merck's doubts about the possible cardiovascular side effects of Vioxx would now be revealed by the federal agency.

CHAPTER 15

Celebrex Meets the FDA

It was like Midas had touched me and I was a pot of gold.
—Margaret Burton, Celebrex user

Dr. Denis McCarthy, professor of gastroenterology and special advisor to the FDA, watched the audience file into the meeting room at the Town Center Hotel in Silver Spring, Maryland, on December 1, 1998. He did not quite know what to expect. For years, he had read stories about Celebrex and Vioxx and heard lectures at medical meetings, but after reading the FDA briefing book on Celebrex, he was left "confused and concerned."[1]

The hype leading up to the advisory committee meeting on Celebrex was extraordinary, and the audience of reporters, drug analysts, pharmaceutical experts, and government officials was stretching out the door.

The Pfizer/Searle team led by Dr. Phil Needleman was already in high gear, reviewing notes and slides and making last-minute adjustments on their laptops. They appeared the models of efficiency—and McCarthy noted they were backed up by some of the best-known experts in gastroenterology and rheumatology.

Drs. Michele Petri and Lee Simon were not on the committee panel. The acting head of the FDA advisory committee was Dr. Steven Abramson. Leading the FDA team across from Searle was Dr. James Witter. Neither man should have been surprised by the presentation, because they had heard it in Hawaii six months earlier.

Shortly after the FDA advisory meeting began at 8:00 A.M., any thought that this would be an ordinary FDA hearing was erased. Phil Needleman started the presentation by introducing the data for Pfizer/Searle.

As always, Needleman was a mesmerizing personality who endowed

Celebrex with the miracle power previously thought to be possessed by magnetized water. Once again he told the amazing story of how his team had made the revolutionary discovery of the cox-2 inhibitors and their years of sweat, toil, and dedication.

New statistics indicated that the menace of ordinary NSAIDs was worse. They were now estimated to be causing 16,000 deaths a year and over 100,000 hospitalizations, a figure that Dr. Witter of the FDA accepted. It seemed that the release of super aspirin could not have come a moment too soon.

The audience loved the story. Needleman's enthusiasm was contagious. About the only people who were not enjoying the show were gathered in a conference room in Merck headquarters watching the video feed.

The Pfizer/Searle team presented its data—and it was outstanding. The company requested approval of Celebrex for osteoarthritis, rheumatoid arthritis, and acute pain.

Finally, it was the FDA's turn. Their manner was completely different—unrehearsed, somewhat awkward. Their slides had none of the elegance of those from Searle. Most in the audience didn't seem to care.

The FDA reviewer stated: "The studies failed to provide evidence of efficacy for celecoxib [Celebrex] in the management of acute post-surgical pain. . . .

"The osteoarthritis studies showed some positive results but still inconclusive evidence of efficacy in the treatment of acute pain.

"And we believe for these reasons, celecoxib at this time has not yet met the requirements to gain the treatment of acute pain indication."[2]

The FDA further stated that no outcomes data existed that would support the fact that Celebrex caused fewer ulcers than other NSAIDs. Even looking at tiny erosions in the stomach, celecoxib was no different from the popular NSAID Voltaren. The FDA recommended that Searle perform a large-scale outcomes trial to gain more proof.

There was a slight pause after the FDA finished—as if no one could quite believe what they had heard . . . super aspirin was not approved for acute pain? Super aspirin was no safer to the stomach than Voltaren? *Super aspirin didn't even seem as good in some ways as regular aspirin.*

The committee broke for lunch and spent several more hours reviewing the studies. Denis McCarthy made numerous comments, mostly talking about the limitations of the small lesions picked up by the endoscope as being predictive of serious ulcers. By five o'clock, the meeting room was empty. "Celebrex is toast," someone in the audience murmured.

And there was more bad news for Pfizer/Searle. Although they ultimately received FDA approval for Celebrex on December 31, 1998, the FDA specifically forbade them from claiming it was safer for the stomach than any other NSAID. They also prohibited the company from making a claim for pain relief and mandated that it clear all advertising in advance with the agency. Five days later, on January 5, 1999, Dr. Garret FitzGerald published his paper in the *Proceedings of the National Academy of Sciences* specifically cautioning doctors and patients about the potential link between super aspirin and heart disease and pointing out that the study supporting this theory had been supported by Pfizer/Searle. Matters were hopeless. Science had spoken.

By June of 1999, six months after the launch of Celebrex, *The Washington Post* reported that the pill had become "the most successful new product in the history of the pharmaceutical business." Over six million prescriptions had been written for the drug and doctors and patients were calling it nothing less than a miracle.

"It was like Midas had touched me and I was a pot of gold," *The Washington Post* reported of Margaret Burton of Olney, Maryland, who started taking Celebrex for her arthritis that year. "I just felt like a different woman. It's like the fountain of youth, to put it mildly."

Dr. Herbert S. Baraf, a Washington, D.C., rheumatologist, hailed the development of super aspirin. "This is an advance in our basic understanding of molecular chemistry. . . . I really believe these drugs will become the standard of care." Stated patient Laurie Schuster of Chicago, "Now I can take my medicine and not have to worry."[3]

Merck watched Pfizer's Celebrex launch covetously. The New Jersey company was now preparing for *its* hearing before an FDA advisory panel. It was also planning an unprecedented strategy to "neutralize" any doctor who might not fully support the upcoming Vioxx introduction.[4]

Neutralizing doctors meant offering them research grants, invitations to national consultant meetings, medical school donations, and various other activities that could prove highly lucrative for doctors who agreed with Merck. For those who did not, it could mean discrediting their research.

A Merck marketing manager, Susan Baumgartner, was assigned the specific task of finding out what it would take to neutralize "problem" physicians and pass the word to the appropriate members of the sales force and the executive ranks.

Two of the most prominent names on the list were Dr. Lee Simon, former member of the Arthritis Advisory Committee, and Dr. Michelle Petri, the committee's former chairperson. Baumgartner was working with another marketer, Carolyn Yarbrough, who had met many of the influential physicians at the Cox in Paradise symposium in July of 1998.

Merck marketing was also planning the largest launch in the history of the company. An all-out three-day sales meeting would kick off the Vioxx campaign, featuring the president of human health, David Anstice. The sales representatives would be offered sizable bonuses and other incentives and provided with tens of thousands of samples to distribute.

Hundreds of physicians were being trained by Merck to be speakers, and noted opinion leaders were secretly flown to Merck headquarters for private media training.

The science department was also part of the blitz. They would start scores of studies and pay consulting fees to even more thought leaders, medical schools, and general practitioners. Some of these studies were little more than marketing exercises, designed to reward doctors for "testing" Vioxx on their patients and reporting results to Merck. The company was also planning huge clinical trials to get FDA approval to market Vioxx for additional indications such as Alzheimer's disease and colon cancer.

Merely by starting such trials, Merck implied that Vioxx worked against these conditions, thus exciting scientists in these fields.

On April 20, 1999, Merck finally presented its data to the FDA Arthritis Advisory Committee. Unlike the first two FDA panels that discussed the super aspirins, this one was decidedly low-key, perhaps because most of the important issues had already been hashed out.

The meeting displayed the Merck machine at its very finest. The presentations were detailed, scientific, and rational. Unlike the Pfizer/Searle meeting where Phil Needleman had all but exhorted his colleagues, the Merck presenters, Drs. Robert Silverman and Beth Seidenberg, were calm and professional—almost matter-of-fact.

Dr. John Wallace was one of the guest FDA experts. By this point in 1999, he had strong doubts that Vioxx was much better than any of the other NSAIDs; in fact, he had begun to worry that it wasn't as good.

More important, Merck was not asking for any extraordinary claim. Nobody could really argue that Vioxx didn't work as well as Aleve for relieving aches and pains of osteoarthritis. As for stomach safety, Merck could prove that it showed fewer tiny stomach erosions than Motrin, but by this time, no one could agree what that meant—if anything.

No company had performed an outcomes study, so neither the FDA nor the panel was going to allow Merck to eliminate the safety warnings about the possibility of serious ulcer complications found in all information inserts (labels) accompanying NSAIDs.

What is remarkable about the meeting, in retrospect, was not what was presented but what wasn't.

Not a single mention was made of Study 023, the FitzGerald study that had questioned the cardiovascular safety of Vioxx. Nor was there a debate of the earlier Merck studies at high doses that had been changed apparently in midcourse because of increases in heart and stroke risk. Nor was it fully learned until years later that two additional studies (one of which was never adequately analyzed or published) showed that Vioxx caused a statistically significant risk of cardiovascular events.

Why weren't these studies debated or the FitzGerald data presented at the meeting? There are a number of possibilities. One was that they were simply lost within the hundreds of thousands of pages of submissions. Because Vioxx had been granted a priority review, the FDA was obligated to analyze five years' worth of extremely complex data in six months. The staff was already exhausted from having to perform the same task for Pfizer, only three months before.

"The pressure on us was simply enormous," an FDA executive says. "We were getting tremendous pressure from the Congress, from medical organizations—hell—even from our families to approve this stuff. It was like a madhouse in here with documents and phone calls—press."[5]

Companies like to boast of the "extensiveness" of their data. This implies that a great number of studies have proven the safety and effectiveness of a drug. But it can also give the drug manufacturer a subtle advantage. If some of the studies are not successful or ambiguous, they can be summarized in such a way that they will be difficult or impossible for reviewers to notice or fully comprehend. Merck admits this strategy with the FitzGerald data, which was included in their Vioxx approval package, but in a less than recognizable form.

Finally, by the third advisory committee meeting to review the cox inhibitors, the FDA had already developed a consensus on the safety and efficacy of the super aspirins and didn't feel there was enough difference between the various studies presented by Pfizer and Merck to warrant anything other than tentative conclusions.

As an FDA member put it: "I guess we had gone through all this stuff with the Celebrex approval and we knew the compounds were pretty much the same. . . . We couldn't get in the way of this marketing battle, that's not our job. . . . So we went with the most obvious data we could. The culture of the agency had changed. One time we would have spent two years on this. You can only do so much in a few months—especially with everyone screaming for super aspirin."[6]

By the end of the meeting, Vioxx won approval for treatment of osteoarthritis, minor changes in indications for stomach safety, and a recommendation for use in acute pain for five days only. After five days, doctors were required to halve the dose. Hardly the stuff of "super aspirin."

"Frankly," John Wallace said, "I didn't think what we recommended was very different from Aleve or Motrin—and from quite a few standpoints, [Vioxx was] not as good. It certainly could not prevent heart attacks like aspirin. And I really didn't think anyone would pay three dollars a pill for something they could get for a few cents and had been proven to lower cardiovascular risk."[7]

It was not until a year later, when the results of the Merck outcomes

trial, VIGOR, were released, that the FDA did a more extensive cardiovascular analysis of Vioxx—but by that time, an extraordinary political
development had occurred at the Department of Health and Human Services (the parent of the FDA), one that no one could have foreseen at the
time, but which demonstrated even further brilliance and power on the
part of Merck.

CHAPTER 16

Payback Time

A view that science is totally
objective is mythical, and ignores
the human element of medical inquiry.
—Ted J. Kaptchuk

No one at Merck had seen anything like it. The Vioxx launch meeting on May 24, 1999, was a multimillion-dollar, three-day extravaganza with live music in a gorgeous San Francisco setting overlooking the Golden Gate Bridge.[1] It featured the music of the Brian Setzer Orchestra, a swing and rockabilly band formed in 1990 by the front man for the Stray Cats. Mingled with talk about cox-2 inhibition and major medical advances were the blaring sounds of "Jump, Jive an' Wail" and "The Dirty Boogie." Merck scientists described the assembly as an important research update for both sales representatives and invited health care professionals. Undoubtedly, it was.

Almost four thousand people, the largest sales force in pharmaceutical history, were gathered to go through the final preparations for the launch of Vioxx.

Along with the Brian Setzer Orchestra was Merck marketing chief David Anstice, who was on hand to deliver what everyone described as a mesmerizing speech. Anstice emerged on the brightly lit stage and exchanged witty remarks with the sales executives leading the meeting.

Then he turned toward the audience, put aside his notes, and held up his hands. "Ladies and gentlemen," Anstice said, "It is now PAYBACK TIME."[2]

The sales reps roared their approval. The bastards at Searle and Pfizer were about to learn what real selling was all about. Anstice waited for the cheers to die down.

"Today, I feel like a kid on Christmas morning. Because I've been presented with a gift that's at the top of every pharmaceutical executive's wish list—it is a winning product. . . . I'm talking about a product that's not just a 'winner.' Vioxx is a champion. A blockbuster. A superstar. Our scientists have handed us the opportunity of a lifetime and it's been passed to us like a gift from the heavens.

"I make this statement because, remember—winners—champions— aren't born. They're made. And this is precisely the case with Vioxx.

"Vioxx was designed, intentionally and deliberately, to be a winner. . . . Vioxx was developed strategically and methodically, to be a champion. . . . Vioxx has been driven and propelled along the road to victory—from day one. . . . When it comes to this market, David Anstice has been in it to win it. You can bank on that."

The sales representatives started to again clap loudly. Anstice quieted them with the motions used by a talk show host. In fact, Anstice had come prepared with a David Letterman Top Ten List. *The Top Ten Reasons Showing We're in It to Win It.*

Anstice began by summarizing the highlights of what Merck had done on behalf of Vioxx. The Merck sales force, like other pharmaceutical sales organizations, was divided into districts, each of which had already drawn up its own plan to sell the drug to capitalize on the huge bonus and incentive program that had been put into place.

"Now some might call such a program extravagant," Anstice said. "Not me. This is a program consistent with the philosophy that we're in it to win it."

Anstice told the crowd that Merck had developed the largest physician speaker team for a drug ever assembled. Hiring physicians to speak for Vioxx had two advantages. First, the speakers themselves were rewarded to prescribe and recommend the pill, and second, other physicians who relied on their colleagues to receive information and feedback would get the same message.

Since 1997, Merck had been putting on workshops and "reaching out" to pain and arthritis specialists, and by the time of launch had recruited 560 doctors to "educate" their colleagues about the wonders of Vioxx.

"We have a legacy in this market," Anstice explained. "Ten or fifteen years ago, we owned this market. Well, I'm here to tell you to get ready—*because history is about to repeat itself!* [Emphasis added.] We are going to own this market once again!" Anstice may or may not have been aware that Merck invented the modern pain market with the manufacture of morphine and cocaine.

Now Merck had assembled a virtual *army* of salespeople, exceeding the extraordinary number Pfizer/Searle had fielded.

"We're topping that number by over 25 percent," Anstice crowed. All told, Merck had recruited almost four thousand people.

This meant that between Pfizer/Searle and Merck, almost seven thousand salespeople were selling super aspirin. Pfizer was considered aggressive in 1951 when they had used eight people. Modern marketing and research techniques make these numbers even more daunting. Today, pharmaceutical manufacturers are able to pull up profiles of virtually every doctor in the United States. The most important "targets" are physicians known as "high prescribers." In private, sales reps call them "whales." These physicians, as the name implies, usually have large practices, see many patients, and write a large number of prescriptions. One such person was Dr. John Braun of Oradell, New Jersey, who would later sue Merck for his own heart attack. Before Vioxx was launched, Braun had received hints from Merck that Vioxx was about to be approved.

His patients, like John McDarby, had already read the articles about the healing powers of the drug, so that if Braun didn't see them himself, it was certain that one of his patients would ask about it. Like most general practitioners, Braun contacted specialists in his area to confirm what he was reading and hearing. The specialists, who had heard either opinion leaders touting super aspirin at medical meetings, or who themselves had been hired as educators by Merck, immediately confirmed what Braun was surmising.

Medical marketing works like a pyramid. A select group of specialists is brought to an exquisite location like Maui, for example, to be given insider views of a new drug. This select group organizes larger groups of specialists in the field. Now a widening number of experts convey the drug information to doctors such as John Braun. The message is reinforced daily by sales reps.

The main way drug salespeople gain entry into a doctor's office is by use of samples, free packets of pills that doctors can distribute to their patients. Merck had manufactured *17 million* samples to be distributed in the first seven months of launch, enough for 25,000 physicians and 375,000 patients.

"Some might call this [distribution of free samples] extravagant," Anstice said. "Not me! I am more than willing to sacrifice a few scripts [prescriptions] to samples in the *short* run to assure we win share in the long run." One of the greatest gimmicks is to institute a huge "clinical trial" in which doctors are paid to prescribe a certain drug under the guise of an important research study. These trials are usually scientifically meaningless and are instigated by the marketing departments. Merck had already launched its ADVANTAGE trial and its goal was to hire eight hundred family doctors to compare Vioxx to another NSAID.

After Anstice explained how to enroll physicians in ADVANTAGE, he reached the number one reason to sell Vioxx.

"It's the best product for patients. And let us never forget that that's what it's all about. The strength of Vioxx is unsurpassed. The safety of Vioxx is also unsurpassed. Vioxx is the only cox-2 inhibitor with demonstrated ulcer rates comparable to placebo." That was true, but Anstice did not explain that neither Merck nor any other company had as yet furnished any *human*-outcomes trials that demonstrated the effect of Vioxx on serious ulcers that cause bleeding and death.

Anstice told the assembly that Vioxx was the equivalent of being handed a blockbuster on a silver tray, whereupon a stagehand brought out a package of Vioxx on a gleaming, ornate platter.

The thrilled group heard Anstice's final words: "Best wishes for a sensational ride down the road to victory!"

This was not the first time pharmaceutical representatives have been sent out to blitz civilization. Nor has their culture changed significantly since Galen's theriac first enraptured the Romans. The thousands of drug salespeople who attended the Vioxx launch meeting left San Francisco about as excited as any representative force in pharmaceutical history. They were armed with glossy brochures, research articles, charts, graphs, Vioxx pads, Vioxx pencils, Vioxx pens, large budgets, and most of all belief. For without belief no medicine works, and all Merck salespeople knew in the deepest part of their hearts that they had a winner that could knock out pain and save lives. For the next few weeks, the largest armada of pharmaceutical power ever assembled (possibly excluding the Roman Marsi, the ships of Venice, and the Royal British Navy) fanned out across the United States, attempting to reach every doctor, every pharmacist, every hospital dispensary, every nurse, everyone connected to the health care system. Commented one rep, "You can only compare it to D-Day. It was thrilling. We were the greatest army the world had ever seen and we were swept up in the path to complete victory."[3]

Nonetheless, Merck was taking no chances. The company had a program to either "neutralize" or "discredit" thirty-six of the nation's most influential arthritis and pain doctors. Perhaps the saddest part of Merck's program was how easily these physicians went along. By neutralization, Anstice explained in court testimony, Merck was bringing thirty-six of the nation's most influential arthritis physicians to a point of "evenhandedness" when giving talks or making presentations about Vioxx.

Anstice later made one admission. "It was an unfortunate choice of words," maintaining that the company had done nothing wrong. "It was all clearly spelled out in the Merck policy guidelines." The company later said that neutralizing meant they were bringing doctors back to a state of being fair and balanced. A list of the names of target physicians were found in Merck internal documents, comprising hundreds of thousands of papers subpoenaed by legal teams, investigators, and congress.[4]

One of the more interesting experts mentioned in the Merck secret memos was Dr. Michelle Petri, who had chaired the first FDA Arthritis Advisory Committee in 1998 to evaluate coxibs. At that time she seemed to recommend that the super aspirins had to actually prove that they were effective by conducting outcomes research.

Three months later, Dr. Petri attended the Cox in Paradise meeting in

Maui, where she again heard the virtues of super aspirin, but this time with the aid of mai-tais and hula dancers. In the document on how to neutralize doctors, Merck does not seem aware that Dr. Petri was chairman of the FDA committee, merely that she "said" she was its head. (Apparently Merck never checked to see if that was true.)

Dr. Petri needed to be neutralized, according to the document, because she was worried about the Vioxx "toxicity and dose-related adverse effects," a fact that proves that at least the former chairperson of the FDA Arthritis Advisory Committee paid attention to the warning given by the FDA's own reviewer, even if no one else did. The Merck memo stated that Dr. Petri "wanted to participate in a Merck study and be more involved with Merck; feels slighted about not having been invited to participate in previous studies for Vioxx"; and refused to meet at a Merck consultants meeting. (No mention was made of her trip to Hawaii, which was partly sponsored by Merck.)

According to the company, Dr. Petri turned down several Merck overtures and wanted a $10,000 grant. "We are currently waiting for her proposals to conduct a study; We are not looking to have her speak at this time." Dr. Lee Simon, who was on the same FDA panel as Dr. Petri, conducted Celebrex studies for Pfizer, and took part in the same conversations in Hawaii, was also on the Merck neutralization list.

"Dr. Simon is looking for $5,000 for a symposium he is organizing in Boston," the document records. "He will also be visited by Dr. Louis Sherwood." This is a reference to a senior Merck medical executive and former academic leader. Sherwood's threats to medical professors eventually proved one of the most embarrassing and damaging in the entire Vioxx scandal.

Some doctors in the Merck document are listed as already "neutralized," among them Dr. Gary Williams, who "is participating in the ADVANTAGE trial and will become a Vioxx speaker"; Dr. John Condemi: "Thought leader in the community and Upstate New York, speaking on behalf of Searle as an advocate and investigator, recently enrolled him in Merck clinical trial after many months of promises and hard effort; not entirely sure if this was too little, too late."

One of the most interesting cases was that of Dr. Max Hamburger. Dr. Hamburger was a senior partner of Rheumatology Associates of Long

Island, one of the largest private practice groups in the United States. According to a Merck document, the physician wanted $25,000 for a symposium he was planning to hold with his associates. Any company that did not provide the money would have trouble getting access to the meeting, which would determine what drugs the group prescribed and recommended.

After being given the $25,000, Hamburger is listed as an "advocate." Merck's memo reports, "Dr. Hamburger was *turned around*." [Emphasis added.]

The most "up front of the doctors" was Dr. Roy Altman, a professor at the University of Miami. Altman is quoted as saying, "Show me the Money!" He was given funding for a $50,000 Rheumatism Fellowship Program.

More ominous is the case of Dr. James McMillan. In bold letters next to his name, Merck writes the word: DISCREDIT. McMillan is accused of having a national impact, "speaking extensively for Searle/Pfizer (200 days this year) numerous reports of biased and inaccurate presentations."

Dr. McMillan is also accused of "gathering information on VIOXX from the Internet." (How Merck knew Dr. McMillan's Web surfing habits is not mentioned.) Curiously, Dr. McMillan was not only a clinical investigator for Vioxx, but for Merck's follow-up cox-2 pain drug, Arcoxia.

Extensively questioned about the neutralization program, David Anstice replied:

"It would not be appropriate nor consistent with our policy if the purpose of a grant was not for that which they are designed for, which is educational and scientific."[5] He provided other amusing answers under oath about the neutralization program, beginning with the case of Dr. Altman.

Later in court, Anstice, who had harangued his troops that he was "in it to win it," seemed to have lost some of his confidence. Of course, neither the "neutralization" document, nor Merck's response that it could not possibly have done what it did because it was against the company's rules, speaks well of most of the physicians. In the doctors' defense, it is hard to stay neutral when two armies are robbing and pillaging, and you are called upon to join one side or the other. With hundreds of millions of dollars flowing, it is easy enough to siphon off a few drops to ensure that your lab is financed, your assistants paid, and that pizza is delivered in a timely manner to the staff: All of which the reps from Merck and Pfizer were happy to arrange.

Nonetheless, sooner or later, the piper must be paid, and despite all its worries, stalling, starts and stops, denials, rationalizations, and quibbles, Merck found itself in the uncomfortable position of actually having to prove that Vioxx could prevent hospitalizations and deaths from ulcers in real human beings. Thus began one of medicine's most entangled and ethically complex sagas.

Part IV

CHAPTER 17

Vioxx Gastrointestinal Outcomes Research (VIGOR)

I just can't wait to be the one to present those results to senior management.[1]

—Dr. Alise Reicin, Senior Director, Merck Research Laboratories

I n January 1999, Merck finally began its VIGOR study, to prove whether Vioxx was really safer than other NSAIDs. The study design was poor from the start. Merck could have chosen among many NSAIDs against which to test its drug, but it deliberately chose naproxen (Aleve). The reason comes directly from *Alice in Wonderland*: According to Merck, "Naproxen . . . was known to produce more severe gastrointestinal effects than many other non-selective NSAIDs."[2] In other words, Merck chose to prove that Vioxx was safer than one of the more dangerous of its competitors.

A good analogy would be that in order to prove you have the fastest horse, you set up a race against a crippled one-eyed mule. Merck justified the decision to test against naproxen for the following reason. Merck's statisticians estimated that if one of those alternate medications were used, perhaps twice the number of patients (roughly 16,000) would be needed to test whether Vioxx was really safer for the stomach.[3]

Put more clearly, it was entirely possible that by running a race against a faster horse, Merck might have lost—or that the race would have lasted forever, resulting in two broken-down mares, proving nothing. According to the principles of a randomized trial, patients in the comparison group should be getting the *best possible alternative* to Vioxx. When Austin Hill designed the first randomized trial for streptomycin, he compared the antibiotic against the optimal therapy that existed at the time for tuberculosis. Merck admits it did not do this for the sake of convenience and cost. It would be as if Austin Hill had put the tuberculosis patients in the non-streptomycin group in poorly ventilated nursing homes in the London slums so that he could gather data more quickly.

After listening to the Merck logic, Stanford arthritis expert James Fries shakes his head in near-disbelief, then shrugs his shoulders—as if to say "drug companies will tell you anything to justify marketing."

Fries continues: "If you look and put yourself in the mind of companies that were developing super aspirin, they first went to the FDA and tried to get these drugs classified as something different from an NSAID, an entirely new class of drugs. And the FDA didn't buy that and didn't allow them to do that.

"But they still wanted the strategy of saying, the regular NSAIDs are old, and we're new. We're different. You know they wanted to get that message out clearly.

"Now the important point is how they designed the studies. They didn't want to go up against the newer, less toxic NSAIDs like moderate-strength Motrin [ibuprofen]—which is much safer than naproxen—because then they would have found that Vioxx, Celebrex, and Motrin all have the same safety."[4] Motrin also cost 35 cents a pill compared to $3 for Vioxx.

The second ethical clinical trial principle Merck violated was that it never formulated a plan for analyzing the heart risks of Vioxx in the VIGOR trial itself. What Merck intended to do was lump any adverse heart events into a large, overall cardiovascular risk database the company had maintained since suspicion of the dangers of Vioxx had arisen in the 1990s.

The drug company had good reason to worry that the trial would not go well. Dr. Reynold Spector, head of clinical sciences at Merck, expressed reservations because the chosen dose of Vioxx, 50 milligrams, was associated with water retention (edema) and high blood pressure (hypertension), both of which are associated with an increase risk of heart disease.[5]

Throughout most of 1999, the debates about the design and ethics of the VIGOR trial took place only among a small number of people within Merck, a select group of investigators, and the FDA. No one else could make comments about the trial because the ethical and methodological issues concerning VIGOR were not made public until years later. As far as bias was concerned—perhaps the most important element to ensure accurate and authoritative results of a randomized controlled trial—there was much to be concerned about.

The leader of the study, Dr. Loren Laine of the University of Southern California Medical School, was caught on a secret tape advising Merck how to explain the results of the study to make it more favorable—and to lessen the safety problems with Vioxx. We were "cagey" about some of the results, is the way Laine put it.[6]

In sum, there was bias in the selection of a comparison drug, bias in the choice of an external trial leader, bias in the analysis and preparation of the results, and an inadequate plan to determine heart attack risk. But that *still* wasn't enough.

In the U.K. Medical Research Council streptomycin trial, Austin Hill went through extraordinary lengths to make sure that only he knew who was assigned (randomized) to each group, throughout the entire process of the experiment.

The VIGOR trial did have a data and safety monitoring board, but it was severely compromised. As revealed on June 8, 2006, in the National Public Radio program *All Things Considered*, the independent members of the board weren't actually outsiders. The head of the safety panel, rheumatologist Michael Weinblatt of the Brigham Hospital in Boston, and his wife owned $73,000 of Merck stock. Soon after agreeing to Merck's plan, Dr. Weinblatt signed a new consulting contract to sit on a Merck advisory board. Merck agreed to pay him $5,000 a day for twelve days over a two-year period. Dr. Weinblatt received an initial check for $15,000 a few weeks later. Another member of the panel, Dr. David Bjorkman, was also a Merck consultant in the summer while VIGOR was ongoing. The committee did not convene until the fall.

The DSMB was blinded, but allowed to look at the data to detect whether one of the therapies was doing so poorly that either it was jeopardizing the lives of patients—or that one therapy was doing so well that withholding it would be unethical.

The committee members did not actually know which of the patient groups was getting a certain pill. They simply saw data marked with a code—group A or group B.

It was of course critical that even though the DSMB was blinded, it had no bias as to the results, or outcome, of the trial.

That is not what happened in VIGOR.

Merck decided that one member of the DSMB would know which patients were taking Vioxx. The person chosen was Merck's statistician, Dr. Deborah Shapiro, who probably had as much at stake in the outcome of the trial as nearly anyone in the company—because she had helped design it. Dr. Shapiro would know which patients were on either Vioxx or Aleve, collect the VIGOR data as it came into the company, and analyze it.[7] Therefore, a pivotal person responsible for getting Vioxx to market was seeing the results, making suggestions, and interpreting what was happening. She was also regularly attending Merck meetings and interacting with colleagues, who must have asked her some very interesting questions.

Almost from the start of the VIGOR trial, excess heart deaths started showing up in the Vioxx group. Even at the first meeting of the DSMB on September 2, 1999, there were eleven deaths in the Vioxx group and six in the naproxen group. By the time of the second meeting on November 18, the Vioxx group showed five additional deaths, four of which were from heart disease.[8]

The DSMB members concluded that these deaths were *not* the result of chance.

Alarmed, the DSMB scheduled a special meeting to take another look at the heart deaths on December 1. The trend toward more Vioxx heart deaths continued. Just as disturbing, the DSMB members were essentially unblinded. They had concluded that group A was Vioxx and that group B was naproxen.

Given the fact that the committee members had the potential for very lucrative consulting arrangements with Merck, bias now played a distinct role.

By December 1, five self-described unblinded DSMB members were using the data prepared by Merck's statistician to determine whether to allow the VIGOR trial to continue. It was shortly after that the committee members learned that the plan to analyze heart disease had never been completed. They demanded that Merck carefully examine the data from the VIGOR trial, a request met with great concern within the company.

Dr. Alise Reicin (the "cool blonde") and other Merck staff members tried to straighten out what was becoming an obvious mess and embarrassment, but were told that "senior management" was not going to listen to what the DSMB was demanding. Much to his credit, Dr. Michael Weinblatt, head of the DSMB, said this was not acceptable.

On January 24, 2000, Dr. Eve Slater, executive director of Worldwide Clinical and Regulatory Development, called a special meeting of Merck experts. The company was under intense pressure to finish the VIGOR trial quickly so that they could submit the results to the FDA. Everyone knew that Pfizer/Searle was completing its own outcomes trial. And still there was no plan for how to analyze the heart attack data. Word of the dispute about the trial was spreading rapidly around Merck. Dr. Thomas Musliner, who had written a memo years earlier warning that the trial could very well be unfavorable to the company, re-sent his skeptical memo about Vioxx safety to key personnel.[9] More fuel was now on the fire.

Ironically, at this point VIGOR was supposed to be completely blinded, yet it seemed that everyone in the company was already involved with how to analyze the results.

Dr. Curt Furberg, professor of preventive medicine at the Bowman-Gray Medical School and an FDA advisor, has sat on at least fifty data and safety monitoring boards. He and his colleagues have carefully analyzed the data from VIGOR from the various meetings held in November and December of 1999.

"We concluded that the committee should have said stop," Furberg says. "They were getting close to the end of the study and saw something that was alarming. Then you have two choices. One is to say stop and the other is to let it run its course. The easy way out is to say let it run its course.

"The effect of not stopping the trial was to not get the proper attention of either the company or the medical community. They lost an opportunity to get the word out that the drug was harmful."[10]

By the beginning of February 2000, Dr. Edward Scolnick, the Merck science chief, was being "pounded" by rumors that the VIGOR trial was a failure.

Vioxx was Scolnick's baby, and the thought of something going wrong was tormenting him to the point that he decided he had to *overtly* break the rules of the trial. "This situation cannot simply follow the 'book,'" Scolnick e-mailed statistician Deborah Shapiro.[11]

He assured Shapiro that this message, which would later become its own subsection of Merck's Martin Report, was strictly confidential. "Get in touch as soon as possible," Scolnick wrote. Merck's research chief had a joke going with Shapiro, about a rabbit's foot she carried for luck, "just in case statistics didn't work out." Dr. Scolnick wrote that he hoped the charm would save the day.[12] Dr. Shapiro was now on the spot. Her predicament perfectly illustrates why a clinical trial member should have neither bias nor a connection with the sponsoring company. Merck's own statistician now had to consider a request from the company's most senior scientist to gain access to information she was forbidden to reveal.

After consulting with colleagues, Shapiro declined Scolnick's demand.

However, on March 9, after the data had been officially unblinded, Shapiro did present the data to Scolnick and his senior staff—and it is fair to say that from that time on, chaos ruled in the world's oldest pharmaceutical company.

CHAPTER 18

Spinning the Results

If you can influence the leaders, either with or without their conscious cooperation, you automatically influence the group which they sway.
—**Edward Bernays, father of public relations and nephew of Sigmund Freud**

D r. Edward Scolnick was home the night of March 9, 2000, when he was quietly able to read in detail the results of the VIGOR study. He must have been mortified.

During the interim analysis, when Dr. Curt Furberg had already said there was adequate evidence to stop the trial, Vioxx had shown double the heart attack rate of naproxen. The final analysis showed that Vioxx had *from four to five times* the heart attack rate of naproxen.

The disconsolate Scolnick had been worried about this for years, because of ever-growing links between Vioxx and heart disease, including the FitzGerald studies. He wrote an e-mail to his senior scientific staff, including Alise Reicin. "The CV [heart attack] data are clearly there. . . . It is a shame, but it is a low incidence and is mechanism-based as we worried it was."[1]

Scolnick said that other outside experts had been right about FitzGerald's concern about Vioxx disrupting homeostasis and its link to heart disease. His conclusion was that the results of the VIGOR study showed that Vioxx could indeed lead to heart disease.

Two days later, a Merck scientist confirmed that the higher the dose of Vioxx, the more likely the side effects related to heart disease were likely to show up—basically the finding of the FDA. The trial dosage of fifty milligrams was just as dangerous as the agency and the advisory committee had suspected.

In order to collect further data, Merck broke the codes on its two Alzheimer's disease trials. However, these trials were being conducted with half the dose of the VIGOR trial (25 milligrams instead of 50) and thus were not comparable.

Merck analyzed other studies, but again, none had the same dose of Vioxx as VIGOR used for as long a period of time—some studies were only six weeks long. Despite these discrepancies, Merck decided to use these studies to justify the safety of Vioxx.

One of the strangest omissions in Merck's safety assessment was their neglecting to reanalyze two key studies known as 085 and 090, which outside investigators later used to demonstrate additional heart dangers of Vioxx.[2] (The FDA also reanalyzed the data and concluded Vioxx should have a distinctive heart safety warning.)

VIGOR could only objectively be interpreted in two or possibly three ways. Vioxx was causing more heart attacks than naproxen; naproxen was protecting the heart; the results were simply chance or bad luck. The bottom line was that VIGOR showed that patients taking Vioxx were four or five times as likely to have heart problems as those on naproxen, for whatever reason. Any other conclusion was simply speculation, and certainly gave no reason for doctors to prescribe the new drug.

Nonetheless, it fell upon Dr. Reicin to somehow figure out why the additional number of heart attacks in the Vioxx group was not worrisome. She must have remembered her memo from years back when she wrote that "she dreaded being the one to present the outcomes study result" to senior management.

After an exhaustive search, Dr. Reicin found a small study done more than a decade before, showing that a drug called flurbiprofen, an NSAID used mostly in Europe, was associated with a 70 percent second heart attack reduction.[3] (Experts later called this study both irrelevant and inconclusive.) Dr. Reicin and others at Merck went on to say that since the molecular structure of flurbiprofen was similar to naproxen, naproxen must also be cardioprotective. Interestingly, when later trying to downplay the significance of the APPROVe trial for Arcoxia (a close chemical relative of Vioxx), Merck stated in a news release "that the results of clinical studies with one molecule in a given class are not necessarily applicable to the others in the class."[4] The release was correct.

As has been shown time and time again, the only way to establish what a drug actually does is to examine its effects in a carefully designed, double-blind, randomized clinical trial (RCT). Not a single such trial ever demonstrated that naproxen reduced the risk of heart attack. In fact, to make that claim would be to violate one of the Food and Drug Administration's most important rules; that *no* claim may be made for a drug unless it has gone through at least one such RCT and the data objectively analyzed and approved by the FDA.

Scientists and drug company executives involved with the development of naproxen were even more dismissive that the pill could prevent heart attacks. Senior Syntex executives, who had worked on the drug, made it clear that if they could have proven that naproxen was protective of the heart, they would have done so. It would have been worth billions.

Given these conclusions about VIGOR, Merck now had to explain to the outside world what the results meant. In time-honored tradition they turned to two people who would craft the results, Dr. Laurence Hirsch and Jan Weiner, the company's public relations experts.

Weiner and Hirsch were among the first to get the results of VIGOR and set about to develop a communications strategy. Hirsch immediately recommended issuing a release that ascribed the VIGOR results to the ability of naproxen to reduce the risk of heart disease. He communicated this to Dr. Eve Slater, who had been playing a pivotal role in the development of super aspirin.

Despite what the company termed full confidence in Vioxx, Merck did take one step that indicated otherwise. Merck informed investigators who were working with their cox-2 drugs in all clinical trials to allow patients to take aspirin if they thought the subjects were at risk of a heart attack. As previously noted, the problem with this change in instructions was that no one had sufficiently studied how Vioxx and aspirin interacted. *It seemed logical* that adding aspirin would help reduce the excess heart disease that had shown up in VIGOR, but it was unproven. And it also might have made matters worse.

Obviously, the company believed that among patients with cardiovascular risk, taking Vioxx alone without aspirin was dangerous (something that FitzGerald had warned about in 1999 and that Merck's internal expert, Dr. Thomas Musliner, had warned about in 1997). The letter to the investigators stated that for patients who were at risk for heart disease, doctors should consider prescribing low-dose aspirin to reduce this risk.

But if patients with cardiovascular risk in clinical trials and their physicians were advised to take aspirin, why weren't all patients and doctors informed?

The letter to the investigators regarding this caution was first characterized as an "important, possibly drug-related safety finding."[5] That sentence was dropped. The final letter also played down the possibility that Vioxx had caused the excess heart attacks. Originally the letter said the heart attacks in the Vioxx group were unexpected. This was later changed to "not entirely" expected. In other words, Merck had its suspicions, which remained unrevealed to doctors or patients.

Who was responsible for drafting these important drug safety advisories? Public relations. Larry Hirsch wrote: "Including the quote from the FitzGerald paper . . . is raising a big, red flag. . . . Couldn't we modulate that a bit by paraphrasing them, rather than directly quoting them?" Hirsch later notes, "I think I have modified the wording in the paragraph with the 'FitzGerald quote' in a way that you will like—it communicates much the same message, but in a far less alarmist way."[6]

This was the strategy that was adopted, and tragically it was the strategy adopted in the new consent form sent to health care institutions and doctors. Any information released to the public either minimized the Vioxx heart risk, or strongly affirmed the pill's safety.

In fact, the corporation considered *not* issuing a press release about the VIGOR study. Merck claimed it was very unusual to issue public information about a study that was "preliminary," a peculiar statement coming from a company that had been putting out press releases documenting the results of Vioxx studies since the first (hardly definitive) findings about the lack of ulcers in test animals.

Nonetheless by March 20, both Hirsch and Weiner were drafting a communications plan. Its main objective was to positively shape public opinion about Vioxx. In fact, in arguing for issuing a press release, Weiner stated that this would give the company "an opportunity to shape perceptions among external publics from the beginning . . . and provide physicians, patients with perspectives from the Company. . . . We control timing, implementation, potentially surprising competitors and pre-empting some of their responses."[7] Nothing was mentioned about the consequences of public health.

A Merck press release about VIGOR was issued on March 27, 2000: It made no mention of the FitzGerald hypothesis and assured patients that Vioxx had the same degree of safety as other NSAIDs and placebo. Merck did draft a background document known as a "standby statement" that did explain the FitzGerald hypothesis—but it was never used.

Another Merck document, "Questions and Answers," included a brief discussion of deaths in the VIGOR trial. In response to a potential question on this topic, Merck was to say that the "number of deaths was small in both groups." That answer was written on March 23, 2000. However, there were 20 deaths in the Vioxx group and 15 in the naproxen group, enough to have alarmed the VIGOR data and safety monitoring board by as early as the previous November.

The first public relations release did not reveal that there were from four to five times more incidents of heart problems and strokes in the Vioxx group compared to naproxen, nor did any materials mention data on high blood pressure or fluid retention.

Dr. Hirsch spelled out that the "communications objectives" should emphasize that the results only applied to patients with rheumatoid arthritis—and only with the highest dose of Vioxx—as well as underscore the substantial gastrointestinal benefits of Vioxx compared to traditional NSAIDs. He also stated that if possible Merck should phrase its words to indicate that there was a "reduction in heart attacks and strokes with naproxen vs. Vioxx," rather than an "increase in heart attacks and strokes with Vioxx."

The goals were textbook public relations: control the reaction to the news, avoid misinterpretation (intentional or otherwise) by audiences and competitors, and meet the needs of customers (investigators, treating physicians, investment community, and employees), in a proactive but low-key, accurate, fact-based manner. In other words, bury the story about the dangers of Vioxx.

The strategy worked. Merck issued VIGOR press releases on March 27 and 28, announcing preliminary results and emphasizing the decrease in ulcers—the primary goal of the trial. News agency stories were brief and followed the Merck emphasis. Headlines included:

> "Merck Says Vioxx Shows Fewer Side Effects" (Reuters)
> "Merck's Vioxx Found Safer on Stomach than Other Pain Drugs" (Bloomberg).

Neither news service mentioned the heart or stroke results. However, a later Reuters story did note that "The [VIGOR] study also indicated patients using the painkiller naproxen encountered fewer thromboembolic events than those using Vioxx, because, unlike the latter drug, [naproxen] blocks platelet aggregation."[8]

According to an internal memo, Merck public affairs expressed satisfaction with the coverage: "We successfully managed discussion of the heart attack data. Dow Jones and *The Los Angeles Times* . . . did not mention cardiovascular events, and other outlets discussed the MI [heart attack] rate with appropriate perspective." Not completely satisfied, the public affairs memorandum concluded, "We have already started planning for the next battle . . ."[9]

The reports from the financial analysts followed a similar pattern as that of the press. J.P. Morgan bought the Merck story that the difference in heart attack rates was due to the beneficial effects of naproxen, not the risk of Vioxx.

Only a few commentators, like Christina Heuer of Salomon Smith Barney, raised questions about both Merck and Vioxx: "Why did MRK release results from a landmark clinical trial in a press release and not a medical meeting? Is the purpose of MRK's press release to 'cloak' bad news?" Heuer asked.[10] Her skepticism barely registered on Wall Street.

David Anstice and Ed Scolnick must have been thrilled as they examined the total number of positive stories. Except for a few isolated mentions, public relations had turned a potentially negative event into a positive. Anstice e-mailed Merck's chairman that "Across the Americas all has been quiet and I think our communications have been clear, well coordinated and reached all relevant parties. The positive study results have been the leading (and even only) story."[11]

Ironically, when Merck was fighting tens of thousands of lawsuits, the company would make the point that the VIGOR trial, right from the start, was *widely publicized and intensely debated.* That is certainly not what David Anstice believed in spring of 2000 or what a look at press databases shows. Merck also maintained that despite the fivefold increase in heart disease in the VIGOR study among patients taking Vioxx, it never occurred to anyone at the pharmaceutical company that this was a strong indication of the drug's link to cardiovascular damage.

No one can accurately assess *exactly* how many lives were lost due to Vioxx, because the heart attack and stroke risk were downplayed, not widely reported and certainly not debated. But this early spin that Vioxx was safe, and that naproxen protected the heart, was accepted by the overwhelming majority of the medical and lay community—until Merck itself pulled the drug from the market.

A year after David Anstice wrote that "Across the Americas all has been quiet," a Texas triathelate named Robert Ernst died in his sleep of heart disease. Neither he nor his widow Carol knew that Vioxx was five times more likely to cause cardiovascular disease than Aleve.

CHAPTER 19

Medical "Interpretation"

Things are not always what they seem.
—**Phaedrus**

Pharmaceutical financial analyst Richard Stover was on a westbound flight with his family, reading what little information he had been able to gather about VIGOR. Since the original positive press reports and scant comments from fellow analysts, he had sensed from his years in the drug business and his extensive coverage of the industry that a major story was being ignored.[1]

Stover, an intense man with a terse but friendly manner, continued to scrutinize a notebook of papers, while trying to frame his own report. Stover worked for Arnhold and S. Bleichroeder, what is known as a boutique investment firm. The company was much smaller than the giant brokerages such as Merrill Lynch or Deutsche Bank, and it allowed Stover the freedom to write more detailed and provocative corporate coverage (sometimes to the dismay of those companies he followed). It was now May 6, 2000, about six weeks since the original VIGOR press release and about two weeks after Reuters had finally published a story casting doubt on the safety of Vioxx.

The Reuters article predicted that Merck would face increased scrutiny by the FDA "because of the number of patients who suffered strokes and heart attacks after taking Vioxx in new clinical trials."[2]

The news service noted that David Saks, manager of Gruntal & Co.'s Medical Sciences Fund, believed the results might even threaten Merck's revenue. The FDA was quoted as saying that Vioxx was "effective and adequately safe."

Merck's PR director Jan Weiner did not deny that there were more heart attacks and strokes in the Vioxx group, but fired back to an inquiring reporter that it was due to the protective properties of naproxen. "That's in the literature," Ms. Weiner said. There was no evidence that Vioxx puts patients at higher risk.[3]

Reuters was one of the few news services that remained with the story. They contacted Roche Holdings, one of the major sellers of naproxen. Roche told the news service that, to their knowledge, naproxen did not prevent heart attacks or strokes. (Like the initial researchers of naproxen at Syntex Pharmaceutical, they made it clear that if they had such proof, Roche could have made billions.)[4]

On May 7, 2000, Merck issued a press release that reached a new level of absurdity. The headline read: "Merck Confirms Favorable Cardiovascular Profile of Vioxx." The story stated: "In response to *speculative* [emphasis added] news reports, Merck & Co. Inc. today confirmed the favorable cardiovascular safety profile of Vioxx. . . . Extensive review of data from the completed osteoarthritis trials and ongoing clinical trials with Vioxx, as well as post marketing experience with Vioxx, have shown no difference in the incidence of cardiovascular events, such as heart attack, among patients taking Vioxx, other NSAIDs or placebo."

In short, Vioxx caused no more heart problems than either a sugar pill or any other NSAID such as naproxen. The next sentence of the release read: "Findings from Merck's large outcomes study showed significantly fewer heart attacks were observed with naproxen compared to patients taking Vioxx." In other words, Vioxx causes more heart attacks than naproxen. (A similar press release would later be described by the FDA as "simply incomprehensible.")[5]

As Rick Stover's flight hit turbulence, he suddenly started to smile—then burst out laughing, his coffee cup clattering on the tray in front of him. His wife stared at him. "Are you all right?" she said.

Stover said, "You know what those guys did?"

"Who?"

"Merck."

"Not really."

"They told the story backward. All I have to do is reverse the headline."

Marion Stover nodded her head while her husband grabbed a pen and starting scribbling out his report. On May 10, 2000, Stover came out with his own VIGOR report, within which he placed a new headline: "VIGOR—A Landmark Trial Demonstrating Unprecedented Degree of Cardioprotection in a Low-Risk Population in an Unparalleled Short Duration of Treatment?"

Stover wrote:

> If one accepts Merck's suggestion that the VIGOR trial was the first trial to show naproxen's cardio protective benefits in more than a quarter of a century, then we believe one has to go on to accept the following statements: Naproxen has been shown to reduce the incidence of heart attack by 80%! WOW!
>
> The VIGOR trial demonstrated this fivefold difference in cardiovascular risk in a remarkably short period of time, e.g., six months. We view these claims—that VIGOR has demonstrated a heretofore unrecognized cardio protective benefit of naproxen—with extreme skepticism.[6]

As further data was released from Merck, Stover's criticisms of Vioxx intensified. Merck noticed. Eventually, Dr. Edward Scolnick, the science chief, threatened "to have Stover boiled in oil" if he ever ran into him at a Merck presentation.[7] Nobody who heard of Scolnick's sentiments took them lightly.

At least one expert physician did agree, at least in part, with Stover. Dr. Gurkirpal Singh, adjunct clinical professor of medicine at Stanford University, found his anger growing markedly after reading the VIGOR press releases. Singh was one of the nation's leading experts on both arthritis and epidemiology and he had been courted by Merck as a speaker since 1998. He also carried a great deal of influence among large pharmaceutical buying groups in the San Francisco area.

Singh had written papers on the ulcer dangers of NSAIDs and was at first enthusiastic about super aspirin. But he was "stunned" to learn that Vioxx had shown a 500 percent greater increase of heart disease than naproxen.

"Clearly the trade off of 500% increase in heart attacks for a 50% reduction in stomach bleeds did not seem attractive," Singh later told a Senate committee. Singh wanted more assurance than a few press releases
that Vioxx was a safe drug before he continued to lecture on the benefits
of super aspirin to physicians.[8]

Nor did Singh accept the notion that naproxen was cardioprotective. He
explained that while naproxen might also prevent the blood from clumping,
and hence lower the risk of clots that blocked the vessels to the heart, preventing heart disease, "naproxen did so only temporarily and incompletely."

Therefore, even before Merck had publicly presented its data to the
FDA, Singh was trying to get answers to key safety issues—such as rates of
high blood pressure, water retention (edema), and heart failure. (Heart
failure is a serious, life-threatening illness in which the heart is literally
starved of oxygen.) Singh pressed Merck for data, but was turned down
numerous times. While the company did present some of the heart disease issues at a meeting for gastroenterologists, it did *not* present this data
to arthritis experts at the following meeting of the American College
of Rheumatology. Thus the most influential doctors who actually prescribed cox inhibitors could not see the full data. Dr. Singh noted, "After
VIGOR was published [in *The New England Journal of Medicine*], it was
like the company had to think of what questions to answer." So Dr. Singh
added a new illustration to his presentations. The slide showed a man—
representing the missing data—hiding under a blanket.

Once again, Merck panicked. The company put together a task force
of scientists and salespeople to monitor Singh and report to headquarters.
Some of Dr. Singh's talks were described as "highly slanted" and "very
skeptical about Vioxx."[9] However, the Stanford professor presented a difficult sales and marketing hurdle, and a Merck representative in Singh's
area worried about interfering with him. Singh had become a major liability for Merck because of the professor's standing both among doctors
and large drug buyers such as hospitals and HMOs. But eventually Merck
had had enough. It assembled a huge dossier on Singh. "The profile of Dr.
Singh is remarkably complete," said Columbia's David Rothman, who reviewed the final document for NPR. "One can't help but almost frame
it in terms of an FBI dossier, except here Dr. Singh is not cavorting with

possible communists, or possible gangsters. Here the dossier is filled with Dr. Singh's take on Vioxx, who is Dr. Singh talking to. It's scrupulously watched and very, very carefully recorded."[10]

Singh learned that if he persisted with his requests, "there would be serious consequences for him."[11]

"Merck can make life very difficult for you, both at Stanford and outside," Singh was informed. At first, Singh didn't believe the threat rumors. He had been involved with scientific disputes before, but they were always handled on a professional level with careful correspondence and respectful debate.

Actually, the threats were part of a larger plan to make sure that negative information about Vioxx was never discussed, much less discredited. Wheels turned and Dr. Louis Sherwood, a top Merck scientist, started making plans.

Rick Stover and Gurkirpal Singh must have felt isolated at the time they first publicly raised serious doubts about Vioxx and the VIGOR study. Only years later, when many more researchers were joining the debate, were more criticisms directed toward Merck.

Dr. Bruce Psaty, professor of epidemiology at the University of Seattle, who analyzed the VIGOR study for a congressional investigating committee, stated that "The rates in heart attack between Vioxx and naproxen were so different, that naproxen was practically conferring immortality on people. Merck said it was several times better than aspirin. And that's just not a credible finding."[12]

Or as Dr. Curt Furberg succinctly put it: "The notion that naproxen could explain the difference between the two groups is absurd."[13]

Absurd or not, the show had to go on. In May 2000, Merck readied itself for the formal presentation of VIGOR at what is known as Digestive Disease Week, one of the world's largest meetings of gastroenterologists.

Dr. Loren Laine, the previous neutral advisor to the FDA about super aspirin and a senior author of the VIGOR study, was going to make the presentation of the data. However, just in case anyone missed the point,

Merck brought in company scientists and hired a squad of PR profession-als to "educate" the press. In addition, Merck had scores of sales reps on hand to neutralize (bring to a balanced position) any doubting physicians.

The VIGOR press release was an unusually long three and a half pages. Nothing was mentioned about heart problems until the third page, and at that point an incredible statement was introduced.

The patients who had the heart attacks *should have been taking aspirin*! Or as the press release states: "4 percent of patients enrolled in the study did meet the criteria for use of aspirin to prevent second cardiac events." Merck found that if the remaining 96 percent of patients were analyzed, no difference in heart problems would have been found between naproxen and Vioxx.[14]

Keep in mind that before anyone either enrolls or is admitted into a clinical trial, he or she is thoroughly examined by expert physicians. And not just any expert physicians, but highly experienced expert physicians. Merck itself hired these doctors and placed in their hands one of the most important drug trials in the company's history.

For the Merck theory about the excess heart disease events in VIGOR to hold true, 327 people should either have been put on aspirin when first screened, or excluded from the trial. Certain diagnoses are difficult to make and require advanced equipment such as an MRI machine or com-plex laboratory work. The diagnosis of cardiovascular risk can be accu-rately assessed by a nurse using a blood pressure cuff (a test available at home), a stethoscope, a blood and urine sample, a scale, and a patient his-tory chart. (When the laboratory tests are analyzed, cardiovascular risk factors like cholesterol levels are actually highlighted, just in case someone should miss them.) It would also help to ask the patient about such habits as smoking and drinking. How could Merck therefore explain that such carefully screened people should have been given aspirin or dropped from the trial?

"This analysis was one of their more absurd explanations for the VIGOR trial," says Dr. James Fries, who, incidentally, was Dr. Singh's boss. "We knew initially that there were more heart attacks in the Vioxx group. Merck offered two explanations, neither of which was good. One was the idea that naproxen was cardioprotective.

"Now this one was pretty funny to me. They invented naproxen right down the road from me at Stanford, Palo Alto, California, at the Syntex pharmaceutical company. I mean I worked with naproxen when they first developed it. And it was clear that Syntex would have loved to have the aspirin market for cardioprotection. . . . You know they had looked at it and there wasn't anything that was positive for it at all. There were a bunch of studies, which kind of indicated that it didn't have it."[15] Syntex actually had reasons similar to Merck for thinking that naproxen might protect the heart—uncannily similar. Both aspirin and naproxen reduce clotting in the blood. In fact, naproxen stays in the blood longer than aspirin.

However, no prospective, randomized, double-blind, placebo-controlled trial ever showed that naproxen lowered the rate of heart disease. In the VIGOR trial, Merck had never set up a plan to analyze patients who "should have been on aspirin." A cardinal principle of the RCT is that data cannot be simply pulled out (or as some say, "dredged") to prove a point that is helpful to the study sponsor after a trial has concluded. The scientific name for such deductions, according to Dr. Ted Kaptchuk of Harvard Medical School, is "auxillary hypothesis bias." This imposing term simply means that the conclusion of a study is changed to explain an unanticipated finding that *would have* been different if the research was performed another way.

As Austin Hill stated in 1937 and has been proven right every time, randomization prevents one group from having all the subjects prone to a certain side effect in the same group. So, if 327 people had indeed been high-risk patients that the investigating physicians didn't recognize as needing aspirin or dropped from the study, they would have been placed in either the Vioxx or naproxen group purely by chance. (This was exactly the reason Dr. Hill mandated randomization in the first place.) Randomization would have prevented all the high-risk patients from being assigned only to one arm of the study.

Merck claimed all the high-risk patients were taking Vioxx, thus "explaining" why this group had more heart disease. That would have been impossible.

"That's why we do randomized trials," Dr. Fries explains. "The observation that high-risk patients had more heart attacks was true, but it doesn't explain the difference between Vioxx and naproxen. In a random-ized trial, the people at greater risk will be in both groups."[16]

There is one additional problem with Merck's conclusion. None of the people who were at cardiovascular risk were informed of the danger of not receiving aspirin. That constitutes a direct violation of medical ethics demanded by the Nuremberg Trials and the Declaration of Helsinki.

So Merck and its investigators failed to make either a routine diagnosis of excess cardiovascular risk of patients who needed aspirin, or they made the diagnosis and failed to warn them: one of the most serious errors in medicine.

Nevertheless, the press, the financial community, and the Digestive Disease Week conference attendees were satisfied with explanations by Merck and Dr. Laine. It is not difficult to see why. While epidemiologists and biostatisticians can review published studies and easily find flaws, a new clinical trial that hasn't been previously published or presented can be done with beautifully prepared slides and limited written information.

A superb professor like Loren Laine can make a carefully rehearsed pre-sentation, emphasizing critical points, downplaying others, and ignoring unhelpful data with the claim that he has "limited time in a busy medical meeting." In the hierarchy of medicine, Laine is at the top, a respected authority whose opinions carry great weight. He was buttressed on the VIGOR presentation panel by other experts reinforcing his opinion and adding to his credibility.

In any case, it would have been difficult to challenge what he was say-ing because the investigators had access to enormous amounts of infor-mation that was as yet unknown to any but a small group, mostly within Merck. In addition, the role of Merck, which had researched, designed, overseen, analyzed, and written the VIGOR results, was kept far in the background, replaced by a panel of renowned academic scholars. The purpose of the trial now appeared to be a question of alleviating an over-whelming public health crisis, not as a way to make huge additional prof-its for a pharmaceutical company.

The venue of the presentation was another point in Merck's favor. The audience was composed of gastroenterologists whose greatest challenge in medicine was treating stomachs and intestines, not hearts or creaky joints.

Cardiac and arthritis experts had that responsibility. Undoubtedly, had VIGOR been first presented at a heart care convention, the reaction would have been far different.

Most important, Merck had created a sophisticated and "reasonable explanation" for the additional Vioxx deaths. In the great tradition of physicians from Galen to Osler, Merck made an important therapeutic conclusion based on a very logical physiological concept.

Many physicians had already accepted the elegant idea that cox-2 inhibition reduced the risk of ulcers. So the main conclusion was not a surprise. As for the heart attack issue, doctors would have to reserve judgment until VIGOR was in a major medical journal that had given it careful and objective scrutiny. Experts speculated that Merck would try to get the study into one of the world's most prestigious and influential publications: *The Lancet, The Journal of the American Medical Association,* or *The New England Journal of Medicine.*

The company risked strict scrutiny from any of the editors of these publications, although the *NEJM* probably had the strictest chief editor among medical publishers: acting editor Dr. Marcia Angell, a stern critic of the pharmaceutical industry, known for her scrupulous vetting of research manuscripts and her condemnation of "commercial drug trials." Even if she accepted the paper, it was likely Angell would commission an accompanying editorial that would not only put the study in perspective and analyze its flaws, but better explain the controversial conclusion about the reason for more cardiovascular events in the Vioxx group.

As it happened, the study did get published in the *NEJM* on November 23, 2000, but instead of clarifying the science, the publication only caused more mystery and accusations. Eventually in December 2005 the *Journal* was forced to withdraw the paper's conclusions based on the discovery of additional information.

In any case, VIGOR survived scrutiny at Digestive Disease Week, because while major medical meetings appear to outsiders as assemblies in which to teach, learn, and exchange knowledge, they are wonderful distractions from the tedium of medical practice. Doctors find themselves treated to luxurious restaurants, invited to private parties and such special events as all-expense-paid excursions with their families to Disney World, leased out entirely for their benefit.

When all is said and done, the brightly colored million-dollar exhibits on gigantic, gaudy stages, where beautiful and sometimes enticing and scantily dressed models stand in front of huge plastic representations of the stomach, intestines, and liver; the gimmicks such as free photographs, free literature, prescribing pads, door posters, and buttons; the groomed salespeople eager to please; and the hustle and bustle of the press room all add up to a modern medicine show. Only the shapes of the elixir bottles have changed, and snakes are left at the door.

CHAPTER 20

Getting Out the Vioxx Message:
The Cyber Obstacleizer

"DODGE!"
—Merck sales training manual

On the morning of September 13, 2000, Dorothy Hamill and Bruce Jenner sat in front of a camera in a comfortable Manhattan television studio. The two had made their debut with Merck's "Everyday Victories" public relations campaigns for Vioxx on *Larry King Live.* If there had ever been any doubt about Hamill's star power, Larry King's show erased it.

Everyone at Merck was thrilled at Hamill's performance—as were over a million others across the country who would drive up Vioxx sales. However, the Food and Drug Administration was threatening Merck with a "Warning Letter," for Hamill's comments about her miraculous recovery with Vioxx and the fact that the program barely made any mention of possible serious side effects.[1]

Merck assembled a top team of marketers, public relations personnel, and its regulatory counsel, Joanne Lahner, to discuss the situation. The Merck team said that the program had presented an "honest view" of Vioxx and, besides, it had only been watched by 1.1 million people, not the 1.5 million that the FDA claimed.

As for informing the audience about side effects, a doctor on the program had told people that "Vioxx was not for everyone" (although neither is mother's milk) and that they should "see their doctor" before taking Vioxx (a sure bet because the pill was only available with a doctor's prescription).

Merck was somewhat contrite. They indicated that although Hamill and Jenner had been "thoroughly trained" about the "proper message" and the scope of what they could say, that the two celebrities "went off on their own." Thus, Merck more or less admitted that their spokespeople knew exactly what to say, but didn't say it; however, there was nothing wrong with what they said anyhow. This response did not seem to amuse the FDA.

Merck said that although they didn't have to, they were putting all further media interviews involving the celebrities on hold as of September 12 until Merck assured the FDA that the celebrities would stay within the agreed-upon deadlines. The FDA backed off on its warning letter.

It was one day after Merck's assurances that Hamill and Jenner began what is known as a "satellite media tour" or SMT. An SMT is a method of getting spokespeople, generally celebrities or doctors, to appear around the country on television news and interview programs while sitting in the comfort of a single television studio and not having to travel anywhere.

The SMT began weeks in advance of the actual broadcast when letters, faxes, and e-mails went out to selected news directors and producers around the country announcing that Hamill and Jenner would be available, via satellite, to have a friendly chat about "an important health issue."

Producers love satellite tours. It allows a local television show to compete with much bigger stations because it appears to the studio audience at home that a local newscaster has a personal rapport with a major celebrity. The news director is supplied with video clips, questions, background material, and sometimes talking points, to make it appear that the local newscaster is an old friend of the stars. WAGA in Atlanta had a virtual love-in with Hamill, Jenner, and Merck's hired doctor:

Announcer: Hello, my name is Marc and I'm an Olympic junkie.
Hamill: Hi, Marc!
Marc: Thank you. Seriously, I love the Olympics, Summer and Winter, and probably won't get enough sleep while the games are on in Sydney . . . But that's okay. The games have given us some wonderful moments and incredibly inspiring athletes and two of my favorites are here this morning, Bruce Jenner, decathlon winner in Montreal, and America's Sweetheart, gold

medalist at Innsbruck Dorothy Hamill, join us here on *Good Day*. You have Dr. James Andrews to help you . . . Does it seem possible it's been twenty-five years?

Jenner: Has it been twenty-five years?

Dorothy: Almost.

Bruce: Twenty-four and a half.

Marc: Has it really?

Dorothy: No, for you twenty-four years.

Marc: People don't want to hear our heroes have maybe lost a step or two.

Dorothy: No, we haven't lost a step or two.

Bruce: We haven't lost a darn thing! Marc, don't start rumors!

Marc: Dorothy, how is the arthritis affecting you?

Dorothy: I'm still skating. I got to the point where I thought I'd have to give it up . . . Everything hurt . . . I'd shuffle to the bathroom in the morning, want to spend the whole day in bed, having chronic pain like that is exhausting. I got to the point where I would drive my daughter to the playground to have a picnic instead of walking to the park . . . My doctor prescribed Vioxx for me and I've had great results. I'm skating two hours a day. I'm going to the gym . . . so it's really changed my life a lot.

So much for Dorothy Hamill being off message in her previous performance and so much for all the additional Merck training. But no one can claim that the video interview was not balanced about the potential side effects of Vioxx, which are elegantly stated by Dr. Andrews:

Dr. Andrews: Vioxx doesn't work for everyone. It may be right for you.

Marc: Thank you so much, Bruce, Dorothy, Doctor for being with us this morning.

Bruce: Thanks for having us.

Dorothy: It was absolutely our pleasure.

Marc: Best wishes to all of you!

Now words appear on the screen as Marc reads the summary: "For a free brochure, 'Everyday Victories: Facing the Challenge of Arthritis,' is available by calling 1-888-36VIOXX or by visiting www.Vioxx.com.[2]

No mention is made that the satellite-video tour has been provided and paid for by Merck or that Hamill, Jenner, and Dr. Andrews are very highly compensated spokespeople for the company.

Similar segments would air around the country. In the Manhattan television studio, Jenner, Hamill, and Andrews sat back and took a break while another television station was contacted. It only took a few minutes to set up a satellite connection and make the necessary technical adjustments. And once again, Hamill and Jenner were having another "spontaneous friendly conversation" with another hard-hitting reporter.

The television station can use the segment live or it can be taped for further use. Or both. A popular satellite tour can draw hundreds of thousands of viewers. These programs are particularly dangerous for patients because the audience does not know that they are seeing a sophisticated commercial, are given no indication of the warnings of a drug, or told that there might be a safer, cheaper, or much better way to treat their condition.

At the end of the day, Hamill, Jenner, and the doctor calmly left the studio, none the worse for wear. In effect, they toured the entire country in several hours and made both producers and the sponsor happy. The FDA never found out.

The wonderful advantage of this satellite technique is not only that it costs very little, it connects Hamill and Jenner with Vioxx. Now the two celebrities can perform around the country, give interviews—but never mention the pill at all. It's not necessary, as the audience has already made the association between the stars and the drug.

At Merck, Dr. Deborah Shapiro was still analyzing the heart safety data on Vioxx. She found, when she broke out the specific number of heart attacks by looking at all the Vioxx trial results, that Vioxx presented a clear danger. She wrote a highly confidential report, titled "VIOXX Preliminary Cardiovascular Meta-Analysis," on October 18, 2000. The "Meta-Analysis" combined the results of all available Vioxx studies. The relative risk of "thrombotic cardiovascular events" (heart-related problems associated with blood clots) was compared among Vioxx users and those given either no drug or another NSAID. Twenty-eight patients had an acute MI (heart attack) versus five on other NSAIDs. Among all patients taking Vioxx or NSAIDs, the rate of heart disease was about double in the Vioxx group.

The results were never shown to the FDA and never presented outside the company, so far as the evidence shows. According to the Martin Report, Dr. Shapiro did not believe the test was valid because of the issue of "heterogeneity." This means that the trials were too dissimilar in terms of dose or length of time to be accurately compared—akin to comparing apples with oranges. But Dr. Shapiro did break out the data separately in various studies and groups, most of which showed a clear heart danger with the Vioxx groups. Neither scientists from the Food and Drug Administration nor any independent researchers were able to examine the data Dr. Shapiro used.

A little over a month after the Hamill broadcasts, on Saturday, October 28, 2000, Dr. James Fries was relaxing in his home near Stanford University. He was more than a little surprised by the identity of the caller.

"Hello. This is Dr. Louis Sherwood of Merck Pharmaceuticals."

Dr. Fries had gotten many calls from pharmaceutical companies, but not at home on a Saturday. "Yes," Dr. Fries said, trying to be courteous. Dr. Sherwood explained that he was a senior vice president at Merck who worked in the medical department and was concerned about an important issue. Fries listened as the man got to his point.

"You have a doctor working in your group named Gurkirpal Singh?"

"Yes, I do."

"Unfortunately," Dr. Sherwood said, "Dr. Singh has an anti-Merck bias and has been giving lectures that were irresponsible and specifically anti-Vioxx." Dr. Fries continued to listen. "We know that Dr. Singh uses a slide in his lecture that shows a person hiding data under his covers and has called Merck 'the Firestone of the Pharmaceutical Industry' " (a reference to the infamous Firestone 500 tire recall of the 1970s).

Dr. Fries is one of the senior epidemiologists and rheumatologists in the world. He had never received a phone call such as this during his entire career. As Sherwood continued, Fries found himself getting more and more angry.

Sherwood accused Singh of trying to obtain information on the VIGOR trial "that would have been inappropriate for him to have."

This was an odd statement for two reasons: Singh was trying to obtain data on the cardiovascular effects of Vioxx that Fries himself had been trying to get. At a recent meeting of the American College of Rheumatology, as rumors had begun to spread in the academic community about the dangers of Vioxx, the company seemed to be going out of its way to prevent scientists from evaluating VIGOR. (The heart data of the VIGOR trial was not presented at the rheumatology meeting). In any case, Dr. Singh's job was to educate physicians about Vioxx. What would be inappropriate about obtaining data about the drug?

Sherwood continued: "Singh is going to flame out and there will be some consequences for both you and Stanford."

Dr. Fries remained polite and promised to investigate the situation. What he found was far worse than he ever imagined.[3]

Matters with Vioxx were not going well overseas. On September 8, 2000, two British health authorities, the Medicines Control Agency and the Committee on Safety of Medicines, reported 1,120 adverse reactions to Vioxx. There had also been eleven deaths associated with the drug. Ironically, the most reported adverse reactions were gastrointestinal: nausea and stomach pain. More distressingly, the drug was associated with bleeding ulcers, five of which were fatal. Three hundred cases related to heart problems were reported.[4] British authorities announced that the safety of Vioxx was under close review.

The New England Journal of Medicine published the VIGOR trial in its November 23, 2000, issue, almost exactly as Dr. Alise Reicin of Merck had drafted it and not long after Dr. Fries had been contacted by Merck's Sherwood. No editorial accompanied the article. No questions were raised about whether naproxen could protect the heart, or whether the heart attacks had all taken place among people who should have been on aspirin, or indeed whether these very people had been given adequate warning.

Important information, such as the number of deaths that occurred in the study and the incidence of high blood pressure and fluid retention, were either distorted or omitted.[5]

If the *NEJM* was "stunned" by the 500 percent or 400 percent increase in heart events with Vioxx, as Dr. Singh and Rick Stover had been, it was never mentioned. This is all the more peculiar because the controversies about Vioxx heart safety had already appeared in the press. And as Rick Stover had put it, the cardioprotective finding about naproxen would have been a medical first.

By the November publication date, Dr. Marcia Angell had left the *Journal* and been replaced by a permanent editor, Dr. Jeffrey Drazen. Drazen said that because of a commercial conflict of interest he could not work on the VIGOR article and instead left it to executive editor Dr. Gregory Curfman.

The editors of the *NEJM* claim, in their "Letter of Concern" published in December 2005, that they were duped by Merck and that information about the number of heart attacks was altered by the company. The *NEJM* claimed it knew this by analyzing a computer disk containing an original draft of the VIGOR study.[6] In a response letter to the *Journal*, Merck claimed that the three additional heart attacks happened after the clinical trial was complete, so that they didn't count and wouldn't have changed the conclusion of the study in any case.[7]

The *NEJM* countered that the three additional heart attacks occurred among people who did not need aspirin and this dramatically changed the conclusion that Vioxx was harmless.[8]

It did appear that Merck often revised the risk of "cardiovascular events" in the Vioxx group. In the first press release, it was "double" the number in the naproxen group.[9] However, when Dr. Laine presented the Results at Digestive Disease Week (May, 24, 2000) it was "four times" (.04). But Merck issued information the following year indicating the number .05, or five times the number of heart events.

Merck reported the controversial three extra cases of cardiovascular disease in the Vioxx group to the FDA, which posted the result on its Web site *before the NEJM publication*, but did not report these events to the *NEJM*. The *NEJM* editors said they were aware of the discrepancy, but thought that the additional heart attacks occurred *after* journal publication.

The following year, when lawyers representing heart attack victims questioned the editors about the different figures, the *NEJM* launched an investigation in which they located the "doctored" disk data.

Upon discovery of the tampering, the editors issued a "Letter of Concern" about the VIGOR study, stating that its conclusions would not have been accepted had the editors known the facts.

But the editors did not "withdraw" the paper, and they allowed Merck and the external investigators to answer the "Letter of Concern." The *NEJM* then "reaffirmed" its "Letter of Concern."

It was later learned that the *NEJM* had issued the first "Letter of Concern" on the advice of a public relations consultant who wanted to distract reporters from investigating why the *Journal* had not published the heart attack data it had known about for years. The *Journal* also admitted that it had sold Merck most of its 929,400 reprints (more than one for every doctor in the country) for $697,000.

Many questions about VIGOR are still vigorously and acrimoniously being argued. It could be claimed, for example, that Merck knew about the cardiovascular risks of VIGOR a year before they were published. It was in November 1999, when the Data and Safety Monitoring Board expressed its first concerns about what was happening in the study and Merck's statistician, Dr. Shapiro (who was fully aware of who was getting the two drugs), started making her analysis.

More mysteries continued to turn up about the VIGOR study. The individual doctors who were doing the actual testing on the patients reported far more cardiovascular disease than was ever reported in the published study. The reason was that the heart events had to be evaluated by an "adjudication" committee. This committee made the final decisions about whether a cardiovascular event (like stroke) had occurred by examining the medical records of patients in the trial. It was later learned that the committee had sharply lowered the number of heart attacks in both the Vioxx and naproxen groups, much more so than is usually seen. This would be in Merck's favor, if the company suspected more heart problems would show up in the Vioxx group, which turned out to be the case. Despite the fact that the adjudication committee had to be strictly objective, it was composed of scientists from Merck.

Once the results of the study were known, Merck warned investigators using Vioxx to begin using aspirin in high-risk cardiovascular patients.

Another lingering mystery is why, after seeing the letter warning the investigators to use aspirin among those with heart risk, didn't the FDA post a warning on its Web site saying exactly what Merck had written to its own investigators? To the contrary, the FDA put out no warning letter or posting about Vioxx and implied on numerous occasions that "no safety problems existed" with the drug. In fact, behind the scenes, as the agency analyzed the data, it was getting very concerned, something that would not be revealed until a year after the study concluded.

Most doctors hadn't the vaguest idea that any of this debate was taking place. None knew about the company's internal memos worrying about the VIGOR trial and its potential findings, nor did they know about the maneuvering behind the *NEJM* publication.

As far as most in the medical profession were concerned, Vioxx was a wonder drug, and all that patients remembered was the smiling face of Dorothy Hamill, telling them they had nothing to worry about, and that their lives could begin anew.

Instead of warning doctors and the public about the concerns raised by the VIGOR study, Merck continued its campaign to "reaffirm" the safety of Vioxx. David Anstice unleashed his army of representatives, by now over 3,500, with documents like "Dodge Ball" and "Obstacle Jeopardxx" to answer concerns physicians might have about Vioxx safety.[10]

The company prepared videos for their sales people such as *Be the Power*. This twelve-minute science fiction film shows characters dressed in *Star Wars* clothes trying to pump up Merck employees to sell more Vioxx. "The trainers show the representatives a yet to be finalized 'cyber obstacleizer'—a machine through which they will be able to enter another world and practice their obstacle handling skills." Inside the machine, the salespeople see a "female obstacle" who says she is afraid that Vioxx causes heart attacks. The representatives are told, "That is not true." At the end of the video the salespeople are told the machine has now allowed them to "be the power."[11]

Salespeople were also given "cardiovascular cards" that showed doctors that patients in Vioxx studies had a *lower* rate of cardiovascular events than "regular" NSAIDs. This was an extraordinary statistical feat. The card was headlined, "Overall Mortality and Cardiovascular Mortality."

The card then provided the following data: total mortality in the Vioxx group was 0.1. But with regular NSAIDs it was 1.1, or ten times the number of Vioxx. Cardiovascular mortality was 0.1 with Vioxx, but 0.8 with NSAIDs. NSAIDs caused eight times the number of cardiovascular deaths than Vioxx.

This was quite an extraordinary piece of literature, considering that the VIGOR trial showed either four or five times the number of cardiovascular events for Vioxx than for naproxen. Merck told their reps not to "bring up the subject of VIGOR," but to allay doctors' fears with the elaborate sales material.[12]

Merck would later argue that it could not mention the results of VIGOR because the FDA would not have allowed it to claim that Vioxx was safer for the stomach than naproxen. If that was the case, then what happened to the 929,400 reprints of the study from the *NEJM?* Merck distributed 45,000 to physicians *before* the FDA allowed it to make the claim that it caused fewer ulcers than naproxen (which was the headline in the study). The fact that physicians received the reprints through Merck's medical department, instead of from sales reps, apparently made it legal.

As Merck's "Martin Report" points out, "Representatives were to serve solely as a conduit for the information and were prohibited from discussing the contents [of the response letter] with the inquiring physician." However, Merck salespeople, not the medical department, were providing the letter to the physicians. So Merck's response to VIGOR, was brought to doctors, by field representatives—in much the same manner as they would deliver any other piece of information from the company. Merck's response was this was deemed to be "the equivalent" of doctor-to-doctor communication, with the sales force merely being "conduits."

The "Martin Report" continues that "the response letter mirrored the language of the [VIGOR] press release, noting that 'significantly fewer thromboembolitic events [heart disease related problems] were observed in patients taking naproxen, which is consistent with naproxen's ability to block . . . platelet aggregation [help protect the heart].' "

Merck admits that the content of this "more detailed reponse letter on the results of the VIGOR trial varied over time," but that ["no version of this letter discussed . . . the possibility that Vioxx might have been responsibe for the between-treatment difference in the incidence of cardio-vascular events in the VIGOR Trial."]

In other words, Merck salespeople were directly handing physicians a letter that did not mention that Vioxx could cause heart disease, even though there were four to five times more heart attacks (according to the FDA) in this group than with naproxen.

This response letter began to be handed out to inquiring physicians on March 27, 2000. Salespeople continued to distribute the release until May 8, 2000—after which when the responsibility returned to the medical department. Still, the "Martin Report" makes clear, that the possibility of the harmful effects of Vioxx on the heart was not mentioned.

On September 17, 2001, the FDA issued a Warning Letter to Merck accusing the company of distributing unbalanced and deceptive information about Vioxx: it made reference to the company engaging "in promotional activities for Vioxx that minimized the potentially serious cardiovascular findings that were observed in the VIGOR study." The FDA alleged that Merck's promotional campaign failed "to disclose that [the naproxen heart protection theory hypothesis was] hypothetical, [had] not been demonstrated by substantial evidence and that there is another reasonable explanation" that Vioxx itself might promote heart attacks.

The "Martin Report" states that, "According to Ms. [Joanne] Lahner [Merck managing counsel], Mr [David] Anstice and Mr. [Raymond] Gilmartin [chairman and CEO] participated in making the decision to institute this procedure, although neither remembered any specific role in doing so."[13]

Merck's decision to distribute the VIGOR study before the FDA had evaluated it was a brilliant marketing move. Salespeople did not directly offer the published *NEJM* article to doctors; however, a good sales rep is clever enough to get into a conversation with a physician whose outcome is: "Doctor, I really can't talk about the VIGOR study, but if you contact our medical department, I'm sure they can help you." The reps target doctors who prescribe large amounts of pain medicines as well as influential gastroenterologists and rheumatologists or pharmacists and physicians who work on committees in hospitals to determine which drugs will be recommended for use by their staff.

The fact that the reprinted articles were sent from a specific "medical division" furthered the illusion that the study was not simply "industry-sponsored," but a full-fledged academic study, whose results represented not only academia at its finest, but the imprimatur of the world's leading medical journal.

A few months after the reprints went out, Merck sent a letter to physicians receiving the reprint stating that the correct number for the difference in heart and stroke events between Vioxx and naproxen was five times (0.5), rather than four times (0.4), as stated in the *NEJM* article itself. This despite the fact that Merck knew the final results before the study was published.

Not until four years later in 2005 was this change reported in the *Journal,* and by this time the 0.4 number had been cited by hundreds of other journals. In its letter, Merck explained that the 0.5 figure included the "total number of heart adverse events," not just those in the "pre-specified cut off point." This is more or less what prompted the *NEJM*'s "Letter of Concern" in 2005.

Why didn't the editors know about the Merck letter changing the number of cardiovascular events?

The baffling answer came out when *NEJM* editor Dr. Jeffrey Drazen appeared on KUOW, a Seattle, Washington, radio show, on August 14, 2005, when he received a live phone call from pharmacist Dr. Jennifer Hrachovec. Drazen seemed startled when he heard Dr. Hrachovec say about VIGOR: "With this study in particular, it bothers me that there are more data from the trial than has ever been published and the *New England Journal* still hasn't published an editorial or any kind of update to [inform] readers and clinicians using this drug and giving it to patients who they think will benefit from a better side-effect profile. My concern is that doctors are still using this and exposing their patients to higher risks of heart problems and they just don't even know that's the case."

Without losing a second of airtime, Dr. Drazen replied that he had to recuse himself from the study (the whole problem wasn't his fault), then went on to say, "We can't be in the business of policing every bit of data that we put out. We think that's the role of people who know the field. And when they think that the field has advanced to the point where something which was true at the time it came out may no longer be true . . . having brought that evidence to our attention in the form of a manuscript or a letter, we can judge whether there's enough new information and put it out if we believe the reanalysis is correct."

In fact, Dr. Hrachovec as well as a physician reviewing Vioxx for a Seattle health insurer had written a letter to the *NEJM*, noting not only differences from the FDA data, but pointing out critical data that had been omitted from the publication. The *Journal*, claiming they had limited space, never published the letter.

Dr. Drazen said that *Journal* editors were *just the middlemen* "in picking what goes out there" and "when there are problems the onus lies with the authors to sound the alert. . . . If you ask me, it is none of our concern about whether Vioxx is a cardiovascular risk in the patients that are on trial. The concern was making sure what was published was correct and people could have set the record straight."[14]

This is not precisely the superlative image the *Journal* likes to project. "Boston, always representative of the high type of medical practice which has prevailed throughout New England, has been singularly fortunate in the type of medical journalism which has characterized that practice," the *Journal* noted in its inaugural issue, February 23, 1928 (Vol. 19, No. 1).

"To Boston belongs the distinction of having published the first journal of medicine in the country, if not in the world, which has continued, despite changes of form and of name in uninterrupted existence until the present day."

The *NEJM* had indeed begun its existence as the *New England Journal of Medicine and Surgery and the Collateral Branches of Science* in January

1812. Two of its first articles were "Treatment of Injury Occasioned by Fire" and "Remarks on Diseases Resembling Syphilis."

Upon the first edition bearing the new name, *The New England Journal of Medicine* noted that the "outlook for the future is as brilliant as the past. May the *New England Journal of Medicine* serve the profession of the future as well as its distinguished ancestors have served it in the years gone by!" These are not the words of humble middlemen waiting around for corrections by appropriate experts from drug companies.

Those who count on the *NEJM* for the last word in medical truth should keep in mind that in the 1928 inaugural, a state-of-the-art lead paper was presented about a woman with headaches who was treated at a Harvard hospital with bloodletting.

In any event, now that the *NEJM* had published the VIGOR study as Merck desired, the company was well on its way to establishing Vioxx as a safer alternative to much less expensive NSAIDs. Heart risks of the drug were "neutralized." By year's end 2000, Vioxx revenues continued climbing dramatically and Merck executives watched as the value of their stock options soared. The company was approaching its goal of regaining its rank as the world's largest pharmaceutical company. Under such circumstances, who could complain?

PART V

Chapter 21

Science in Reverse

"Bury me on my face," said Diogenes; and when he was asked why, he replied, "Because in a little while everything will be turned upside down."

—Diogenes, "Liberties"

Dr. James Fries was furious. He thought *The New England Journal of Medicine* VIGOR article did a poor job of addressing the medical community's concerns about Vioxx toxicity and did not carry the information he and many others were struggling to uncover and analyze. But Fries was more startled when he learned that Merck had been making serious, unheard-of threats to the country's leading physicians. He said, "They got people fired and made up an enemies list.[1]

"And this wasn't some isolated incident or a loose cannon. It was very wide within Merck. At least five or six top people left Merck because of fear that the whole VIGOR story was going to blow up their career."

Fries called Dr. Louis Sherwood and the two exchanged heated words. Sherwood denied there were any problems with Vioxx, "because they occurred only in the high dose," a statement Fries recalls as a "bizarre contradiction."

Finally, Sherwood more or less backed off, but Fries wrote a detailed letter of the threats to medical professors and addressed it to the head of Merck, Raymond Gilmartin. Merck replied that they would "investigate the intimidation."

"It didn't stop though," Fries states. "Some of it maybe." Dr. Fries bumped into Sherwood at another medical meeting and later the two had another agitated phone call. "That was when I said, 'Lou, you ought to be ashamed of yourself.'"

Sherwood said he had been a top academic professor and could use his power any way he wanted. Fries hung up as Sherwood started his next sentence.

Fries exhaled slowly and thought about the list of experts who had been threatened. The name he wondered about most was Dr. David Yocum. Merck had gone after the new head of the FDA Arthritis Advisory Committee? Surely the Food and Drug Administration of the United States had to take *some* action.

Dr. David Graham is associate director for science and medicine in the Office of Drug Safety, the division of the Food and Drug Administration responsible for keeping track of the side effects of drugs that have been approved by the agency. Graham is a slender man with a gaunt face and slight body who has been in and out of the spotlight for most of his twenty-year career with the FDA.

Graham originally studied neurology in medical school, but changed his mind, and switched to a specialty in epidemiology and the design and analysis of clinical trials. A devout Catholic, Graham has six children and took up the study of biblical Greek so that he could read the New Testament in its original language.[2]

Almost no one disputes Graham's brilliance, but his take-no-prisoners style within the FDA has caused deep fractures—and his testimony in front of the Senate committee investigating Vioxx caused many in the medical and legal community to label him a "bomb thrower" and "panic monger."

Graham shrugs off the criticism. He takes his job as an FDA safety officer as seriously as his religion and feels a sense of responsibility to what he refers to as his *patients*, "the people in the United States" who take prescription medication.

Shortly after VIGOR was published in the *NEJM*, the study came to Graham's attention. He read it over and over, focusing on the details. The conclusion made no sense. How could Merck, the outside academic investigators, and the *Journal* have come to the conclusion that there was nothing to be concerned about regarding the heart risks of Vioxx? Graham found himself questioning how the outcome of the study could be explained by the fact that naproxen protected the heart.

"It simply defied the scientific basis by which we analyze clinical trials. That's not my opinion, it's basic to how we form our conclusions," Graham explains.

In any experiment evaluating therapies, there must be at least two groups. The first group is known as the "experimental group" and consists of the medical treatment under study. The experimental group in Ben Franklin's study was magnetized trees. The experimental group in Austin Hill's first randomized, blinded trial was the tuberculosis drug streptomycin.

The experimental group in VIGOR was Vioxx. If a therapy works, the experimental group must show an effect. If it does not, the therapy is a failure. The experimental group must be compared to a "control group." In Franklin's study, the control group was an un-magnetized tree; in Austin Hill's study, the control group was tuberculosis patients given bed rest, fresh air, baths, and good diets.

In the VIGOR trial the control was the group taking naproxen. At the completion of the trial, results in the experimental group, Vioxx, are compared to the findings in the control group, naproxen.

The way the comparison is done, Graham explains, is like creating a fraction or a ratio—that is, the number of events in the experimental group (Vioxx or streptomycin), divided by the events in the control group. How did Austin Hill learn that streptomycin cured tuberculosis? He compared the number of cures in the streptomycin group (30) with the number of cures in the bed rest group (3).

He was able to create a simple fraction 30 (experimental group), divided by 3 (control group): $^{30}/_3$ or 10. Hill could then conclude that streptomycin was ten times more effective than bed rest.

Graham explains: "When Merck analyzed the data for the number of ulcers in the VIGOR trial, they did it the right way. They found that the rate in the Vioxx group was .5 for every hundred patients in the trial. The rate in the control group (naproxen) was 1."

So the ratio is .5 divided by 1, or ½. That means twice as many people taking naproxen got ulcers, compared to Vioxx. The experimental drug (Vioxx) was twice as safe for the stomach as the control drug, naproxen. Or at least that's what the initial data seemed to indicate.

But when Merck analyzed the number of heart attacks and strokes, the company did not use the same method. Graham describes what Merck did: "For the heart attacks and strokes, what Merck should have been forced to present was the rate of heart attacks in the Vioxx group (5 per hundred), compared to the rate in the naproxen group (1 per hundred). And that is a five times increased risk of heart attacks in the Vioxx group compared to the naproxen group. The fraction would look like 5/1."

Graham immediately recognized that Merck had turned the clinical trial results upside down. Instead of using the fraction 5/1 (as they had appeared to have done with the rate of ulcers), they used ⅕. "The *New England Journal* allowed Merck to do that. And what that does is to allow Merck to misdirect the audience. Merck was able to claim that the risk with naproxen was only ⅕ of that of Vioxx and that's because naproxen *lowers* cardiovascular risk. It allows Merck to avoid having to say the words: 'The risk is *higher* in Vioxx than it is in naproxen.'

"What Merck should have done is present the data properly—that there was a fivefold increase of heart attack in the Vioxx group compared to naproxen. Then in the next paragraph they could have given their interpretation. They could have explained why they thought Vioxx didn't increase the risk of heart disease.

"That's legitimate. You can do that in a paper as long as you're honest about the way you've presented the science." Graham is definitive: "In my view, Merck was neither honest nor transparent."

If Austin Hill had flipped his data, he would have concluded that bed rest did not seem as effective as streptomycin for curing tuberculosis, not that streptomycin effectively cured the disease. Hill might have gone on to say that he didn't know why this was so, but that there was still no proof of streptomycin's value as a cure.

Ben Franklin could have concluded that magnetized trees as well as regular trees were "equally effective" as cures. "Regular trees are just as effective as magnetized trees for the cure of nervous affliction," Franklin might have logically deduced. If Merck could conclude that naproxen lowered the risk of heart disease, Franklin could have deduced that touching an ordinary tree lowered the rate of anxiety. The doctor could have ascribed this result to the fact that the ordinary tree worked the same way as a related shrub.

As Graham delved deeper into the VIGOR study, his anger only increased: "The *New England Journal of Medicine*, their editorial board, and the outside reviewers they commissioned allowed Merck to make a false claim." Graham sees the controversy over whether there were four times the deaths or five times the deaths as a red herring. "Either way, Vioxx presented a serious health hazard," Graham concludes.

The story of Franz Anton Mesmer and how he created "observation bias" should now be clear. Mesmer was essentially a magician who misdirected the mind. He created belief in his patients, and the belief itself created the cure. By skewing the words in the *NEJM* article and using experts to give it validity, Merck was able to harness the authority of the *Journal* and those who read it. Reporters and financial analysts were given constant briefings using the data, and the experts were induced to believe what really wasn't there. Merck managed to pull off the impossible. They convinced the world that magnetized trees had the power to cure.

In fact, given the millions of people who were taking Vioxx, Graham worried that the country *really did* face a health catastrophe. The people most likely to use Vioxx for arthritis would be older and probably have more risk factors for heart disease in the first place—hence be more susceptible to any harmful effects of a cox inhibitor. But Graham needed more proof than reworking the VIGOR study's statistical method. He thought the best course of action would be to remove Vioxx from the market until the dispute could be resolved, or at least that Merck be given one year to conduct a study to prove that their drug was not harmful to the heart.

Dr. Graham told the Senate Finance Committee that the FDA did not ban the high-dose (50 mg) formulation or its use. This was the dose used in VIGOR and recommended for acute pain. "I believe such a ban should have been implemented." The reason is simple. Because a patient had a bottle of 50 mg pills, it would be simple to take two: one in the morning, one at night. That means 100 mg a day, close to the amount Merck used in its initial Vioxx study that produced such dangerous side effects.

However, Dr. Graham had jousted with his FDA colleagues before and was certain the agency would let the safety issues of Vioxx slide. Graham concluded he would have to take matters into his own hands to stave off the looming disaster to his "patients." Within days of analyzing the VIGOR study, he called colleagues at the health care group Kaiser Permanente in California, which has one of the largest drug safety databases in the country. Graham hoped he could use this information to conclude whether Vioxx was causing heart disease as he suspected. He further believed he did not have much time to make his case, because a deadly drug was being used by an ever-increasing number of people.

By the fall of 2000, Merck and Pfizer had both published studies in prestigious medical journals (*NEJM* for Vioxx and *JAMA* for Celebrex) "proving" that super aspirin was safer for the stomach than other NSAIDs. However, despite the successful publications and all the accompanying lectures and distributions to doctors, the drug companies had to prepare meticulously for their toughest presentation yet—another FDA advisory committee hearing to at last review the *human* evidence of whether or nor Vioxx and Celebrex were really safer than similar pills. This time Merck and Pfizer were required by law to make sure that all of the information about the studies was available.

Furthermore, the FDA reviewers and outside expert advisors were not only free to analyze and question any statement or conclusion the companies might have. It was their job. This was not like publishing in even the best medical journal. The FDA was thorough, tough, and empowered by statute to enforce its decisions. At least, that is how the system is supposed to work.

Even before the two-day arthritis advisory committee hearing began, it was shrouded in controversy. A day before it was to convene in the Gaithersburg, Maryland, Holiday Inn on February 8, 2001, Dr. David Yocum (who had been threatened by Merck) was forced out of his chairmanship and not allowed to participate by the FDA because he had *one patient* who had been in a Merck Vioxx trial. Dr. James Fries had confidentially told *USA Today* about the Merck threats to investigators. The paper agreed not to run the story but to keep track of those who had been intimidated.

Yocum was furious with the FDA. He knew that people with far greater conflicts of interest had been happily making decisions about Vioxx for years. Not inconsequentially, Yocum was skeptical about the super aspirins. "When you look at people under the age of 60, the risk of a significant GI bleed is very, very small, if you adhere to taking NSAIDs with food and not drinking alcohol with them," Dr. Yocum told *USA Today*.[3]

Dr. Eve Slater, then Merck's senior vice president of corporate relations and regulatory liaison and increasingly Merck's highest-ranking point person on Vioxx with both the press and the FDA, explained that the company had done thorough research to explain why naproxen protected the heart. It worked similarly to aspirin, Slater explained. She was countered by an FDA researcher who worried that Vioxx might be disrupting homeostasis, an ancient concept first made prominent by the Roman medical authority Galen, and centuries later by Dr. Garrett FitzGerald. According to FDA official Robert DeLap, "People have a lot of organ systems and one does not know if a drug that perhaps produces less of a certain side effect in the gastrointestinal system might produce other adverse effects."[4]

Some of those effects included high blood pressure and water retention—edema—not fully reported in the *NEJM*, nor anywhere else, although they are serious enough to cause heart failure. Slater was reassuring. "The edema numbers will be reported in spades to the advisory committee," Slater said. "There was no specific reason why it was not reported. There was no effort on anybody's part to put an important number under the rug." Slater evidently didn't think it was an important issue. "You're beginning to count the number of angels on a pin," she said. If left untreated and severe enough, high blood pressure and water retention may cause health complications or death. These were the figures so anxiously sought by Dr. Singh and Dr. Fries. It was the data that Dr. Singh was told "was none of his business."

The first day of the advisory meeting was bad enough. Pfizer/Searle presented the results of their outcomes trial, CLASS. It had already been presented in *The Journal of the American Medical Association* to much acclaim, and showed that Celebrex was far safer for the stomach than "regular NSAIDs."

The study reported in *JAMA* was six months long. The study presented to the committee by the FDA showed data at nine months and at a year. During this extended period of time, there were far more ulcers in the Celebrex group. The committee members, many complaining of either deceit or fraud, were "flabbergasted."

The *JAMA* said they were unaware of the additional data before they published the paper, but said they had to "trust the investigators with what was submitted." The infuriated and still confused advisory committee turned down Pfizer's request to be able to claim more Celebrex stomach safety than any similar NSAID. Super aspirin number one was decisively shot down.

The VIGOR study was presented the next day. Dr. Alise Reicin showed the results. As usual, her poise and finesse were outstanding, her demeanor confident. Behind her sat ten of the world's leading cardiologists, gastroenterologists, rheumatologists, and statisticians—a small cheering section provided as a courtesy from Merck just to make sure all questions could be properly answered. In fact, the presence of the renowned panel was really more important than any other factor. These professors were the equivalent of the French Academy of Sciences or the British Royal Society, to which all doctors aspire as the heirs to Galen, Harvey, Osler, and their prestigious universities.

One doctor who was not present was Grant Cannon, associate chief of staff for Academic Affiliations of the Salt Lake City Veterans Administration Medical Center, and lead author of a study published in *Arthritis and Rheumatism* comparing the stomach safety of Vioxx and a popular NSAID similar to naproxen called diclofenac. The study involved 784 patients with an average age of sixty-three who had osteoarthritis of the knee and hip. Merck released a press release touting the study. "Vioxx Relieved Signs and Symptoms of Osteoarthritis for One Full Year—Study Confirms Safety of Vioxx in Extended Use."[5] The VIGOR study only lasted nine months.

Dr. Cannon said that the study, which used a Vioxx dose of 12.5 to 25 milligrams, was "welcome news to physicians and patients looking for the right medicine for osteoarthritis."[6] But the study had an outcome no one expected. There was no difference in symptomatic ulcers in either group. Vioxx not only failed to prevent serious bleeding ulcers and death, it didn't even prove any better at stomachaches. Nor did Merck explain why it was so important that Vioxx, which cost about $3 a pill, should be used instead of a common over-the-counter drug like Motrin that costs about ten cents.

Even more disturbing, the Vioxx dose was not the often-used dose of 50 mg. If that dose had been used, could Vioxx actually have caused more ulcers than an ordinary NSAID? Speculation, of course, but given the number of novel theories tossed around in the Vioxx debacle probably not unfair.

Merck did point out that the number of heart-related incidents was similar in both groups. But again, this was at a lower dose than the 50 mg which was used in the VIGOR study. Merck scientists had known since 1996 that the cardiovascular risk was dose-dependent, in other words, determined by the amount of the drug taken. And as pointed out earlier, dosage creep is common with people in pain.

The diclofenac study also partly put to rest all the speculation about whether the finding of tiny erosions in the stomach correlated with serious ulcer. At least as far as diclofenac was concerned it did not. The concern expressed by many scientists that these erosions meant very little in terms of actual clinical experience seemed confirmed.

But none of these speculations about Dr. Cannon's research was addressed at the FDA Arthritis Advisory Committee. The diclofenac study simply disappeared. Merck never again raised the issue that, even at a low dose, Vioxx was no more safe for the stomach than another popular similar medication. The cox-2 hypothesis continued to be widely accepted.

Making no mention of the diclofenac study, Dr. Alise Reicin addressed the Food and Drug Administration and the panel of advisory committee experts (without the skeptical Dr. Yocum) and reviewed the dreaded NSAID hospitalization and death numbers and the benefits of super aspirin. Dr. Reicin artfully attributed the heart disease results in the

VIGOR study to the benefits of naproxen. No one asked her why if Vioxx was safer for the stomach than one NSAID, it had been found no safer for the stomach than another.

Nor did Reicin provide information about the Vioxx side effects—exactly. These were somehow mixed with two other studies that no one or scientific body, including the FDA, had seen before. Dr. Reicin also talked about the benefits of Vioxx proved by an unknown experiment on a green monkey.[7]

"A green monkey?" one of the financial analysts asked, looking through all his notes for the nonexistent details. Reicin also made a less than convincing case that Merck had gone through a patient base of 28,000 people, who showed no more heart attacks on Vioxx than other NSAIDs. Except that the 28,000 did not include the naproxen patients, ignoring the results of one of the largest gastrointestinal trials ever conducted. That wasn't all they omitted.

Dr. Reicin did not mention the analysis of heart disease events performed by Dr. Deborah Shapiro, the Merck statistician, which showed more complications in the Vioxx patients than in those taking other NSAIDs. The data remained secret until it was discovered during legal proceedings and investigations of Merck.

The FDA review was done by Dr. Maria Lourdes Villalba, who found that Vioxx did indeed cause fewer serious ulcers than Aleve. But the number of serious events was the same as would be expected from the general population, from 2 percent to 4 percent. Dr. Villalba found a significant increase in heart disease among the Vioxx patients. She also observed that it should have been the investigators, not Merck, who made the judgment as to who needed aspirin.[8]

Villalba cast serious doubt on the naproxen theory. There were 58 percent fewer deaths in the naproxen group than with Vioxx. Aspirin could only have been expected to cause 25 percent to 30 percent fewer deaths. This was the same conclusion that Robert Stover had reached a year earlier, which earned him the threat of being boiled in oil.

Dr. Villalba noted that Merck had submitted other studies showing the cardiovascular risk of Vioxx. And finally she gave the long-sought numbers for high blood pressure and water swelling and their consequences.

Ten patients in the Vioxx group had serious problems caused by high blood pressure, compared to one patient taking naproxen. Sixteen patients had serious congestive heart failure (a fatal disease), compared to three in the naproxen group. (These were the numbers that Dr. Singh had been chastised for trying to seek.)

How did Merck public relations treat this information? At a meeting of the American Geriatrics Society, Merck publicized a study by Merck researcher Gregory Geba, M.D., with the suggested headline "Little Risk of Hypertension with Cox-2 Blockers." The story emphasized the safety of Vioxx and Celebrex with regard to high blood pressure and implied the drugs had no adverse effect. "The vast majority of patients do not have elevations," Dr. Geba stated. Significantly, the report was delivered to doctors who were treating patients at increased risk of heart disease.[9]

Besides hypertension and edema, the FDA reviewer revealed another shocking fact. There were two deaths from bleeding ulcers in the Vioxx group and one in the naproxen group and *overall, there were more serious adverse events taken as a whole with Vioxx than naproxen.*

The entire purpose of super aspirin was to reduce serious ulcer complications, especially death. If there were 16,500 ulcer deaths a year from NSAIDs, it was clear that neither Celebrex nor Vioxx was going to reduce that number at all. As Dr. Eric J. Topol, writing in the *NEJM,* December 30, 2004, summarizes the matter: "It is hard to imagine that the small protection from gastric or duodenal ulcers in the VIGOR trial is an acceptable trade-off as compared with twice the incidence of death, heart attacks and strokes." Indeed, Dr. Targum, the FDA reviewer of the VIGOR, wrote in her report ". . . [that] naproxen . . . would be the preferred drug." But what about the claim of "100,000" hospital admissions? The VIGOR study revealed that the number of perforations and obstructions were the same with naproxen or Vioxx, although the paper is cleverly written to group these together with bleeding (which is a potentially serious stomach complication). However, the total number of hospitalizations was higher with Vioxx than with naproxen. So substituting Vioxx for naproxen would not reduce the number of hospital admissions at all—just the opposite—especially since Vioxx caused five times as much heart disease. (Perhaps gastroenterologists might have seen fewer patients given Vioxx, but the rest of the hospital staff would see more.)

The whole purpose of developing the cox-2 inhibitors was to prevent hospital admission and death. The VIGOR study announced with such fanfare proved neither.

Finally, the FDA reviewers threw cold water on Merck's analysis of the 28,000 patient-study analysis that Dr. Reicin cited to prove that heart disease was the same in Vioxx as other NSAIDs, calling the data misleading and unscientific. Merck had committed an elementary statistical error based on "heterogeneity," meaning that the groups of studies were too different to properly analyze or make any real deductions. In other words, it was like comparing apples with oranges.

The advisory committee did listen to the FDA presentations, then ignored them. One cardiologist spent his time presenting his own (self-admittedly poor) analysis of the results. Another committee member gave a slide presentation on the dangers of bleeding ulcers. There were jokes about who were sexier: cardiologists, gastroenterologists, or rheumatologists.

Although many committee members made obscure and largely uncertain recommendations, they did stumble on some very significant information, almost by accident. One committee member was probing why the VIGOR trial had not been stopped earlier, given the fact that more heart attack deaths occurred in the Vioxx group. Dr. Reicin began answering the question, then decided to call James Neaton, Ph.D., a biostatistician who sat on the VIGOR data and safety monitoring board (DSMB).

Dr. Neaton said that the trial had not been stopped because: "I think that there was speculation on the part of some people on the board that this could be a protective effect of naproxen." Protective effect of naproxen? The board was speculating on this, according to Neaton, at least two months *before* the results of the trial were known. During this period the DSMB was unaware of which patients were taking Vioxx and which naproxen.

But Dr. Edward Scolnick and others at Merck have stated under oath that they had no idea naproxen could be protective of the heart *before* the results of VIGOR became known. Merck says that it made the association when it looked at previous research papers on a similar drug (flurbiprofen) and came to the conclusion after examining previously blinded clinical trials. All this happened in March 2000. Neaton said the DSMB was speculating on it the previous November or December 1999.

Besides which, how could three independent outside observers, who were not even supposed to know which patients were getting Vioxx, know about the naproxen hypothesis? There are three conclusions, all bad:

- Merck knew in advance that naproxen was protective and failed to inform patients, therefore deliberately putting them at risk.
- Merck knew in advance that Vioxx was poisonous, therefore deliberately putting patients at risk.
- Merck informed the independent DSMB about the possibilities of these possible conclusions *before the study was over* and both the Merck statistician and the DSMB ignored data that showed a clear pattern of harm to patients.

Dr. Edward Scolnick wrote to his team after the advisory committee hearing, "I was nervous from start to finish. You all were FANTASTIC. You made them look like grade d high school students and you won big huge and completely. You should be proud happy and . . . exhausted, enjoy and bask in the warmth of having done an impossible job superbly! Great job."[10]

Merck put out a self-congratulatory press release and, once again, never mentioned that Vioxx might be associated with heart disease. The statement read: "The Advisory Committee agreed with Merck and the FDA that results from the VIGOR study should be included in the labeling for Vioxx." The release quoted Dr. Eve Slater, who seemed to be gaining power and prestige with every advance of Vioxx.

"Merck is confident that the data presented today support the excellent safety profile of Vioxx, and *we* look forward to further discussions with the FDA to complete the review of our application to modify the labeling for Vioxx," said Slater, senior vice president clinical and regulatory development, Merck Research Laboratories.[11]

Vioxx had made it through an impossibly tough day. The advisory committee had recommended that Vioxx be given a label that stated it was safer for the stomach than a "standard" NSAID (although it recommended against removing the warning that such medications could cause severe bleeding and ulcers). But by and large, the committee did not reject the naproxen hypothesis and downplayed the association of Vioxx and heart disease. It asked for more data on Vioxx, but mandated no definitive studies. The FDA review team and many others in the agency were enraged. "I think we lost all perspective of our role to guard the nation's safety," David Graham said.[12] The FDA cardiovascular division vowed a complete reanalysis and a warning label for Merck. It became a case of Goliath vs. Goliath.

The talks between Merck and the FDA became brutal. The FDA insisted on a heart attack warning. Dr. Edward Scolnick at Merck told his staff that the company should not handle this matter in the usual way. Scolnick continued in an e-mail on October 4, 2001, "It is too important. There [sic] are never routine ways to do things in situations like this."[13]

In a later e-mail, Scolnick boasted, "if necessary, he would go to contacts he had made in the Department of Health and Human Services," regarding the FDA/Vioxx standoff.[14]

He never made it quite clear how he could do that, but it would become evident soon enough that the top medical authority in the government's health apparatus would be a person with whom both Dr. Scolnick and Merck were well acquainted.

CHAPTER 22

Losing Their Minds

The investigator or the investigation team should discontinue the research
if in their judgment, it may, if continued be harmful to the individual.
—**Declaration of Helsinki:**
Recommendation for Conduct of Clinical Research

In his *New Yorker* article, Dr. Jerome Groopman had promised
that cox-2 inhibitors would go beyond curing pain to possibly preventing Alzheimer's disease and cancer. He cited an Alzheimer's expert at Harvard who thought Vioxx and Celebrex would reduce the incidence of the
disease by half. Merck and Pfizer intended to scientifically prove these
claims, and, in 1998, the same year the Groopman article was published,
Merck announced with great fanfare the first of three Vioxx trials for the
prevention and treatment of mild Alzheimer's disease.

However, on March 21, 2001, Merck science chief Dr. Edward Scolnick received the first of many shocks regarding those trials. The memo
regarding the trial known as 091, a study of the efficacy and safety of a 25
milligram dose of Vioxx on slowing the progression of Alzheimer's disease (AD), read, "in the analysis of the first AD progression trial there was
an imbalance in the number of deaths observed, with more deaths occurring in the MK-0966[Vioxx] group compared to the placebo group."[1]

According to Dr. Bruce Psaty, writing in the *Journal of the American
Medical Association,* when the most accepted statistical test is applied to
the Merck Alzheimer's data, there were thirteen deaths in the Vioxx
group as opposed to three in the placebo group.[2]

After Dr. Scolnick got the news, he decided to investigate further, and
his staff added data from the ongoing Study 078, which was measuring

the progression of patients from memory loss and other "mild cognitive impairment," or MCI, to Alzheimer's disease.[3]

MCI is common among the elderly and, in fact, the characteristics are so vague they could be considered normal for many. MCI more specifically refers to a condition of forgetfulness, and slowness of thinking, but not enough to cause serious danger. It has been estimated that a third of all adults develop MCI—tens of millions of people.

The results of the 078 trial could thus have a tremendous impact on public health, because many Vioxx users (especially those with osteoarthritis) are elderly and thus potentially susceptible to MCI and milder Alzheimer's. The data in 078 was bleak. There were 21 deaths in the Vioxx group and 9 in the placebo group. If the deaths in the studies are combined, there are 57 deaths in the Vioxx group and 29 in the placebo group. Even more strikingly, considering that Merck was using these studies to prove Vioxx was safe for the heart, there were 21 deaths from heart disease with Vioxx and 6 with placebo—a three-fold increase.[4]

This was a time in which all of Merck marketing, including its huge sales force, was putting out papers showing the safety of Vioxx. Two of the doctors who were subject to this blitz were Dr. John Braun (who was treating the heart attack victim John McDarby) and Dr. Brent Wallace, who was treating sport and health enthusiast Robert Ernst, who had found love with a new wife, Carol.

The Alzheimer's data was known to Merck in April 2001—more than three years before Vioxx was taken off the market and just at the time when the FDA was giving Merck its new label allowing the company to make additional safety claims.

According to a Merck internal document, on December 5, 2001, the FDA sent a letter to the company asking about the ethics of continuing study 078 based on the excess mortality seen in study 091. The letter from the FDA is quoted by Dr. Bruce Psaty in his Alzheimer's *JAMA* article: "Please clarify whether the safety monitoring board and the IRB (institutional review board) overseeing these studies are aware of the excess of total cause mortality in the Vioxx 25 mg group as compared to placebo . . . Have these oversight groups commented on the ethics of continuing study 078 in light of the mortality data?"[5]

Merck had a small problem. This study of people with mild cognitive impairment did not have a safety monitoring committee.

Another highly confidential Merck document reveals the company called an "URGENT teleconference: Topic: Need to Set up External DSMB for Ongoing Vioxx AD [Alzheimer's Disease] Prevention Trial"[6] when this oversight was discovered in April 2001. Nothing was done. Merck concluded that the data "had not identified a safety issue."[7] It was another *incomprehensible* conclusion, among so many in the Vioxx tragedy.

Merck did not inform the medical review boards of its finding of increased deaths and allowed the study to continue for about two additional years. During this period, the trial participants had to be given a new consent form for them to continue. The increased risks of fatality in the Vioxx group were not revealed. Failure to stop the trial caused 20 additional deaths in the Vioxx group and 12 in those assigned to placebo.

Given the fact that in each analysis, more deaths were occurring in the clinical trial group receiving Merck's drug, what was the implication for the elderly in America and throughout the world who were taking the drug? The answer is unknown, but the possibilities are alarming.

Dr. Psaty writes in *JAMA* that given the mortality findings and the Alzheimer's disease findings "in our judgement [the data would] have prompted a DSMB [patient safety board], if it had existed, to stop the trial early."[8]

Dr. David Graham was unimpressed by Merck's claims about the lack of Vioxx side effects after the VIGOR study was completed and published—nor was he fazed by the conflicts swirling in the FDA bureaucracy above him. On August 13, 2002, Graham headed up an FDA team assigned to further investigate the heart risks of Vioxx by using the huge database of Kaiser Permanente health care (California). The FDA supervisor was Dr. Peter Honig, the designated federal agency expert who oversaw Graham's work.

In July 2002, Merck finally revealed the results of 091, the Alzheimer's study that had caused so much alarm. The company presented the results at the Eighth International Conference on Alzheimer's Disease in Stockholm,

Sweden. Merck stated that Vioxx had failed to show any improvement in patients with mild to moderate Alzheimer's, but the company made no mention of the excessive deaths in the Vioxx group. Merck said that the data indicated that Vioxx was generally well tolerated by people with Alzheimer's disease.[9]

The statement was true. The drug was well tolerated, unless the subject died first. Merck public affairs did its usual masterful job of getting out information. It did not reveal any.

The excess numbers of deaths in the Vioxx group only became known three years later when it was posted on the FDA Web site in 2005. Still, Merck *did* make a presentation and put out a press release about one part of the study. On November 20, 2002, four months after the Stockholm Conference, Dr. Alise Reicin delivered a talk at the American Heart Association. Merck released information to the press indicating that "Rofecoxib [Vioxx] Has [a] Good Cardiovascular Safety Profile in Older Patients with Alzheimer's or Cognitive Impairment."[10]

Dr. Reicin once again mentioned the 28,000-patient pooled data study that found no difference in heart disease with Vioxx and other NSAIDs—just as long as the 4,000 subjects given naproxen were not counted. She then stated that in the Alzheimer's study, serious heart events were actually *lower* in the Vioxx group than with placebo. "This analysis provides further evidence that Vioxx is not associated with an increased risk in the development of cardiovascular adverse events," Alise Reicin said. "The rate of confirmed serious cardiovascular thrombotic events was similar in the two groups."[11] However, Dr. Reicin did not mention that the difference in heart events was 21 in the Vioxx group and 6 with placebo, an increase of 3.5 times. Nor did she mention the difference in death rates: 57 in the Vioxx group and 29 in the placebo.[12] These figures were both published in the *JAMA* article by Dr. Psaty, based on both Merck's own analysis and those performed by an independent expert.

Not until late 2003 did the FDA start to *fully* examine the raw data from the Alzheimer's studies. While, as noted before, the FDA published a chronology of the reports, a complete analysis was not performed.

One of the authors of the late-posted FDA summary was Dr. James Witter, M.D., Ph.D., who had been studying the data on cox-2 inhibitors even before attending a cox update symposium ("Cox in Paradise") in Hawaii in 1998.[13]

Commented Gurkirpal Singh, director of the post-marketing drug surveillance program at Stanford University, "You would think physicians would want to know Merck had evidence indicating that patients taking Vioxx in two clinical studies were twice as likely to die as those taking placebo. It's a very important finding."[14] In testimony before a House subcommittee he stated, "As early as 2001, the FDA already knew that in two Alzheimer's disease studies, patients on Vioxx were almost twice as likely to die as those on placebo; updated safety data confirmed these findings. Yet, the FDA never released their analysis in any scientific meeting or any other communication to the public. Once again, the drug company continues to claim safety of its drug, the FDA knows otherwise, but the prescribing physicians and patients remain blissfully unaware. And the band plays on . . ."[15]

Pfizer was also deceptive. After Vioxx was removed from the market, Pfizer told *The New York Times* that no completed study had ever shown any increased heart-related risks related to Celebrex.[16] But on February 1, 2005, Pfizer "acknowledged" that in its study to test Celebrex on Alzheimer's patients in 1999, the number of patients suffering heart attacks was almost four times that of those taking a placebo."[17]

The complete data in the Pfizer study were never published or made available to physicians and patients. Despite the fact that the results were made available to the FDA in June 2001, this was four months after the agency's Arthritis Advisory committee had been convened to assess the safety of Celebrex. Committee members and others in the scientific community expressed the opinion that they would have loved to have known about the data years before it became public, and that it would have influenced their opinions about the drug's safety.

Pfizer did claim that the study had been presented in Sweden in 2000, but that the safety data may not have been included. Out of 285 patients taking Celebrex, 22 suffered heart attacks, compared to 3 of 140 patients taking placebo. Pfizer said that its own study was flawed and that the results might have been due to chance.[18]

The aptly named term for what Pfizer claimed is called "rescue bias." Rescue bias occurs often in pharmaceutical drug trials when results don't turn out as expected. The company therefore "rescues the situation" by condemning or belittling its own study by finding selective faults in the experiment."[19]

The unanswered question remains: What happened to the Nuremberg and Helsinki ethics codes forged after World War II? The Helsinki provisions, incorporated into United States law, provide for "particular concern and care" for the elderly and infirm, especially those who might not understand the principles of "informed consent." People with Alzheimer's and cognitive impairment should have been scrupulously monitored and the medical community kept fully and immediately informed. Neither happened.

CHAPTER 23

Path of Destruction

They care more about profits than health.
—**Professor Joan-Ramón Laporte,**
Fundació Institut Català de Farmacologia

The more Dr. Eric Topol of the Cleveland Clinic examined the Vioxx data from the Arthritis Advisory Committee posted on the FDA Web site, the more concerned he became. As his young colleague Dr. Debabrata Mukherjee had pointed out, Merck's conclusions did not add up, especially when Topol examined additional Vioxx studies. He was now joined by Dr. Steven Nissen, also at the clinic, who was a member of the Arthritis Advisory Committee and at first was not certain there was a problem.

Topol and his team started doing something no one had done. They ignored Merck's analysis of the Vioxx data and whenever possible went to the original raw results (in other words, the side effects before they were reinterpreted or "adjudicated"). "In the published VIGOR article," Dr. Topol says, "Merck reported that there were twenty cardiovascular events in the Vioxx group and four in the naproxen group. But when we examined the FDA charts, we found there were forty-five major cardiovascular events versus nineteen. These serious heart problems weren't even mentioned in the *NEJM* article and were glossed over in Merck presentations.

"The VIGOR authors claimed there was no difference in deaths between the two groups, but it was actually increased by 47 percent in the Vioxx arm. At three points in the paper they said the death rate was the same, but they didn't actually report the data—very deceptive."[1] The deaths were explicitly stated in data presented to the FDA. They read:

Overall deaths in Vioxx group—22
Overall deaths in naproxen group—15
Hospitalizations in Vioxx group—338
Hospitalizations in naproxen group—265

Hospitalizations from heart problems:
65 in the Vioxx group
24 in the naproxen group

Heart attack deaths:
9 in a Vioxx group
5 in a naproxen group

Vioxx did score better in gastrointestinal problems—49 with naproxen and 29 with Vioxx.[2]

The FDA data that was omitted clearly shows 22 deaths with Vioxx and 15 with naproxen. The words in the *NEJM* say the following: the overall "mortality rate and the rate of death from cardiovascular causes was similar in the two groups." Not true. And no mention that three times the number of people were hospitalized for heart ptoblems in the Vioxx group. "The heart attack rate was erroneous," concludes Dr. Topol.[3]

By May 2001, in the heat of the battle between the FDA and Merck, Topol and his team finished their analysis. They distinctly raised the possibility that Vioxx could cause heart attacks and called for a large-scale clinical trial to resolve the controversy. The researchers did mention the theoretical possibility that Vioxx might even *protect* the heart by reducing inflammation in the blood vessels, but when Dr. Topol examined the Vioxx data more closely, he ruled this possibility out. (Some key Vioxx studies were never made public by Merck or posted by the FDA—and much information became available only years after the studies were completed.)[4]

In mid-May, Dr. Topol made the decision to show Merck the Vioxx paper, which was planned as a publication for *The Journal of the American*

Medical Association. This article was different from many of the other threats to the reputation of Vioxx. Doctors actually read *JAMA* and they pay attention to studies coming out of the world-famous Cleveland Clinic and its chief of cardiology.

Topol reiterated the conclusions of Dr. David Graham. "Vioxx was in the experimental arm and the only proper conclusion was that there were more deaths in this group," Topol stated. "Merck flipped this completely upside down. This complete turnaround had never been done before in my experiences of interpreting clinical trials, and I've been doing this for twenty years, and I'm not aware that it's ever been done before or since. It was really an extraordinary deception."[5]

When Topol's manuscript arrived at Merck, the company exploded. Dr. Alise Reicin and Merck's head of cardiovascular research, Dr. Laura Demopoulos (a former colleague of Topol's), tried to alter or at least tone down the publication's conclusions. Merck also orchestrated a huge public relations campaign to counter anything negative in Topol's paper—or as Topol puts it, Merck planned "a path of destruction"—certainly nothing new for a company that had "neutralized" doctors, and threatened medical schools as well as professors of medicine.

Dr. David Graham and several other members of the FDA staff in the Office of Drug Safety held a video conference call with executives from Kaiser Permanente to work out a way of analyzing the Kaiser database. All agreed it was a matter of utmost importance for the public interest to know the heart risks of Vioxx, and contract negotiations between the agency and the health care provider began.

The result was that the FDA itself started progress toward a study of the super aspirins. The study was eventually entitled "Risk of Acute Myocardial Infarction and Sudden Cardiac Death in Patients Treated with Cyclo-Oxygenase 2 Selective and Non-Selective Non-Steroidal Anti-Inflammatory Drugs."[6]

Graham received permission to examine not only the higher dose of the drugs, but lower doses as well. Already, Graham felt the 50 mg dose (used in VIGOR) should have been removed from the market. "If the low dose turns out to cause heart attacks, this is going to be a catastrophe," Graham said.[7]

Alise Reicin and Laura Demopoulos had been talking quietly with Eric Topol. The Merck physicians were sitting in his well-appointed office at the Cleveland Clinic, clutching research documents and manuscripts. Although usually perfectly composed and restrained, Dr. Reicin's voice began taking on an edge. "There's no evidence of what's in your article," Reicin finally said. "There's no question about the safety of Vioxx," she continued.[8] Topol tried to keep matters friendly, but Reicin wasn't interested in a medical debate.

"Dr. Topol," Reicin said, "VIGOR was a trial in patients with rheumatoid arthritis and you'd expect them to get more heart attacks."

"Well, that may be true, Alise, but why would there be an imbalance?" Topol replied. All the subjects had been *randomized*. Because patients were assigned to each group purely by chance, any of the side effects would occur in equal numbers.

Reicin ignored Topol. "Naproxen inhibits platelets and that must be the explanation."

"Well, there's no real proof of that," Topol said.

"We analyzed 28,000 patient records," Dr. Demopoulos added.

"Could we examine the data? We'd like to see it," Topol replied.

"It's proprietary, we can't," the Merck doctors replied almost in unison.

Topol pointed out that if Merck was analyzing its own data it might have biases. (He was not yet aware how much of the VIGOR trial had this problem.)

In any case, finally realizing they weren't going to get their way, Reicin and Demopoulos made some cordial small talk and left.

The Merck campaign to discredit Dr. Topol's work began.

Dr. Loren Laine, author of the VIGOR study, probably never expected that the secret rehearsal tapes he was making for Merck would ever be

seen, much less used in a court of law and played years later in front of
the FDA and its advisors. Laine sat in a studio, surrounded by public relations and marketing professionals from Merck, television producers
(DWJ Television), and Ogilvy public relations. The objective was to make
a short video that resembled a television news segment (known as a video
news release or VNR), to be released nationwide to broadcast stations.[9]
Its purpose was to contradict the upcoming Topol article.

It was the beginning of yet another Merck blitz of information touting
the safety of Vioxx: conveyed by prominent Merck-contracted physicians
and consultants, in medical journals, talks, media interviews, and medical
Web sites. The strategy of the attack was to convey that Topol's article
was hopelessly flawed, lacked critical information and was alarmist and
misguided. Never mind that it said more or less exactly what the FDA review staff had concluded and that if it lacked data, it was because Topol
was unable to obtain and verify it from the pharmaceutical company that
protected its confidentiality.

Dr. Laine began his taped, on-camera studio rehearsal with the familiar
story that cox-1s were the good guys and cox-2s were the bad guys. Interestingly, Laine himself had cast doubt on this theory at the Arthritis
Advisory Committee in 1998, when he had been the independent gastroenterology expert assigned to give advice to the agency and other committee members. (It was already known that cox-2 played a vital role in
many body systems.)

The taping continued with the Merck PR advisors then asking Dr.
Laine about the "kidney findings in the VIGOR study."

Laine says: "Well, that's actually not going to be—I mean the only thing
that's in the *New England Journal* article says there's no difference in kidney
[renal] failure or renal dysfunction. . . . So I don't think you really want to
go there, do you? Because there are no data on blood pressure or edema
[water retention] in the study. And the only thing it says specifically, and we
were cagey about this, was related to kidney failure or kidney dysfunction."

Laine advised Merck not to mention this data: "Because if you're
bringing up high blood pressure and water retention, it's nowhere in the
study. . . . It's not what's in the article." And it wasn't.

This was the data that Drs. Singh, Fries, and many others had tried to get—in vain—and had been held back by Merck. The reason was clear. Twenty-eight patients in the Vioxx group had to drop out of the study because of high blood pressure–related adverse side effects, versus six in the naproxen group. There were nineteen cases of congestive heart failure in the Vioxx group, versus nine in the naproxen group. Twenty-five patients in the Vioxx group had to drop out because of adverse side effects, versus thirteen in the naproxen group.

Laine points out the VIGOR study was "extremely large, actually one of the largest randomized trials ever done in the field of gastroenterology." He clained that Vioxx could be used to reduce the risk of sudden serious ulcer development. However the FDA never removed the bold, black warning that these stomach complications could occur with *any* NSAID, *including* Vioxx. Nor did the advisory committee ever recommend the change.

Professor Laine told millions of potential viewers in a Merck-distributed video news story that Vioxx had fewer side effects in the stomach than naproxen, but neglected to mention that Vioxx caused more overall side effects than naproxen. He made *no mention whatsoever* of the fact that there were five times more heart problems in the Vioxx group than the naproxen group. (One of the consultants who first analyzed the tapes observed facetiously that Laine was altering the old advertising slogan, "Why trade an upset stomach for a headache?" to "Why not trade an upset stomach for a heart attack.")[10] Or, as Dr. Topol stated in a more serious manner in *NEJM,* "It is hard to imagine that the small protection from gastric or duodenal ulcers in the VIGOR trial is an acceptable trade-off, as compared with twice the occurrence of death, heart attacks, and strokes."

Adding a more personal touch, Laine explains that he sees patients who were taking aspirin, Motrin, and naproxen (Aleve) all the time "and it's very common for us to see patients presenting with internal bleeding."

He is asked how he usually treats pain and responds jokingly, "I'm a gastroenterologist, so how would I know?"

Dr. James Fries, who challenged Merck's threats to physicians, laughs also. "We don't see a lot of bleeding here at Stanford."[11] He refrained from making any comment about the University of Southern California Medical School, where Laine practices.

The published VIGOR study, of which Laine was one of the lead authors, states in the first paragraph the by now classic assumption that there are from 15,000 to 16,000 deaths from NSAIDs each year and over 100,000 hospitalizations. In the video outtakes, with the camera running, Laine states: "These numbers are totally incorrect . . . I know these numbers but they are totally wrong . . . and to say these events are due to NSAIDs is also incorrect . . . those figures are totally bogus." Laine says he can provide many reasons for the inaccuracy, but never elaborates. Nonetheless, the professor finds a good way of modifying the statement by saying: "As long as we say it's *estimated* or *reported*, it's not me saying it."

So the large number of deaths and hospitalizations caused by NSAIDs have been "estimated or reported," Dr. Laine writes in the *NEJM*—and tells millions on television and in medical lectures—it's just that Laine himself knows the figures are "incorrect" and "totally bogus."[12]

Finally, Dr. Laine clarifies why it took so many patients to complete the study. He explains that this is because the *stomach and intestine side effects are so rare* that a huge number of patients were necessary to get a result. "That's the right answer," Laine tells the PR people. "I'm not sure you really want the right answer." He never gives the right answer, although Merck alludes to the same problem. If the company had compared Vioxx to a different, less toxic NSAID, no difference in stomach trouble would have shown up without testing extraordinary numbers of people—*if stomach trouble had shown up at all.*

Professor Frank Wollheim, from the University of Lund in Sweden, who reported on the Cox in Paradise meeting, also had some comments on these figures. "No patient of mine ever died from taking Motrin," he says, "and I can't remember anyone having to go to the hospital. Maybe Swedes have stronger stomachs."[13]

Next to be rehearsed was Dr. Laura Demopoulos, senior director, cardiovascular clinical research, Merck & Co., who had argued with Eric Topol about the safety of Vioxx at the Cleveland Clinic. The whole basis of Merck's legal defense for Vioxx can be summarized as follows: Until the results of the APPROVe [colon cancer prevention] trial were known in

September 2004, Merck had no reason to believe that Vioxx could be harmful to the heart.

However, in the outtake of Dr. Demopoulos on camera, she stated in 2001, "that one possible explanation for the VIGOR result is that Vioxx caused heart troubles. We all say it ourselves. I mean we've said it in lots of different places . . . There isn't a single person in the company who's going to say that's not a possible explanation [of the VIGOR results]."[14]

So there is a slight discrepancy between the official Merck explanation of what it knew and when about Vioxx and that of Dr. Laura Demopoulos.

Either no one had an inkling of the Vioxx dangers or everyone did.

As a cornerstone to rebut Merck's own findings in the VIGOR trial, Demopoulos explains that Merck is publishing a study of 28,000 patients in an important medical journal, the American Heart Association's *Circulation*, proving the safety of Vioxx. The external author was leading cardiologist Dr. Marvin Konstam, chief of cardiology at New England Medical Center and professor of medicine at Tufts University, who took a key role in convincing other academics both of the validity of the Merck heart event analysis and the safety of Vioxx.

But in the taped outtakes, Dr. Demopoulos explains that this figure of 28,000 *does not* include the patients in VIGOR, thus deleting the results from 8,000 patients. "It's not correct to say that we showed no increased risk versus naproxen," Demopoulos explains while the camera is rolling. This was the same conclusion reached by the FDA reviewer. Reading press releases carefully, a reader can notice in fine print that Vioxx is no more dangerous to the heart than "non-naproxen" NSAIDs—although the company had already admitted that it never adequately tested Vioxx against other less poisonous NSAIDs.

Dr. Demopoulos concedes that Dr. Topol has raised valid points and that there is no definitive proof that naproxen reduces heart attacks. A large-scale study is needed to prove that. She stares at the camera and says to her boss, Dr. Scolnick, "Ed, give me the money!"

She then says such a study is being planned and should be done.

The final, edited Merck Vioxx video news release leaves the interesting comments of Dr. Laine and Demopoulos on the cutting room floor. The three-minute report simply condemns Topol's study, repeats bogus numbers, omits crucial data, and says not a word about the possible danger of Vioxx causing heart disease. "Eric is going to be really angry now," Dr. Demopoulos states.

After Dr. Topol published his *JAMA* article, he sometimes wished he had never heard the word Vioxx. At nearly every medical meeting he went to, he had to defend his work. In some circles, he was simply thought of as an arrogant traitor. There was not much he could do without additional data, which neither Merck, nor anyone else, was likely to provide him, and at every meeting he attended, Dr. Alise Reicin would be presenting yet another paper on the safety of Vioxx.

And then there was the seemingly constant reminder of Dorothy Hamill, America's Sweetheart, whose health had so dramatically improved. When the FDA had first approved direct-to-consumer advertising, it had done so with the understanding that "significant side effects" would be prominently displayed in all advertising media. Apparently the agency did not consider heart attacks a serious side effect. Merck and its advertising agency, DDB Needham, didn't regard the possible risk of heart disease as significant enough to mention, either.

In the many commercials made with Dorothy Hamill, and in the thousands of times they ran on television, the possibility of heart risk was *never* mentioned. The commercials were brilliant. No expense was spared to film Hamill, smiling radiantly at the camera, lacing up her skates and thanking the heavens (and Vioxx) for her ability to skate again. The advertisements had a genuine warmth to them and they certainly instilled trust. Who could possibly imagine that the beloved Olympic champion with the famous hairdo could be selling anything dangerous, as Dr. Topol implied?

An article entitled "The So-Called Advantages of Celecoxib and Rofecoxib: Scientific Fraud" was published in the July–September 2002 issue of a prominent, independent drug bulletin in Spain, *Butlletí Groc*. The article, written by Professor Joan-Ramón Laporte, the bulletin's editor, noted the irregularities in the conduct and analysis of the VIGOR trial and the Celebrex long-term arthritis safety study (CLASS).[15]

The *British Medical Journal* summarized Dr. Laporte's objections: "The bulletin said the results of the VIGOR trial generated doubts on the cardiovascular effects of Vioxx. It referred to a *Lancet* commentary that had 'raised the possibility that the company was already aware of the likelihood of this adverse effect, and suggests that a selection bias may have been introduced which may have led to an underestimation of the cardiovascular safety of Vioxx.'"[16]

Such bias had indeed been suggested by Merck executive Brian Daniels and in fact Merck had used every statistical trick to prevent VIGOR from showing any harm to the heart in the Vioxx group. Analyst Richard Stover had been one of the first to note this. Dr. Gurkirpal Singh told the Senate Finance Committee, "It appears . . . that in early 1997, Merck scientists were exploring study designs that would, in fact, exclude people who may have had a weak heart. . . . So that the heart attack problem [with Vioxx] would not be evident." Singh continued: "We need to know how a drug behaves in people who are going to take it—even if it, I quote [from a Merck document], 'kills the drug.' It is better to kill a drug than kill a patient."[17] *Butlletí Groc* was essentially the first medical journal to state this outright as early as 2002.

Professor Laporte was no kinder to Pfizer. He pointed out what the FDA committee advisors had already observed: that the CLASS study published in *JAMA* showed that Celebrex was safer to the stomach after six months. However, the study was designed to last one year, and at that time, as the FDA demonstrated, Celebrex was no more superior than a standard NSAID in terms of stomach safety.

While Pfizer let the *Butlletí Groc* accusation go, Merck decided to sue the Spanish drug bulletin. Laporte also believed that the only reason he thought Pfizer was not jumping in was that the company believed any open hearing would make the Celebrex results seem worse. However, Merck demanded that the medical publication retract its article on the Vioxx outcomes trial and reproduce a text prepared by the company. This is an extraordinary action in the scientific world. First of all, the drug giant itself had been accused by the *NEJM* of distorting or eliminating data in the VIGOR trial and had disavowed the paper's conclusions. Second, Merck has constantly referred to itself as a company that welcomed "vigorous" free and open scientific debate.

Dr. Laporte was furious. "I feel this is an attack on independent information on drugs," the professor said. "The pharmaceutical industry has almost a monopoly on information on drugs and therapeutics."[18] Professor Laporte said that the text Merck wanted him to run was "mainly propaganda" for Vioxx.

The Spanish doctor was now entering a long line of scientists and researchers whom Merck had tried to intimidate or neutralize: James Fries, Eric Topol, John Wallace—to name just a few. Professor Laporte had concluded his article by stating that the data presented by Merck and Pfizer to European regulatory authorities (similar to the FDA) was based on distorted information. He wrote: "The obvious commercial interests that led to the manipulation of the scientific results and the disregard of patients' health undermined trust in the scientific rigor of the published studies." Merck argued in court in Madrid that the company had a constitutional right to "rectify" Laporte's comments.

Merck only succeeded in angering medical experts worldwide, some seven hundred of whom sent letters of support to Dr. Laporte. One noted professor wrote the court saying that "large transnational pharmaceutical companies have a history of unjustified bullying of their critics."[19]

The Spanish court agreed to listen to the case and eventually ruled against Merck. Professor Laporte was jubilant and hailed the decision as a victory for scientific freedom.

Perhaps the greatest irony of the situation is that both the published VIGOR study and the CLASS study are still considered the most authoritative publications about Vioxx and Celebrex and continue to be cited by physicians today. Once information is printed in a prestigious scientific journal, widely distributed and quoted, backed up by company speakers, and touted by drug representatives, the message generally sticks—no matter what the later evidence.

In fact, among many physicians and researchers, cox-2 drugs still are regarded as miracle compounds.

CHAPTER 24

The Drug Warriors

It helps to have friends in high places—to know important people to
help you get what you want.

By late 2001, the battle between Merck and the FDA was reaching fever pitch. Merck refused to accept the FDA's demand to put the
risk of heart attacks for Vioxx in the warning section of its proposed new
label and the FDA refused Merck's demand to play down the Vioxx heart
risk. It was a standoff—like two gunslingers pointing loaded pistols at each
other's head. With billions of dollars at stake, Merck indicated it would
turn to its government contacts "at the highest levels" to ensure the success
of its most important drug, Vioxx. Nonetheless the battle raged on.

On September 21, 2001, the Public Health Service of the Department
of Health and Human Services sent a scathing warning letter to Raymond Gilmartin, chairman of Merck. It was signed by Thomas Abrams,
director of the Division of Drug Marketing, Advertising and Communications of the Food and Drug Administration (a component of the Department of Health and Human Services).

The letter was unusually broad and harsh, making severe accusations
against Merck. It was also unusual in its tone and language. Most government communications, no matter how serious, are written in a careful bu-
reaucratic style. But the Merck warning letter had an altogether different
style almost irreverently sarcastic:

> We have identified a Merck press release entitled, "Merck Confirms
> Favorable Safety Profile of Vioxx," dated May 22, 2001 that is false and
> misleading. . . . Additionally, your claim in the press release that Vioxx has

"a favorable cardiovascular safety profile," is *simply incomprehensible,* [emphasis added] given the rate of MI [heart attack] and serious cardiovascular events compared to naproxen. The implication that Vioxx's cardiovascular profile is superior to other NSAIDs is misleading; in fact, serious cardiovascular events were twice as frequent in the VIOXX treatment group (101 events, 2.5%) as in the naproxen treatment group (46 events, 1.1%) in the VIGOR study.

Merck's heart safety claims were not just wrong, but incomprehensible.

"Your minimizing [the potential risks of VIOXX] and misrepresenting the safety profile raise significant public health and safety concerns. Your misrepresentation of the safety profile of Vioxx is particularly troublesome because we have previously . . . objected to promotional materials for Vioxx that also misrepresented Vioxx's safety profile." A formal letter from the Department of Health and Human Services accusing a drug company of "significant public health and safety concerns" is about as serious a statement that this government division can make, short of severe fines or removing a drug from the market. The letter continued with a list of specific legal violations that Merck had committed and required the company to respond by October 1, 2001.[1]

The fact that public relations was so harshly criticized must have come as a nasty blow to the executive in charge of this function, Dr. Eve Slater. Slater was also in charge of regulatory affairs, the company's top liaison with the FDA. How exactly was Merck going to answer these charges and what would they do with Slater?

Merck's answer was to claim "freedom of speech" guaranteed by the Constitution in making its "incomprehensible" safety claim. It also made it clear that the "other side of the story" (heart disease risk) had been published in various newspapers and financial analyst reports, so it had a basic right to defend itself by telling *its* side of the story. Merck even averred, somewhat curiously, that it was a pharmaceutical company, not a newspaper, one of the few assertions no one has questioned.[2]

The person ultimately in charge of evaluating Merck's legal response was Daniel Troy, chief counsel of the FDA. Daniel Troy had been appointed to his post just before the letter was written, in August 2001, and because of the lack of a permanent FDA commissioner had assumed enormous power at the agency. "In his first meeting with the FDA staff, Troy browbeat us," an FDA worker said. "It was humiliating because of his alliances with drug companies. He left no doubt that he had access 'to the top' and that he intended to use his powers." The mood in the agency changed almost overnight.[3]

Before joining the FDA, Troy had been the lawyer hired by the tobacco industry to fight the FDA's right to regulate cigarettes. Not only was Troy a tobacco lawyer, he had represented several drug companies, including Pfizer. Troy had argued for *less* FDA regulation of promotion and advertising and even helped the pharmaceutical industry defend its legal positions while he was FDA chief counsel. This put him in direct opposition to senior members of the FDA.

In October, about the time that Merck's response to the warning letter was due, Troy began changing the legal policy of the FDA and Health and Human Services. On November 29, 2001, as Tom Abrams was reviewing Merck's response letter, Health and Human Services issued instructions that the FDA would henceforth have to clear all its warnings to the drug industry through the Office of Chief Counsel (Daniel Troy).

But the policy was not yet official. It was then that Merck pulled off one of its greatest political maneuvers in its storied history. Edward Scolnick, Merck's powerful research chief, had vowed to fight the FDA's effort to put the heart risks about Vioxx in the warning section of the drug's label. He had promised to do anything he could. This battle between the FDA and Merck continued for over a year until an abrupt change in 2002.

President George W. Bush had contemplated appointing a brilliant woman to be the new FDA commissioner: Dr. Eve Slater, Merck's point person for VIGOR and a close friend of Edward Scolnick's. Congress refused the appointment on the grounds of Slater's relationship with the pharmaceutical industry.

The president then made a clever end run. In December 2002, Slater bid a sad farewell to Merck. She was going to miss Dr. Scolnick, Ray Gilmartin, and all her many other friends at the company. But she wasn't going very far and would certainly stay in touch. On January 25, 2002,

Dr. Slater had the great honor of becoming the assistant secretary of health at the HHS "as the Secretary's primary advisor on matters involving the nation's public health and overseeing the U.S. Public Health Services."[4] The primary advocate for Vioxx, Merck's most profitable drug, was now responsible for the Food and Drug Administration. In the past, the agencies HHS supervised had been relatively autonomous. But the Bush administration, under new Secretary Tommy Thompson, wanted centralized control. The FDA's power was crippled by the lack of permanent positions; nearly everyone was an "acting" executive. Therefore, HHS and a permanent appointment like Daniel Troy ensured even greater power.

Dr. Slater was not the only "stealth" appointment. On February 25, one month later, Dr. Lester Crawford was appointed FDA Deputy Commissioner. Since there was no "permanent commissioner," Dr. Crawford was de facto head of the FDA, although a weak one.

On January 31, 2002, the deputy director of HHS, along with the Office of Chief Council, implemented the new policy that warning letters would have to be cleared by Daniel Troy. That meant Merck had little to worry about. Troy was adamantly pro-industry and favored many of the techniques used in the Merck marketing campaign. That same January, Merck made a few minor changes in its Vioxx promotion policy, based on the demands of the Warning Letter, but by and large, Merck the company was let off the hook and never again received a Vioxx warning—an amazing about-face by the FDA considering the severity of the charges, but understandable given the new leaders of the HHS. Merck's public affairs department was not censured for its "incomprehensible" promotion, nor did the company change its overall sales and marketing practices.

Shortly after Dr. Slater's arrival in Washington and Dr. Crawford's appointment, the logjam between Merck and the FDA began to clear and the Merck company and the government reached an astoundingly quick resolution of the imbroglio. On April 11, 2002, the FDA gave Merck its new label with just about everything the company wanted.[5] ("A miracle" is how Merck's research chief Edward Scolnick characterized it.)

The heart risks were minimized. The danger of heart attack did not appear in the "Warning" section, as the agency had previously continually demanded. The heart risks would now appear in the less important "Precaution" section. The official FDA-approved Vioxx label's description of the VIGOR study emphasized the favorable ulcer safety finding. The FDA said that in VIGOR there was a "significant reduction" of risk of developing ulcers, including serious bleeding.

Under "Other Safety Findings," the FDA noted that the VIGOR study "showed a higher incidence of adjudicated serious cardiovascular events" in the VIOXX high-dose group. A chart was thrown in to show the number of events, but the label also stated that the number of deaths from heart events was seven with Vioxx and six with naproxen. In other words, no difference. It did not show the table deleted by Merck from the *NEJM* VIGOR paper showing increased total mortality and hospitalization in the Vioxx group.

What happened to the language in the FDA's own warning letter? That FDA document stated there were twice as many cardiovascular events in the Vioxx group. This sentence was downplayed in the new information label.

In fact, the FDA said that in two other studies with the lower 25 mg dose, Vioxx was safer than a sugar pill regarding some cardiovascular effects, but more dangerous in terms of causing overall death. However, and most important, the FDA said the significance of these two studies, when combined with the VIGOR study, "was unknown."[6]

Even more disturbingly, not a single mention was made about the deaths in the Alzheimer's study, despite the fact that it was over a year since Merck had analyzed the data.

Neither physicians nor patients read drug labels in any case, but now that the FDA had approved wording stating that the heart risk of Vioxx was of "unknown significance," the Merck sales force, its advertising agency, and its public affairs division were off and running. Because of the vague statements in the label, the company had license to claim just about anything it wanted.

News of Merck's victory over the FDA quickly spread through the company in the second week of April 2002. The company's triumph was complete. There was just enough of a warning so that Merck could claim it had adequately disclosed the heart risks of Vioxx—but not enough of a warning to affect sales. With Daniel Troy firmly in charge of enforcing advertising and promotion, Merck submitted to the FDA for approval one of the largest advertising programs in pharmaceutical history. The only person missing from Merck's celebration was the woman who had tirelessly defended the company against its critics and fought with the FDA for years as Merck's liaison to the agency. She had been involved with some of the most outrageous public affairs releases since Merck had promoted the benefits of cocaine in the nineteenth century, when it was legal. Dr. Eve Slater was busy in Washington, protecting the public health. The new assistant secretary of Health and Human Services had only been on the job for four months and later admitted she didn't know a thing about politics or have anything to do with the FDA. Also absent from the celebration was Carol Ernst, whose husband had died of heart disease on May 6, 2001. This was two weeks after the HHS warning letter that Merck was responsible for "significant health and safety concerns."

One day after the agency gave Vioxx a virtually clean bill of health the story of Vioxx took another grim twist, a twist some believe was even worse than what had happened before.

CHAPTER 25

FDA vs. FDA

And who shall guard those self-same guardsmen?
—Juvenal, Roman poet

The FDA completed its study of the heart disease risks of the super aspirins (using the Kaiser Permanente database) in the summer of 2004. By this time, Dr. Wayne Ray from Vanderbilt University, director of the division of pharmocoepidemiology, and professor of preventive medicine, one of the world's experts on pharmacology and cox inhibition, had joined with Dr. David Graham to perform the analysis. Ray was also one of Merck's consultants. The data showed that both the "high" dose (50 mg) of Vioxx and the low dose increased the risk of heart attack and sudden death. The study also showed that naproxen was *not* protective of heart disease.

Dr. Graham now had a new boss at the FDA. In yet another astonishing "coincidence," Dr. Peter Honig, the expert who oversaw the Vioxx FDA study, and Dr. Graham's boss, was now a senior vice president at Merck. Graham presented the results to his new supervisor, Dr. Paul Seligman, and Seligman's deputy, Anne Trontell, along with Graham's recommendations that the high dose be withdrawn from the market and the low dose not be used. "I was basically recommending withdrawal of both high and low dose and that created an uproar in the FDA," Graham says. That was an understatement. Graham wanted to present the data at the International Conference on Pharmacoepidemiology and Therapeutic Risk Management in Bordeaux, France, in September 2004, but needed clearance from FDA upper executives. They pressured Graham hard to change his recommendations. Management did not want Graham and

Ray to question the Vioxx label change they had made in 2002 that in essence said that the cardiovascular risk of Vioxx was "uncertain."[1]

Graham explains: "The FDA created obstacles and review channels that did not exist in the past. There was a lot of name calling, suggestions were made that I not be allowed to present or that I present with different conclusions—or that I also present FDA's conclusions—it was all over the board." A top FDA official overseeing Vioxx, Dr. Jonca Bull, asked Graham why he had done the study in the first place. "We relabeled this drug in 2002, so nothing more needs to be done," Dr. Bull said. It was a Kafkaesque question: Dr. Graham did the study because the FDA had doubts about Vioxx safety.

The FDA sent Graham's manuscript to Merck, allowing the company to prepare a detailed rebuttal. "It was important that Merck know, but not the public," Graham says sardonically. He decided to present his data in September 2004 in Bordeaux with a few modifications from his initial conclusions.

At that time the FDA still had not fully reviewed the Alzheimer's disease data, study 091 and study 078, despite the fact that 091 had been completed in 2001 and 078 completed in April 2003. Then another bombshell exploded.

When a secret analysis of the Alzheimer's data was performed by Merck itself, the company found that *more* subjects taking Vioxx with slight memory impairments (MCI) became worse and developed Alzheimer's *at a faster rate* than those taking the placebo. The results were statistically significant. The conversion rate to Alzheimer's disease from MCI was 6.4 percent with Vioxx, vs. 4.5 percent taking nothing at all.[2] Once again the public health implications were startling. Given the fact that so many people have mild cognitive impairment, this meant that 2 percent more of them were more rapidly developing Alzheimer's disease when they took Vioxx.

There was also the distinct possibility that Celebrex was also putting this same population at risk. Pfizer's claim that its trial was "small" and "poorly conducted" was not a legitimate excuse. For if the company was in possession of a study of any sort indicating Celebrex caused damage to Alzheimer's patients, they certainly should have started a larger study to make certain of the drug's safety and then published the data so that it could be replicated.

The interpretation, as stated before, was simply "rescue bias," as was that of the FDA regarding Dr. Graham's study. Bad results? Blame the study.

Not only was Vioxx putting Alzheimer's disease patients and MCI patients at risk of more deaths, the drug was actually accelerating onset of the tragic and debilitating disease of Alzheimer's. Merck's response was to keep the information secret from the public. The corporate relations department, which in most companies is obligated to be the "conscience of the company," devised a means of further deceiving patients, in case the "results became public prior to the presentation of the data." A series of questions and answers was developed that attempted to ignore the results. Among other things, Merck said the primary results of the study really meant nothing, because they were inconsistent with other parts of the study.[3] This is another example of "rescue bias"—or blaming the study for the results.

The scientists at Merck who interpret data have a way with words that is unrivaled. This standby statement with the questions and answers was never used because the results remained secret. The company, which time and again used the slogan "putting patients first," placed them dead last.

The new Alzheimer's data was submitted to the FDA in July of 2003, according to an FDA chronology posted in 2006. On December 17, 2003, the FDA received more heart disease information from Merck on the Alzheimer's trials, and on January 28, 2004, the agency finally concluded what Merck had known for months and years: "That subjects [with Alzheimer's disease and mild cognitive impairment] given Vioxx experienced more deaths as well as a deterioration of mental functioning."[4] The FDA decided it needed *another* review by a different division before considering regulatory sanctions or even making an announcement. The agency further decided to delay any public notification until the latter part of 2004, at which time they planned a meeting with Merck.

John McDarby was at home in Woodcliff Lake, New Jersey, with his wife when he suddenly began feeling "disaffected" and that something was wrong. It was April 15, 2004. Trying to walk it off, John stepped outside briefly, then returned to the living room where he became disoriented and collapsed. Finding her husband sprawled on the floor, his wife dialed 911, and within minutes the scream of an ambulance could be heard. Paramedics rushed to the incapacitated man and attached an oxygen mask.

Later when asked about the experience, McDarby said that he couldn't remember the questions he was asked in the ambulance or at the hospital. However, the immediate aftermath of the attack itself stayed vividly in his mind. "When I hit the floor my body went completely numb and I have never recovered."

Only a few months later, Dr. John Braun, McDarby's physician, suffered a cardiac arrest. When he learned the probable cause—Vioxx—he was perhaps more startled than anyone.

On June 9, 2004, yet another division of the FDA confirmed the fatal Merck 2001 findings of the Vioxx Alzheimer's data. Moving with "all due speed," the agency decided to do *further* analysis and set up a meeting with Merck. The date was to be September 27, 2004.

Much to the consternation of his FDA supervisors, Dr. David Graham presented the Vioxx study the FDA itself had commissioned him to perform. The data was presented at the International Conference on Pharmacoepidemiology in Bordeaux. Graham had further infuriated his supervisors by informing them that he had submitted his manuscript to *The Lancet* for publication.

In a mind-bending, bureacratic, Washington, D.C., statement, the FDA said that its own analysis still needed to be confirmed by the FDA, but Kaiser Permanente, the huge California health care group that had provided the database for the analysis, acted decisively. The group removed Vioxx from its list of approved drugs and discouraged its physicians from using it. As this was taking place, on September 8, 2004, the FDA's Center for Evaluation of Drugs and Research, with the apparent blessing of Dr. Lester Crawford and Daniel Troy's Office of Chief Counsel, announced that Vioxx had received government approval for treating children with rheumatoid arthritis. The release stated that Vioxx "now has more approved indications for medical conditions than any other COX-2 specific inhibitor."[5]

One glaring exception was an indication to treat mild memory impairment.

In this and other press releases and medical talks, Merck had referred to the 50 mg dose of Vioxx as a "supra therapeutic" dose, implying it was an unnaturally high dose. (This was the dose used in the VIGOR trial.) However, in a September 2004 press release, Merck pointed out that for some conditions like migraine headache, taking just such a dose would be helpful. They also added that "chronic use of that dose" was not recommended, even though the company knew this was an amount commonly used by patients.

And why did the company make an easy-to-take 50 mg tablet? According to researchers at the Vanderbilt University Medical School, ". . . Patients are often being prescribed the highest 50-mg dose by their doctors for daily pain relief." The researchers found that many people took the dose for more than the recommended period of five days and were taking Vioxx for everyday problems. The study, which was conducted by Marie R. Griffen, M.D., MPH, professor of medicine and preventive medicine, looked at the medical records of forty thousand patients taking NSAIDs. About 15 percent of Vioxx users were taking at least 50 mg a day, according to a report published on *WebMD Medical News,* on July 14, 2004. The irony was that Merck had done a brilliant educational job convincing people that the pain of arthritis was acute and sometimes lifelong, but warned that for patients with "acute pain," Vioxx was not recommended for more than five days. If pain is "acute" and occurring for long periods of time, what dose did Merck think patients would use? What did Dorothy Hamill do after her fifth day? She had been in such pain she could not get out of bed, nor properly care for her daughter. The commercials don't say.

Less than thirty days after the juvenile rheumatoid arthritis approval, on September 27, Merck was scheduled to meet with the FDA about the final results of the Alzheimer's studies. But at 8:32 that morning, the company informed the agency that it planned to remove Vioxx from the market because of increased risk of heart attack and stroke. The Alzheimer's meeting was canceled and Merck scheduled a high-level meeting with the FDA on the 28th to discuss the "new" findings that Vioxx could increase the risk of heart disease. The FDA expressed "shock" about the heart disease findings as did so many in Merck senior management.

The FDA agreed with Merck's decision to remove Vioxx from the market. The questions about the pill's link to worsening the condition of patients with forgetfulness and Alzheimer's disease, however, have never been completely analyzed in front of an independent FDA advisory panel. An analysis using the original Merck data was not published until April 2008, just about seven years after Merck examined it.

Chapter 26

After the Party

Party is the madness of many for the gain of a few.
—Alexander Pope

When **Ray Gilmartin** and Peter Kim stood in front of the microphones in the Bijou Room of the Hilton hotel on September 30, 2004, they announced to the world that Merck was taking Vioxx off the market because the company always put people ahead of profits. Both said that the company only had definitive evidence of heart-related dangers of Vioxx a week before.

Merck made it clear, however, that this would not affect the fate of its follow-up drug, Arcoxia, because "the results of clinical studies of one molecule in a given class are not necessarily applicable to others in the class."[1] This statement is all the more ironic because Merck justified the safety of Vioxx based on studies related at least in part on the results of clinical trials from other molecules or drugs. In the Vioxx chronology section of its Web site, Merck still implies that the drug naproxen has a protective effect on the heart because of a study done with another drug, indobufen, in 1993. Also on the Web site, Dr. Edward Scolnick, the now retired head of Merck research, talks about how his staff used this study as part of its assessment that naproxen protects the heart. So Merck established another new scientific principle: "It is not scientifically valid to make conclusions about one drug, based on the results of another," unless the other drug can turn a negative study into a positive one. By the same token, if one of a pharmaceutical company's drugs is poisonous, then no such conclusion can be drawn on a similar drug made by the same company.

The removal of Vioxx from the market caused shock, disbelief, and anger. Although many were disturbed that Merck had sold the drug so long, a surprising number of patients, researchers, financial analysts, and lawyers objected to its removal. Especially disappointed were experts in the field of Alzheimer's disease. "We should not give up on this," said Dr. Linda Van Eldik of Northwestern University. "Inflammation is a key player in the damage in Alzheimer's. . . . I would hate to stop this area of research, because I think it's really important."[2]

Dr. Timothy Hla, professor of cell biology and director of the Center for Vascular Biology at the University of Connecticut, wrote that the removal of Vioxx from the market was causing a crisis: "Cox-2 inhibitors appear extremely promising to prevent and/or treat cancer and Alzheimer's disease. They control inflammation in the brain."[3] Obviously the news that Vioxx *worsened* the condition had not made it to the specialists, despite Merck's claim that the data had been "fully and publicly" reported.

At the *fifth* meeting of an FDA advisory committee to assess the safety of super aspirin, eight months after Vioxx was removed from the market, patients and doctors alike lined up at the microphone in the public comment portion of the gathering to complain of the loss of Vioxx. Dr. Max Hamburger, now president of the New York State Rheumatology Society (who had accepted thousands of dollars from Merck and Pfizer to allow them to promote super aspirin to his group), said that he had polled New York rheumatologists and that they were in favor of returning Vioxx to the market. Dr. Hamburger maintained that the public did not understand that all pain drugs have risks and that physicians needed Vioxx to continue research.

Dr. John Klippel of the Arthritis Foundation agreed about maintaining the freedom of patients to have access to the "widest range of therapies." Dr. Klippel did not mention that he had appeared on television and made numerous appearances with ice skating star Dorothy Hamill, whose statements exaggerating the benefits of Vioxx nearly led to an FDA warning letter.

These physician comments were made during a special meeting of the Drug Safety and Risk Management Advisory Committee over three days: May 17, 18, and 19 of 2005. The committee was chaired by Dr. Alistair Wood, who seemed to view the proceedings with a certain macabre sensibility. Much of the meeting days was predictably taken up by FDA officials explaining why they had acted in a timely and judicious manner; Merck and Pfizer executives explaining why they had acted in a careful scientific and ethical manner; and FDA advisors reflecting on how they had done their very best to analyze complicated data to assist in the valuable job of protecting the public's health.

The meeting was controversial even before it began. The FDA intended to ban the participation of the advisor Dr. Curt Furberg, the epidemiologist who had raised doubts about super aspirins. After negative publicity and considerable negotiations, Dr. Furberg was allowed to attend. And it took the intercession of Congress to allow Dr. David Graham to present his data without threat of retribution.

The advisory meeting itself was not without either humor or interesting revelations, mostly originating from Dr. Wood. When a top Pfizer medical director said he did not know the results of a huge negative Celebrex study published two days before in *The New England Journal of Medicine,* Dr. Wood said that the executive's statement did not pass the "laugh test." He held up his copy of the *Journal* and offered the Pfizer physician a copy so that he could bring himself up to date.

Wood also tried to put to rest the idea that naproxen could protect the heart. He questioned Dr. Marvin Konstam, "author" of the now infamous 28,000-patient study conjured up by Merck and published in the journal *Circulation* reaffirming the safety of Vioxx. This was the study that FDA reviewers implied was flawed and unscientific because it was like comparing apples to oranges. This study helped convince physicians that naproxen was helpful to the heart. Dr. Konstam explained that when the VIGOR study had first been analyzed "there was *not a hint of a problem* [emphasis added], which I think led me at that time and I think led others at that time to say this may be contributed by a significant beneficial effect of naproxen." Not a *hint* of a problem when VIGOR clearly showed there were five times as many heart attacks in the Vioxx group?

Dr. Wood refused to let Konstam get by. "Just let me make sure I understand. Are you saying this is still your position?"

"No, no. That was the position at that time," Konstam replied. He continued on with more explanations, but was stopped by Wood again.

The chairman asked: "But just to be *absolutely clear*, you are not saying you still believe the VIGOR study was due to a totally protective effect of naproxen, are you?"

"No, no," Konstam said again. "I am not."

This meant that the lead author of the study published in *Circulation*, the journal of the American Heart Association, used over and over to defend the safety of Vioxx, was denying the study's scientific basis.

Wood did not spare Pfizer's Celebrex CLASS research either. He pointed out that the CLASS study published in *JAMA* had been "discredited because the paper failed to disclose all the data and that was now the subject of critical and apologetic comments from the editor of *JAMA*, Catherine DeAngelis, herself." This meant that at least four major papers from three major medical journals were either discredited or no longer valid.

No matter—a survey of physicians taken after the FDA session found that most continued to believe the articles were valid and many thought Vioxx had been unfairly withdrawn. No wonder. Bear in mind that because of the high standards of the journals, they could be made available to doctors under FDA "safe harbor" rules, despite the fact that they were either misleading or simply inaccurate. The terms most often heard at the advisory meeting with regard to the failure to warn of the serious side effects of Vioxx were the data were "uncertain," "muddy," and "inconclusive." Dr. David Graham, in one of the meeting's few moments of drama, pointed out that if everyone was "uncertain" about the safety of a drug, it should not have stayed on the market until further data became available to ensure public health.

Little debate ensued on this crucial issue, perhaps because, as *The New York Times* revealed in a front-page story a few days after the special session was held, many of the advisors had ties to the pharmaceutical industry.[4] The FDA seemed surprised that such associations should have either caused the panel members to be prevented from serving—or that the ties should have been made public. In an exceptional piece of perverse logic, the agency read a prepared conflict of interest statement that said: "it has been determined that the topics of today's meeting are issues of broad applicability and there are no products being approved."[5] This statement was issued despite the fact that the committee had to vote on the safety of *five* very specific billion-dollar drugs and recommend whether they should either stay or be removed from the market.

Vioxx remains off the market to this day and its successor, Arcoxia, never received FDA approval.

By 2007, more than three years after Merck took Vioxx off the market, the company's market value had doubled—its stock at sixty—higher than before Vioxx was removed. Business professors and public relations experts, instead of bemoaning Merck's fate, cited the company for its brilliant legal strategy and its talent in maintaining its outstanding image. Unfortunately, Merck got in ethical and potentially legal trouble again when it failed to release the results of a study about Vytorin, its cholesterol drug, in a timely manner. The company was involved with a controversy about the results with its own outside chief investigator. In June 2008, the company's stock price hovered around $40. Although the company has offered to pay about $5 billion to patients injured by Vioxx and has agreed to pay over $650 million to resolve federal and state allegations about improper Medicaid rebates, doctor kickbacks, and other questionable marketing practices, the company is resolute: "The settlements do not constitute an admission by Merck of any liability or wrongdoing."[6]

"At Merck we are dedicated to the highest standard of ethics and integrity," said Bruce Kuhlik, newly appointed executive vice president and general counsel.[7]

However, according to reporter Ed Silverman of *Pharmalot,* on May 20, 2008, Merck paid $58 million in order to reach a deal with attorneys general from 29 states and Washington, D.C., to "fully resolve" investigations under state consumer protection laws related to marketing the notorious Vioxx painkiller.

Specifically, the drugmaker was cited for allegedly launching an aggressive and deceptive advertising campaign which misrepresented the safety and improperly concealed the increased risks associated with Vioxx, according to Pennsylvania attorney general Tom Corbett. "Using Merck's Vioxx, which was a prescription pain relieving drug, carried an increased risk of having a heart attack or another serious cardiovascular side effect," Corbett says in a statement. "Merck allegedly knew about this, but continued to misrepresent the safety of their product in their advertisements until they finally admitted that Vioxx caused serious side effects and pulled the product from the market in 2004."

Merck's senior executives have walked away with tens of millions of dollars in profits, lucrative job opportunities, and highly rewarding consulting contracts. Raymond Gilmartin left Merck with over $40 million in compensation. Dr. Edward Scolnick retired and now has a multimillion-dollar, state-of-the art medical research center across from the Harvard Medical School named after him.

Pfizer's Celebrex remains on the market. The FDA forced the company to put a large "black box" warning on the label that no one reads, and the pill still sells respectably. Television advertising, which was temporarily halted, has resumed. No one from Merck, Pfizer, the Food and Drug Administration, any university, or any physician has ever been so much as reprimanded—except for a few salesmen who did not understand either company ethics or the law.

The person who seems to have suffered the worst is Dr. Eric Topol. In December 2005, the Cleveland Clinic removed Topol from his job as provost of the medical college that he had founded, a move that also meant he was no longer on the conflict-of-interest committee. At the time, Dr. Topol told *The New York Times* that his willingness to take on Merck was at the heart of his removal from that job, an accusation Merck denied.[8] He also accused Merck of a "persistent pattern" of trying to discredit him. In February 2006, Dr. Topol left the clinic altogether and is currently the head of the Translational Science Institute and Genomic Medicine program for Scripps Health. To this day, Dr. Topol believes that the fines Merck paid were merely a slap on the wrist and will not prevent future misconduct.

Most important of all, the many questions surrounding the development and marketing of Vioxx and the future of medicine itself have not been resolved. Medical advances and the accompanying adoption of modern ethics seem to have been continually marching forward since the end of World War II. The reign of the quacks and pharmaceutical chicanery are well behind us as we enter the twenty-first century of biostatistical medical science—or . . . is something more chilling at play?

Dr. Andrew Marks, chairman of the Department of Physiology, director of the Center for Molecular Cardiology, and professor of physiology and cellular biophysics at Columbia University, made the following comments in the prestigious *Journal of Clinical Investigation* (January 4, 2006), which provide a frightening commentary on the future of drug development:

> Is all the excess, glory, and fortune jeopardizing the very important and necessary rights of patients to truly informed consent? We pride ourselves in having come so far and learned so much in the past sixty years about how to respect patients' rights, but when a giant company like Merck tries to hide data about a blockbuster drug because it may be harming some patients, we must ask ourselves—how far have we come?

The Widow

Vioxx was produced and sold legally. The drug was approved by the Food
and Drug Administration, and its label did warn of coronary side effects.
—"The Vioxx Hex," *The Washington Post,* September 16, 2005

Throughout the summer of 2005, the courthouse in Brazoria
County, Texas, was packed for the trial of *Carol Ernst versus Merck
Corporation.* The world's leading medical experts battled each other on
whether or not Vioxx had contributed to the death of Ms. Ernst's husband,
Bob. The legal talent was also formidable. Representing Merck were the corporate powerhouses Fulbright & Jaworski and Williams & Connolly; representing Ms. Ernst was the dazzling trial attorney Mark Lanier and his staff.

The Ernst family endured months of pre-trial preparation and the gru-
eling trial itself. Through it all, Carol Ernst was steadfast, almost calm—
although this exterior demeanor masked pain she had lived with for what
seemed like an endless period of time.

At the close of the proceedings, after all the experts had their say, corporate executives had carefully defended their decisions, and opposing
medical professors had carefully elaborated the evidence for and against
Vioxx, Carol Ernst took the witness stand.

She was cross-examined by one the nation's foremost defense attorneys,
Gerry Lowry, who launched a vigorous attack on Carol Ernst's testimony,
her character, and her late husband's character and life. Courtroom experts speculated that the tough words were an indication that Merck was
playing hardball with any witness, no matter how potentially sympathetic.

Carol Ernst was aware that the fight would not be easy, that she was up
against a corporation many regarded as the "gold standard" in the pharmaceutical industry.

Nonetheless, it was finally Carol's turn to speak to the jury, the court, and the world:

> It makes me feel bad about [my husband] Bob's death even more as I've listened to all of what Merck has had to say in this trial. The company chose not to share with patients and doctors the risks of Vioxx. Everyone would agree that they should have the right to know of drug risks so that they can make a determination whether to take a drug or not.
>
> If Merck had acted responsibly, I would not have to be here . . . the jury wouldn't have to be here. . . . There is no reason for this to have to happen to anyone.

Carol Ernst won her case and was awarded $253 million. The trial court reduced the judgment to $26 million, a cap under Texas laws. Merck appealed.

Carol Ernst returned to her hometown of Keene, Texas. The gratitude and sense of justice she felt at the conclusion of the trial began to wear away. Three years later she had not received a penny, but her optimism remained. Had not Merck made a settlement offer to thousands of people like her for almost $5 billion? And hadn't much of that settlement occurred because of the victory of her and her attorney? Had not Merck settled health care fraud charges in February 7, 2008, brought by the Justice Department regarding Merck's Vioxx marketing practices? Even on May 20, 2008, Merck agreed to pay a multi-state investigating task force $58 million for downplaying the risks of Vioxx in its commercials. Hadn't those been the very commercials she and her husband had seen?

The money in Carol Ernst's case seemed insignificant, especially to a corporation worth around $60 billion that was scrambling to regain its reputation.

On May 29, 2008, the Fourteenth Court of Appeals reversed the finding of the jury in the case of *Carol Ernst vs. Merck & Co., Inc.*:

> The judgment of the trial court [Brazoria County, Texas] is reversed and judgment is rendered that appellee [Carol Ernst] take nothing.

FOLLOW-UP

David Anstice, formerly President, Human Health—The Americas; member of the Management Committee, Merck & Co. He is now executive director of strategy initiatives, Merck & Co.

Lester Crawford was given the title of FDA Commissioner and confirmed by the Senate. He resigned three months later and a year later was indicted on criminal charges of conflict of interest.

Francesca Catella-Lawson left the University of Pennsylvania to take the position of Associate Director, Clinical Research Gastrointestinal Group, Clinical Sciences, Merck Research Laboratories.

Kenneth C. Frazier, formerly Senior Vice President and General Counsel; member of the Management Committee, Merck & Co., was promoted to Executive Vice President and President, Global Human Health, Merck & Co.

Raymond V. Gilmartin resigned as Chairman of the Board, President, and Chief Executive Officer; and member of Management Committee, Merck & Co. He is now a Professor of Management Practice, Harvard Business School.

Alise Reicin was promoted from Senior Director, Pulmonary-Immunology Group, Merck Research Laboratories, to Vice President of Clinical Research at Merck & Co.

Edward M. Scolnick retired from his position as President, Merck Research Laboratories; member of Merck's Board of Directors; and member of Management Committee.

Eve E. Slater left the Department of Health and Human Services one year after taking the position. She is now Senior Vice President of World Wide Policy, Pfizer Corporation.

AUTHOR'S NOTE

For many years I have worked in the pharmaceutical industry. It is a fascinating enterprise, with its own set of rules of conduct and ethics.

I doubt much reform will occur, but not for the reasons generally given. Since drugs were first discovered, they have been sources of hope, belief, inspiration, power, and relief of life's ills and pains. Despite the efforts of modern science to make drug research and testing an objective, scientific enterprise, we are conditioned to continually gaze ahead in search of the next miracle pills. They appear and disappear like clockwork, some for good, some for bad—and all expensive. But when we are in need we keep begging our doctors for a cure—any cure—and most of all for some hope. And as long as that human impulse exists, Franz Anton Mesmer and his successors will be there to provide it—in whatever guise suits the age.

I have spent a great deal of time since my employment in 1984 as director of public affairs of the Squibb Corporation (now Bristol-Myers Squibb) facing ethical medical issues and addressing them in a *practical* way. Most questions are not easy to solve—and poring over the rules and regulations of the FDA, reading the Helsinki Agreement, and studying the history of the conduct and practice of medicine seldom provide a simple answer.

My wife, Susan, died of brain cancer in 2002. She suffered for eighteen months and endured the best medical science could provide. We were never told the hazards involved in her experimental therapy. In the end, I wondered if treatments and care had regressed, rather than moved forward.

I was forced to take a hard look at my profession and beliefs. The doubts of Andrew Marks remain in my mind.

In 2005, I became fascinated with the Vioxx story. Working with attorneys attempting to elucidate Merck's actions, I spent two years reading confidential Merck records and talking to Vioxx researchers. In addition, I have read the reports of members of the Food and Drug Administration, patients, drug salesmen, and practicing physicians, but am still left with the question: Why did Merck undertake so many activities that could put patients at risk?

There are a few possible answers. Perhaps the company and its advisors really believed they had a safe product whose benefits outweighed its risks. Or maybe it was a simple issue of delusion, denial, and greed.

And finally there is my own conclusion, with which the reader may or may not agree, but informs the title of this book: *Poison Pills.*

According to the ancient Greeks, who saw the duality of remedies, medicine's greatest pills are poisons. Sometimes only the barest dose separates a miracle drug from a poison. The English word for pill comes from the Greek, *pharmakon.*

The philosopher Socrates wrote that *pharmakon "acts as both remedy and poison."* He also warned of an even more dangerous phenomenon. He wrote that pills, by their seductiveness, may make one stray from natural, habitual paths and laws. When this happens, as with Vioxx, the consequences may be tragic.

ACKNOWLEDGMENTS

In order to write this book, I had to review thousands of pages of legal documents, watch numerous trials, and speak to scores of scientists, health care providers, pharmaceutical executives, and attorneys. In addition, many books, medical journals, news reports, tape transcripts, and videotapes were used.

Most of all, I drew on my experiences in the pharmaceutical industry to place all the data in perspective. I have worked as a medical journalist, director of public affairs for Squibb Corporation, later Bristol-Myers Squibb, and owned my own communications company where I did extensive work for Merck & Co. I have known some of the people in this book, including Ken Frazier, who was responsible for the legal review of the videotapes and written material my company produced on behalf of Merck and Astra Merck, a joint venture.

I acknowledge his honesty and integrity and above all, sense of humor. I have tried to portray him and all the others in this story as honestly as possible. I worked for Jan Weiner, Merck's director of public affairs. She was a "worthy competitor" when I was at Bristol-Myers Squibb, and a fair and scrupulous person for whom to work.

This is a work of nonfiction. No names or characters were invented. All quotes are as reported to me and checked as much as possible with other sources. All the data presented in this book is backed by either professional analysis or in medical journals. However, many discrepancies still remain in terms of facts and figures. Even various prestigious medical journals contain contrary statements.

More problematically, some of the data in this story have never either been properly published or carefully analyzed. I have relied as best I could on experts, first-hand accounts, and reports—and used my own judgment in making conclusions.

My greatest thanks and appreciation go to the scientists, physicians, pharmacologists, and financial analysts who spent hours giving me firsthand information of their experiences with Vioxx and took me behind the scenes. It was particularly gratifying to see so many in the medical community willing to have the time, effort, and courage to be interviewed for this book.

My sincerest gratitude to Professor John L. Wallace, who provided a wealth of scientific papers and lecture notes as well as personal stories regarding Vioxx, and cardiologist Dr. Eric Topol, one of the first to confront Merck's data and a tireless investigator who put his reputation on the line at many points. Drs. Donald Young and M. Kerry O'Banion spent hours explaining the discovery of cox-2 and the patent battle that followed. I appreciate the efforts of Dr. Curt Furberg and Dr. Bruce Psaty, two of the nation's foremost epidemiologists, both of whom wrote important commentaries on Vioxx in leading medical journals, and Dr. Eric Ding, who authored a critical study on Vioxx and arrhythmia. Also thanks to Dr. Richard Logan, epidemiologist at the University of Nottingham, and Dr. Frank Wollheim, emeritus professor at the University of Lund.

All Americans owe a debt of thanks to Dr. David Graham, whom I spoke to on a number of occasions. As an FDA safety officer, he aptly considers his patients to be the American public and fights for them. That is very good news indeed! Thanks also to friend Barbara Ryan, of Deutsche Bank, who was untimely awakened by the Vioxx withdrawal, and financial analyst Richard Stover, whose reporting on Vioxx was so sharp that he was threatened with being "boiled in oil."

Many others contributed to this book for background information only, including members of the Food and Drug Administration. Will Wiest of the Ritz-Carlton hotel in Maui provided me with extensive information about the resort. I hope to get there myself.

I thank Dr. Adeoye Olukotun for helping review the manuscript as well as Dr. Steven Jubelirer, a leading blood expert from the University of West Virginia Medical Center.

I owe a special debt of gratitude to Dr. James Fries, professor of medicine at Stanford University. Dr. Fries is not only a brilliant doctor and scientist, his work on collecting data on arthritic patients (ARAMIS) has done the world a great service in understanding how best to treat and not to harm patients with pain. Dr. Fries talked to me at length at a time when he was caring for his dying wife. He both wanted to set the record straight and act as a true professor by imparting his wisdom. Enough said.

For second-hand accounts, it is necessary to acknowledge Merck's own investigation into the Vioxx story: "Report of the Honorable John S. Martin, Jr. to the Special Committee of the Board of Directors of Merck & Co., Inc. Concerning the Conduct of Senior Management in the Development and Marketing of Vioxx." Wherever possible I relied on this extensive document for information. I would request that Merck post the Martin Report in a format that is easily searchable online.

Several excellent sources were used for background material. Foremost, I would like to acknowledge Professor Thomas Dormandy's book, *The Worst of Evils: The Fight Against Pain.* It is an immensely readable and compelling account of pain control through the ages and is written with considerable wit and insight. I have quoted from Dr. Dormandy's account of the invention of anesthesia, surely one of the most entertaining accounts of a major medical advance ever written.

I also highly recommend *The Devil's Doctor* by Philip Ball. It relates the story of one of the most controversial medical figures in world history, Paracelsus. The book gives an excellent account of the origins of modern pharmacy and how the ideas of Galen gradually lost their absolute control. Mr. Ball has also given an excellent account of what medicine was like in the Renaissance.

I found the best account of American medicine in the nineteenth century to be *The Toadstool Millionaires: A Social History of Patent Medicines in America Before Federal Regulation* by James Harvey Young, Ph.D. It is a veritable cornucopia of quackery, yet makes many valuable points about the evolution of drug regulation (or lack thereof), advertising, and merchandising. Despite numerous changes of laws, the reader of this book might well be surprised at how little has actually changed.

Another excellent source for historical materials can be found in the

Wellcome Institute for the History of Medicine. Some of the authors whom I found in this invaluable archive include historians and professors Vivian Nutter, Roy Church, Roy Porter, and J. P. Griffen, among many others. The account by Professor Church of the career of S.M. Burroughs in the nineteenth century gives an excellent sense of the origins of modern drug marketing.

The ties between Merck, Freud, and the development of cocaine have been well researched in works by Paul Gootenberg, editor of *Cocaine: Global Histories,* David Musto, Joseph S. Spillane, and Steven Karch. For anyone unaware of the origins of the cocaine trade, Merck's contribution to its formation, and the American experience with this drug, the works of these scholars will prove startling.

Understanding the origins of modern drug testing is difficult indeed. But two excellent Web sites provide an outstanding trove of articles. Please see www.jameslindlibrary.org and that of Ted Kaptchuk, Associate Professor of Medicine, Harvard Medical School, who has written and lectured on many aspects of the efficacy and philosophies of clinical trials (www.osher.hms.harvard.edu/pe_faculty.asp). I read Dr. Kaptchuk's work enthusiastically, quoted from it, and can recommend his studies to anyone with an interest in medicine.

I need to thank the wonderful staff at the National Library of Medicine, where I spent many fascinating days examining original medical journals. I have made extensive use of articles appearing in *The Journal of the American Medical Association, The Lancet, British Medical Journal, Journal of the Canadian Medical Association, The New England Journal of Medicine*, and many others. The Princeton University Library provided a good refuge on many cold nights.

I found it surprising how different the original articles are from the conventional portrayal of medicine.

With that in mind, I relied on timely reports. Among many excellent reporters who have written about Vioxx are Alex Berenson, Melody Peterson, and Gina Kolata of *The New York Times,* Heather Won Tesoriero of *The Wall Street Journal*, and Ransdell Pierson from Reuters. Many other journalists also did fine and timely reporting from newspapers worldwide.

Reports appearing on National Public Radio by Snigdha Prakash and Vikki Valentine were particularly illuminating.

Before starting to write this book I worked for a number of law firms as an expert witness for those who had been injured by Vioxx. This gave me access to a huge number of documents, all of which have been made public since I read them. Two lawyers who have worked tirelessly for their clients include Eric Weinberg and Chris Placitella. Both provided me with background information and analysis of the Vioxx case. The Lanier Law firm, which represented Carol Ernst, in particular Richard Meadow, aided research as did attorneys David Buchanan and Michael Coren. I received payment for these services. My mother owned stock in Merck & Co., but sold it subsequent to the Vioxx withdrawal. I currently own stock in BMS, Lilly, and Abbot laboratories.

Many people worked tirelessly both on the proposal and the actual book. Barbara Lowenstein, my agent, guided me through the initial writing as did attorney Don Veix. Thomas Dunne, publisher, shepherded this book from beginning to end. My editor, Joel Ariaratnam, had the special patience to coax the best work from me. In fact, everyone at Thomas Dunne/St. Martin's Press has treated me with the respect and dignity most authors can only wish for.

My research assistants, Genevieve Stein-O'Brien and Blanche Brann, did an amazing job of rescuing me from a task that at times seemed insurmountable.

Special people need to be warmly thanked for their constant support. Pamela McGrew, an inspiration, constructive critic, and guide, fed me, loved me, and took me in on days when the written word failed. And lastly there is my mother, Ruth Nesi—a wise old soul. She is my harshest critic. She read the first manuscript when she was eighty-four and told me I had a real page-turner. It was my first inkling that readers might really like this book.

Notes

PRELUDE: THE WIDOW

Although Carol Ernst was not interviewed by the author in person, all quotes and feelings ascribed to Ms. Ernst are well documented in various news accounts and court transcripts.

1. Court TV, "Widow Testifies She Recommended Her Husband Take Vioxx," August 5, 2005.
2. Alex Berenson, "In First of Many Vioxx Cases, a Texas Widow Prepares to Take the Stand," *The New York Times,* July 13, 2005.
3. Richard Stewart, "Jurors Shed Tears During Vioxx Testimony," *The Houston Chronicle,* August 5, 2005.
4. Gardiner Harris, "Court Considers Protecting Drug Makers from Lawsuits," *The New York Times,* February 26, 2008.
5. Linda Johnson, "Despite $4.5 Billion Vioxx Deal, More Merck Suits," AP, March 7, 2008.
6. Alex Berenson, "For Merck, Vioxx Paper Trail Won't Go Away," *The New York Times,* August 21, 2005.
7. Brenda Sapino Jeffreys, "Merck Ponders Grounds for Appeal in Wake of $253 Million Vioxx Verdict," *Texas Lawyer,* August 22, 2005.
8. CNBC-TV, *Kudlow & Company,* August 23, 2005.
9. "The Vioxx Hex." Editorial, *The Washington Post,* September 16, 2006.
10. Eric Ding, et al., "Adverse Effects of Cyclooxygenase-2 Inhibitors on Renal and Arrhythmia Events: Meta-Analysis of Randomized Trials," *The Journal of the American Medical Association,* October 2006; 296: 1619–1632. Joint first authors (published by *JAMA* via priority early release, September 12, 2006).
11. Eric Ding, interviewed by the author, October 2006.

12. Richard Epstein, "Ambush in Angleton," Editorial, *The Wall Street Journal,* August 22, 2005.

13. Marc Kaufman, "Merck Found Liable in Vioxx Case," *The Washington Post,* August 20, 2005.

14. See CNN-TV, *The Situation Room,* August 19, 2005, Angleton Court transcript and other contemporary reports of Ernst sentiments.

Chapter 1. Shooting Stars

1. Dorothy Hamill, "Everyday Victories" (Merck television commercial for Vioxx).

2. Barbara Ryan, pharmaceutical analyst and managing director, Deutsche Bank, interviewed by the author, September 2006.

3. James S. O'Rourke, "Merck & Co. Communication Lessons from the Withdrawal of Vioxx," *Journal of Business Strategy* 27 (2006): 11–22.

4. Dr. Peter Kim, Merck & Co. press release, "Merck Announces Voluntary Withdrawal of Vioxx," September 30, 2004.

5. Heather Won Tesoriero, "Vioxx Doctors Wooed by Merck Are Now Its Docs," *The Wall Street Journal,* March 10, 2006.

6. D. Mukherjee, E.J. Topol, et al., "Risk of Cardiovascular Events Associated with Selective COX-2 Inhibitors," *JAMA,* 2001; 286: 954–959.

7. James Witter, M.D., Ph..D., Team Leader, DAAODP, Maria Lourdes Villalba, M.D., Medical Officer, FDA Memo (Update of Cardiovascular Thrombotic Events in Alzheimer's Studies 078 and 091), March 12, 2002.

8. John Wallace, Ph.D., MBA, professor of pharmacology and therapeutics, University of Calgary, Alberta, Canada, e-mail response to author query, May 29, 2008.

9. Bruce M. Psaty, M.D., et al., *The Journal of the American Medical Association,* 2008; 299 (15): 1813–1817.

10. Raymond Gilmartin, CEO, Merck & Co., conference calls, September 30, 2004.

11. Dr. Peter Kim, Merck & Co. press release, "Merck Announces Voluntary Withdrawal of Vioxx," September 30, 2004.

12. Ibid.

13. Senate Finance Committee Transcript, November 18, 2004.

14. Merck & Co. Research Management Committee, No. 96–19, October 10, 1996.

15. John Wallace, Ph.D., MBA, professor of pharmacology and therapeutics, University of Calgary, Alberta, Canada, e-mail response to author query, May 29, 2008.

16. Garret FitzGerald, M.D., University of Pennsylvania, press release, "New Cox-2 Inhibitors May Elevate Cardiovascular Risk," January 14, 1999.

17. John Wallace, Ph.D., MBA, professor of pharmacology and therapeutics, University of Calgary, interviewed by the author, September–October 2006.

18. *Larry King Live,* CNN-TV, January 31, 1999.

19. Ibid.

20. Thomas Abrams, director of Drug Promotion and Marketing and Communications, FDA, as quoted in Merck & Co. internal memo, September 15, 2000.

21. Phil Kloer, "WAGA Show Helps Celebs Pitch Merck's Arthritis Drug," *The Atlanta Journal Constitution,* September 16, 2000. See also WAGA transcript "Good Morning Atlanta," September 13, 2000.

22. Hollister H. Hovey, "Merck Faces Rocky Path After Vioxx Withdrawal," Dow Jones News Service, September 30, 2004.

23. James Cramer, *The Street.Com,* September 30, 2004.

Chapter 2. Super Aspirin and Poison Pills

1. Jerome Groopman, "Super Aspirin: New Arthritis Drug—Celebra," June 15, 1998. http://www.jeromegroopman.com/articles/super-aspirin.html.

2. James Fries, M.D., professor of medicine, Stanford University Medical Center, interviewed by author, September–October 2006.

Chapter 3. Cox in Paradise

1. Jerome Groopman, www.jeromegroopman.com.

2. Ibid.

3. Frank A. Wollheim, M.D., interviewed by the author, October 2006.

4. "RxNews: Are New Painkillers Really Safe?" *Healthfacts*, February 1, 1999.

5. Ibid.

6. Letter from Professor James Fries, Stanford University Medical Center, to Raymond Gilmartin, CEO of Merck & Co., January 9, 2001.

Chapter 4. The Pharmaceutical Miracle

1. "What the Doctor Ordered," *Time* magazine, August 15, 1952.
2. Thomas Dormandy, *The Worst of Evils: The Fight Against Pain,* New Haven: Yale University Press, 2006.
3. James Fries, M.D., interviewed by author.
4. Vivien Nutton, "The Drug Trade in Antiquity," *Journal of the Royal Society of Medicine*, February 8, 1985.
5. Ibid.
6. J. P. Griffin, "Venetian Treacle and the Foundation of Medicines Regulation," *British Journal of Pharmacology,* 58:3, 317–325.
7. Dormandy, *The Worst of Evils.*
8. Ernest Jones, *The Life and Work of Sigmund Freud,* New York: Basic Books, Inc, 1953.
9. Paul Gootenberg, "Between Coca and Cocaine," The Woodrow Wilson Center, February 2001.
10. James Harvey Young, Ph.D., *The Toadstool Millionaires: A Social History of Patent Medicine in America Before Federal Regulation,* Princeton: Princeton University Press, 1961.
11. *Merck Manual 2005 Edition,* Merck & Co.
12. Paul Vallely, "The History of Cocaine," *Independent Newspaper* (London) March 2, 2006.
13. Dr. Marcia Angell, *The Truth About Drug Companies: How They Deceive Us and What to Do About It,* New York: Random House, 2005.
14. Philip Ball, *The Devil's Doctor,* New York: Farrar, Straus & Giroux, 2006.

Chapter 5. The Evolution of Ethics in Modern Medicine

1. *Merck Ethics Manual,* Merck & Co.
2. "From experience to design—The science behind Aspirin," www.creatingtechnology.org, http://www.creatingtechnology.org/biomed/aspirin.htm.
3. Charles Darwin, *The Descent of Man and Selection in Relation to Sex,* Chicago, Rand McNally, 1874.
4. C. Kaldjian and A. Sofair, "Eugenic Sterilization and the Qualified Nazi Analogy: The United States and Germany, 1930–1945," *Annals of Internal Medicine* 132: 312–319; 2000.
5. J. McTavish, "What's in a Name? Aspirin and the American Medical Association," *Bulletin of the History of Medicine,* 1987; 61: 364–365.

6. Dr. Pope of the Leicester Infirmary and Fever House, *The Lancet*, April 13, 1889, p. 728.

7. F. Roberts, *The Lancet*, October 14, 1899.

8. *Buck v Bell* 274–US200 (1927).

9. Editorial, "Feeble-Mindedness and the Future," *The New England Journal of Medicine*, 1933; 208: 852–3.

10. Consent Form, Merck & Co., December 4, 1998.

11. Garret FitzGerald, M.D., University of Pennsylvania, *Healthfacts*, February 1, 1999.

12. Thomas Musliner, M.D., internal Merck & Co. memo to Friedman, Nies, Spector, November 21, 1996.

Chapter 6. The Advertising Miracle

1. A. Cramp, M.D., "Truth in Advertising Drug Products," *JAMA* lecture, September 16, 1920.

2. Jane Brody, "Hailed and Feared, Cortisone Now Safer and More Varied," *The New York Times*, January 20, 1981.

3. Edward Kendall, "The Development of Cortisone as a Therapeutic Agent," Nobel Lecture, December 11, 1950.

Chapter 7. Super Aspirin is Born

1. Groopman.

2. Dormandy, *The Worst of Evils*.

3. The results of the BYU and the generic case are unknown as of early 2008; both Pfizer and Merck retained the rights to their respective drugs.

4. Dormandy, *The Worst of Evils*.

5. Groopman.

Chapter 8. Discovery

1. M. Kerry O'Banion, M.D., Ph.D., professor of neurobiology and anatomy, University of Rochester, interviewed by the author, September–October 2006.

2. Donald Young M.D., professor of medicine and biochemistry, University of Rochester, interviewed by the author, September–October 2006.

3. Andrew Pollack, "Battling Searle, University Gets Broad Patents for New Pain Killer," *The New York Times*, April 12, 2000.

4. Donald Young, M.D., interviewed by the author, September–October 2006.

5. Groopman.

6. Donald Young, M.D., interviewed by the author, September–October 2006.

CHAPTER 9. THE EPIDEMIC BLOSSOMS

1. Young, *The Toadstool Millionaires.*

2. *British Medical Journal,* December 3, 1983, 287 (6404:1725).

3. Ibid.

4. Merck & Co. press release, July 7, 1996.

5. Searle press release, July 8, 1996.

6. Ibid.

7. "Super Aspirin Could Help Prevent Bowel Cancer," *Cancer Weekly,* October 27, 1997.

8. Ibid.

9. Groopman.

10. Carolyn Abraham, *Toronto Globe and Mail,* September 8, 1998.

11. Ibid.

CHAPTER 10. THE WAR BEGINS

1. Alice Foote MacDougall, *Women's Words,* edited by Mary Bliss, New York: Columbia University Press, 1996.

2. Merck & Co. internal e-mail, Scolnick to McKinney, June 1, 1998.

3. Fran Hawthorne, *The Merck Druggernaut,* New York: Wiley, 2003.

4. Lee Simon, et al., 'Preliminary Study of the Efficacy of the Safety and Efficacy of SC-58635," *Arthritis and Rheumatism,* September 1998; 41(9), 1591–1602.

CHAPTER 11. BURSTING THE BUBBLE

1. John L. Wallace, Ph.D., professor of pharmacology and therapeutics, University of Calgary, Alberta, Canada, interviewed by the author, September–October 2006.

2. Ibid.

3. *Environmental Health Perspectives,* vol. 104, no. 6, June 1996.

4. Dr. Robert J. Langenbach, Ph.D., principal investigator, National Insti-

tute of Environmental Health Sciences—National Institutes of Health, interviewed by the author, September–October 2006.

5. Masferrer, et al., PNAS, April 12, 1994; 91(8); 3228–3232, communicated by Philip Needleman, December 21, 1993.

6. Ibid.

7. Langenbach, Ph.D., interviewed by the author.

8. Ibid.

9. Ibid.

10. Ibid.

11. Wallace, Ph.D., interviewed by the author.

12. Ibid.

13. Ibid.

14. Ibid.

15. "New Super Aspirins May Give Pain Relief Without Stomach Upset," CNN-TV, November 6, 1998.

16. Merck & Co. Memo, Research Committee No 96–10, Blue Bell: October 10, 1996.

17. John L. Wallace, Ph.D., interviewed by the author.

18. *Kudlow & Company,* CNBC-TV, August 23, 2005.

19. Martin Report, Merck & Co., discussion with FitzGerald.

20. Ken Shinmura and Robert Bolli, et al., "Cyclooxygenase-2 Mediates the Cardioprotective Effects of the Late Ischemic Preconditioning in Conscious Rabbits," *PNAS,* Vol. 97, No. 18, 10197–10202, August 29, 2000. Submitted to *PNAS* by Dr. Eugene Braunwald.

21. Martin Report, Merck & Co., "Approval of Vioxx."

22. Martin Report, Merck & Co. Internal Document.

23. Anne Wilde Mathews and Barbara Martinez, "E-Mails Suggest Merck Knew Vioxx's Dangers at Early Stage," *The Wall Street Journal,* November 1, 2004.

24. Ibid.

25. Martin Report, Merck & Co., discussion with FitzGerald.

26. Ibid.

27. Frank A. Wollheim, M.D., interviewed by the author, October 2006.

28. Garret FitzGerald, M.D., University of Pennsylvania, press release, "New Cox-2 Inhibitors May Elevate Cardiovascular Risk," January 14, 1999.

29. Ibid.

30. Ibid.

CHAPTER 12. THE VIOXX MYSTIQUE AND HYPNOTIZED WATER

1. Wallace, Ph.D., interviewed by the author.

2. James Lind, *A Treatise of the Scurvy,* London: A. Millar, 1753.

3. Stephan A. Schwartz, "Franklin's Forgotten Triumph: Scientific Testing," *American Heritage*: 65–73; October 2004.

4. U.S. Military Tribunal, Transcripts of the Proceedings in Case 1, pg. 177, testimony of Karl Brandt.

5. *"The Merck Manual: A Century of Medical Publishing and Practice,"* CBE *Views,* Vol. 22, NR3, 1999.

6. A. D. Blackader, "Drugs and Medicinal Agents Considered from the Professional, Economic and National Standpoints," *The Canadian Medical Association Journal,* July 1916.

7. *The Merck Manual,* Merck & Co.: Rahway, NJ, p. 316.

8. "Doctors, Drugs, and Dollars," *Time,* August 4, 1961.

CHAPTER 13. IS SUPER ASPIRIN SAFE AND EFFECTIVE?

1. A. S. Elstein, "Human Factors in Clinical Judgment: Discussion of Scriven's Clinical Judgment," In: Engelhardt, H.T., Spicker, S. F., Towers, B., *Clinical Judgment: A Critical Appraisal,* Dordrecht: Reidel, 1979.

2. Ted Kaptchuk, "Effect of Interpretive Bias on Research Evidence, *British Medical Journal,* June 28, 2003; 326: 1453–1455.

3. Transcript of FDA Arthritis Advisory Committee meeting discussing safety issues surrounding cox-2 inhibitors, March 24, 1998.

4. Letter of Concern, Merck & Co., Musliner memo.

5. Dr. Loren Laine, FDA Advisory Committee transcripts, 1998.

6. Dr. Lee Simon, FDA Advisory Committee transcripts, 1998.

7. Leona Malone and Dr. Michele Petri conversation, FDA Advisory Committee transcripts, 1998.

CHAPTER 14. THE COOL BLONDE

1. Martin Report, Merck & Co. internal memo, Scolnick to McKinney.

2. Martin Report, Merck & Co. internal memo, Briggs to Simon, et al.

3. Alex Berenson, "Plaintiffs Find Payday Elusive in Vioxx Cases," *The New York Times,* August 21, 2007.

4. Alice Reicin, Martin Report, Merck & Co., "GI Outcomes Trail Protocol," February 25, 1997.

5. Thomas Ginsberg, "Vioxx Memo Warned of Wishful Thinking," *The Philadelphia Inquirer,* October 18, 2005.

6. "Lawyer Grills Vioxx Researcher at Trial," *Court-TV News,* October 14, 2005.

7. Austin Bradford Hill, "Principles of Modern Statistics," *The Lancet,* 1937.

8. Iain Chalmers, "Fisher and Bradford Hill: Theory and Pragmatism?" *International Journal of Epidemiology,* 2003; 32:922–924.

9. H. Bastin, "Down and Almost Out in Scotland: George Orwell, Tuberculosis and Getting Streptomycin in 1948," The James Lind Library: 2004.

10. Iain Chalmers.

11. Ibid.

CHAPTER 15. CELEBREX MEETS THE FDA

1. Dr. Denis McCarthy, professor of gastroenterology at University of New Mexico School of Medicine and special advisor to FDA, interviewed by the author, September–October 2006.

2. Transcript from the FDA Arthritis Advisory Committee Meeting, December 1, 1998.

3. J. Gillis, "With 'Super Aspirin,' Drug Companies Are Feeling No Pain," *The Washington Post*, June 26, 1999.

4. "Physicians to Neutralize," Merck & Co. Memo, MRK-AF 102101416, July 23, 1999.

5. Anonymous FDA executive.

6. Ibid.

7. Wallace, Ph.D., interviewed by the author.

CHAPTER 16. PAYBACK TIME

1. Merck & Co. internal document, re: Launch Meeting; April 16, 1999.

2. Merck & Co. internal document, "Vioxx Launch Meeting Remarks of Anstice to Representatives," May 24, 1999.

3. Anonymous.

4. "List of Physicians to Neutralize," Merck & Co. memo, July 23, 1999.

5. David Anstice, trial transcript.

Chapter 17. Vioxx Gastrointestinal Outcomes Research (VIGOR)

1. Alex Berenson, "For Merck, Vioxx Paper Trail Won't Go Away," *The New York Times*, August 21, 2005.

2. The Martin Report, Appendix D.

3. Ibid.

4. James Fries, M.D., interviewed by the author.

5. The Martin Report, Appendix D.

6. Merck outtake video, Tape "B25213 LAINE" by DWJ Television, Ridgewood, NJ.

7. The Martin Report: Appendix D.

8. Ibid.

9. Ibid.

10. Dr. Curt Furberg, clinical trial expert, Wake Forest University, interviewed by the author, September–October 2006.

11. The Martin Report, Appendix D.

12. Ibid.

Chapter 18. Spinning the Results

1. Anna Wilde Mathews and Barbara Martinez, "E-Mails Suggest Merck Knew Vioxx's Dangers at Early Stage," *The Wall Street Journal*, November 1, 2004.

2. Senate Finance Committee Hearings, November 18, 2004.

3. Martin Report, Appendix E

4. Merck & Co. press release, "Vioxx Withdrawal," September 20, 2004.

5. Martin Report, Merck & Co., Appendix E.

6. Ibid.

7. Ibid.

8. R. Pierson, "Merck's Vioxx Seen Facing FDA Scrutiny on Heart Attacks," Reuters, April 27, 2000.

9. The Martin Report, Appendix F.

10. Martin Report, Merck & Co., Appendix E.

11. Merck Internal Document, "Positive Public Relations"—Anstice to Gilmartin, March 30, 2000.

Chapter 19. Medical "Interpretation"

1. Richard R. Stover, senior analyst at Arnold and S. Bleichroeder, Inc., interviewed by the author, September–October 2006.

2. "Eleven Deaths Among UK Vioxx Users," Reuters Health, September 8, 2000.

3. Ransdell Pierson, "U.S. Regulators Likely to Sensitize Vioxx Adverse Affects," Reuters, May 1, 2000.

4. Reuters Health, September 8, 2000.

5. FDA Warning Letter to Merck, NDA 21-042, Vioxx (rofecoxib) tablets, MACMIS ID # 9456, September 17, 2001.

6. Richard R. Stover, "Cox-2 Inhibitor Update," Arnold and S. Bleichroeder, Inc., May 10, 2000.

7. Merck & Co. e-mail, Scolnick to Anstice, "Analyst Report on Vioxx," December 5, 2001.

8. Gurkirpal Singh, Testimony to House Subcommittee on Health of the Committee on Energy and Commerce, November 18, 2004.

9. Anna Wilde Mathews and Barbara Martinez, "E-Mails Suggest Merck Knew Vioxx's Dangers at Early Stage," *The Wall Street Journal*, November 1, 2004.

10. Snigdha Prakash, National Public Radio, "Documents Suggest Merck Tried to Censor Vioxx Critics," June 9, 2005.

11. Gurkirpal Singh, Testimony to the Senate Finance Committee, November 18, 2004.

12. Dr. Bruce Psaty, M.D., Ph.D., interviewed by the author, September–October 2006.

13. Dr. Curt Furberg, M.D., Ph.D., professor of public health science, Wake Forest University, interviewed by the author, September–October 2006.

14. Merck & Co. Press Release, "Vigor Results," May 2000.

15. James Fries, M.D., interviewed by the author.

16. Ibid.

Chapter 20. Getting Out the Vioxx Message

1. Merck & Co. internal memo, letter from Abrams, FDA, September 15, 2000.

2. WAGA-TV, transcript of Dorothy Hamill and Bruce Jenner on Channel 5, September 13, 2000.

3. James Fries, M.D., interviewed by the author, October 2006.

4. Reuters Health, September 8, 2000.

5. Gregory D. Curfman, et al., "Expression of Concern," *The New England Journal of Medicine,* December 29, 2005; 353: 2813–2814.

6. Ibid.

7. Alise Reicin, "Response to Expression of Concern," *The New England Journal of Medicine,* March 16, 2006.

8. "*New England Journal of Medicine* Confirms Letters of Concern," *The New England Journal of Medicine,* March 16, 2006.

9. "Merck Informs Investigators of Preliminary Results of GI Outcomes Study with Vioxx," press release, March 27, 2000. Also see Merck Q&A, Martin Report, Appendix E.

10. Martin Report, Merck & Co, Appendix G.

11. Ibid.

12. Ibid.

13. Ibid.

14. Puget Sound Public Radio, August 14, 2001.

Chapter 21. Science in Reverse

1. James Fries, M.D., interviewed by author.

2. Graham, interviewed by the author, September–October 2006.

3. Rita Rubin, "FDA Action Could Give Boost to Celebrex," *USA TODAY,* February 6, 2001.

4. Ibid.

5. Merck press release, "Study Confirms Safety of Vioxx in Extended Use." May 3, 2000.

6. ACR Meeting: "Vioxx Comparable to Diclofenac, Ibuprofen in Osteoarthritis," November 10, 1998 (accessed www.pslgroup.com/dg/co636.htm).

7. John Gartner, "Vioxx Suit Faults Animal Tests," *Wired,* July 22, 2005.

8. Transcript of FDA Advisory Meeting, February 8–9, 2001.

9. Roberta Friedman, Ph.D., "Little Risk of Hypertension with COX-2 Blockers," Presented at AGS, May 16, 2003.

10. Merck internal memo, Edward Scolnick, M.D., to Team, February 8, 2001.

11. Merck & Co. press release, "Response to FDA Advisory Committee Meeting," February 2001.

12. David J. Graham, M.D., interviewed by the author.

13. Merck & Co. memo, Scolnick to Kim, et al., October 4, 2001.

14. Merck & Co. internal memo, April 6, 2001, Superior Court of New Jersey, McDarby Appeal, Docket No. A-0076-07T1, May 29, 2008.

CHAPTER 22. LOSING THEIR MINDS

1. Merck & Co. internal memo, from Block to Scolnick, March 21, 2001.

2. Bruce Psaty, et al., "Reporting Mortality in Alzheimer Disease," *JAMA,* April 16, 2008.

3. Merck & Co. internal memo, from Chen to Bain, April 8, 2001.

4. Bruce Psaty, *JAMA,* April 16, 2008.

5. Ibid.

6. Merck & Co. internal memo, from Eddowes to Reicin, et al., April 18, 2001.

7. Bruce Psaty, *JAMA,* April 16, 2008.

8. Ibid.

9. Martin Report, Merck & Co.

10. Jill Stein, "Rofecoxib (Vioxx) Has Good Cardiovascular Safety Profile in Older Patients with Alzheimer's of Cognitive Impairment," report from *PSL Group Medical News,* November 20, 2002.

11. Ibid.

12. Bruce Psaty, *JAMA,* April 16, 2008.

13. James Witter, FDA memo re: "Cardiovascular Data in Alzheimer's Studies," March 12, 2002.

14. Gurkirpal Singh, M.D., "Daily Health Policy Report: 2002 Study Submitted to FDA Showed Possible Heart Risks Related to Vioxx," *Kaisernetwork.org,* February 10, 2005.

15. Gurkirpal Singh, M.D., Testimony to House Subcommittee on Health of the Committee on Energy and Commerce, February 10, 2005.

16. Alex Berenson and Gardiner Harris, "Pfizer Says 1999 Trials Revealed Risks with Celebrex," *The New York Times,* February 1, 2005.

17. Ibid.

18. Ibid.

19. Ted Kaptchuk, *British Medical Journal,* June 28, 2003; 326: 1453–1455.

Chapter 23. Path of Destruction

1. Eric Topol, M.D., interviewed by the author, September–October 2006.

2. NEJM, Dec 30, 2004.

3. Topol Interview - Also see FDA Advisory Committee Briefing Document, NDA 21–042, 5007 VIOXX Slides February 8, 2001.

4. Topol.

5. Topol.

6. David Graham, M.D., Ph.D., et al., "Risk of Acute Myocardial Infarction and Sudden Cardiac Death in Patients Treated with Cyclooxygenase 2 Selective and Non-Selective Non-Steroidal Anti-Inflammatory Drugs: Nested Case-Control Study," *The Lancet,* 2005; 65: 475–481.

7. David J. Graham, M.D., interviewed by the author.

8. Eric Topol, M.D., interviewed by the author.

9. "B25213 Laine," Merck & Co. outtake video.

10. Anonymous.

11. James Fries, M.D., interviewed by the author.

12. "Laine," Merck & Co. outtake video.

13. Frank A. Wollheim, M.D., interviewed by the author.

14. "Demopoulos," Merck & Co. outtake video.

15. Joan-Ramón Laporte, *"Las Supuestas Ventajas de Celecoxib y Rofecoxib: Fraude Científico,"* Editorial, *Butlletí Groc,* July–September 2002.

16. Liza Gibson, "Drug Company Sues Spanish Bulletin over Fraud Claim," *British Medical Journal,* January 24, 2004.

17. Gurkirpal Singh, Testimony to House Subcommittee on Health of the Committee on Energy and Commerce, November 18, 2004.

18. *British Medical Journal,* January 24, 2004.

19. Ibid.

Chapter 24. The Drug Warriors

1. FDA Warning Letter to Merck, NDA 21-042, Vioxx (rofecoxib) tablets, MACMIS ID # 9456, September 17, 2001.

2. Merck & Co. internal document, "Response to FDA Warning Letter," November 29, 2001.

3. Anonymous FDA executive.

4. Press release, U.S. Department of Health and Human Services, last revised April 22, 2002.

5. Merck internal e-mail, Scolnick to Staff, January 25, 2002.

6. FDA, "Revised Merck Label," April 11, 2002.

CHAPTER 25. FDA VS. FDA

1. David J. Graham, M.D., interviewed by the author.

2. MRK-AD0329040, "Standby Statement: Trials of Vioxx in Alzheimer's Disease," July 31, 2003.

3. Ibid.

4. James Witter, M.D., Ph.D., Team Leader, DAAODP, Maria Lourdes Villalba, M.D., Medical Officer, FDA Memo RE: Cardiovascular Data in Alzheimer's Studies 078 and 091, March 12, 2002.

5. Merck & Co. press release, "Vioxx Approval for Juveniles," September 8, 2004.

CHAPTER 26. AFTER THE PARTY

1. Merck & Co. news release, "Merck Announces Voluntary Withdrawal of Vioxx," September 30, 2004.

2. Rob Stein, "Studies on Painkillers in Jeopardy," *The Washington Post*, December 26, 2004.

3. Timothy Hla, Editorial, "A Balanced Look at COX-2 Drugs," *The Boston Globe*, March 25, 2005.

4. Gardiner Harris, "F.D.A. Limits Role of Advisers Tied to Industry," *The New York Times*, March 22, 2007.

5. Transcript of Joint Meeting of Drug Safety and Risk Management Advisory Committee, February 16, 2005.

6. Merck & Co. press release, "Settlement with Patients," www.merck.com.

7. *ZoomInfo* People Information, as accessed May 15, 2008.

8. Reed Abelson and Stephanie Saul, "Ties to Industry Cloud a Clinic's Mission," *The New York Times*, December 17, 2005.

SELECT BIBLIOGRAPHY

Ball, Philip. *The Devil's Doctor*. New York: Farrar, Straus & Giroux, 2006.

Bastin, H. "Down and Almost Out in Scotland: George Orwell, Tuberculosis and Getting Streptomycin in 1948." James Lind Library, 2004.

Berenson, Alex. "In First of Many Cases, a Texas Widow Prepares to Take the Stand." *The New York Times*, July 13, 2005.

Berenson, Alex, and Gardiner Harris. "Pfizer Acknowledges It Failed to Reveal Celebrex Cardiac Risk Found in 1999 Trial." *The New York Times*, February 1, 2005.

Blackader, A. D. "Drugs and Medicinal Agents Considered from the Professional, Economic and National Standpoints." *Canadian Medical Association Journal*, July 1916.

Bolli, Roberto. "Cyclooxygenase-2 Mediates the Cardioprotective Effects of the Late Phase of Ischemic Preconditioning in Conscious Rabbits." *PNAS* 97 (2000): 10197–10202.

Bombardier, C., et al. "Comparison of Upper Gastrointestinal Toxicity of Rofecoxib and Naproxen in Patients with Rheumatoid Arthritis." *The New England Journal of Medicine* 343 (2000): 1520–28.

Bresalier, R. S., et al. "Cardiovascular Events Associated with Rofecoxib in a Colorectal Adenoma Chemoprevention Trial." *The New England Journal of Medicine* 352 (2005): 1092–1102.

Brodie, Jane. "Hailed and Feared, Corisone Now Safer and More Varied." *The New York Times*, January 21, 1981.

"A Class Act," *Chembites e-zine*, www.chemsoc.org/chembytes/ezine/2001/gauthier_aug01.htm.

Chalmers, Iain. "Fisher and Bradford Hill: Theory and Pragmatism?" *International*

Journal of Epidemiology 32 (2003): 922–24, http:ije.oxfordjournals.org/cgi/content/full/32/6/922.

Cramp, A. "Truth in Advertising Drug Products." *The Journal of the American Medical Association* lecture, September 16, 1920.

"Doctors, Drugs, & Dollars." *Time*, August 4, 1961, http://www.time.com/time/printout/0,8816,895515,00.html.

Dormandy, Thomas. *The Worst of Evils: The Fight Against Pain*. New Haven: Yale University Press, 2006.

"Eleven Deaths Among UK Vioxx Users." Reuters Health, September 8, 2000, http:/www.medscape.com.

Epitomes of the British Medical Journal, January to April 1899. Quoted in Ann Anderman, *A History of Aspirin* (MJM 1996) 2.

Ernst, Carol, interviewed by Mark Lanier, *McNeil/Lehrer NewsHour*, PBS, August 22, 2005.

"Feeble-Mindedness and the Future" (editorial). *The New England Journal of Medicine* 208 (1933): 852–53.

Foster, Steven D. "Botanical." Answers.com, http://www.answers.com/topic/botanical.

Friedman, Roberta. "Little Risk of Hypertension with COX-2 Blockers." PSL Group, DG Dispatch, May 16, 2003.

Gillis, Justin. "With 'Super Apirin,' Drug Companies Are Feeling No Pain." *The Washington Post*, June 26, 1999.

Graham, David. Testimony, Senate Finance Committee *FDA, Merck and Vioxx: Putting Patient Safety First*. November 18, 2004, http://finance.senate.gov/hearings/testimony/2004test/111804dgtest.pdf.

Griffen, J. P. "Venetian Treacle and the Foundation of Medicine's Regulation." *British Journal of Clinical Pharmacology* 58: 331–25.

Groopman, J. "Super Aspirin: New Arthritis Drug—Celebra." *The New Yorker*, June 15, 1998.

Hamill, Dorothy. Interview with Bruce Jenner. *Good Morning Atlanta*, WAGA TV, September 13, 2000.

Hill, A. "Principles of Medical Statistics." *Journal of the American Statistical Association*, 43, no. 243 (September 1948) 492–93.

Hine, Tommy. "The Toughest Jump of All: After the Gold, Too Many Blues." *Dallas Morning News*, January 31, 1999, http://apse.dallasnews.com/contest1999/writing/100-250.hartford14.html.

Hla, Timothy. "A Balanced Look at COX-2 Drugs." *The Boston Globe*, March 25, 2005.

Jeffreys, Brenda Sapino. "Merck Ponders Grounds for Appeal in Wake of $253M Vioxx Verdict." Law.com, September 22, 2005, http://www.law.com/jsp/article.jsp?id=1124442316408.

Jones, Ernest. *The Life and Work of Sigmund Freud.* New York: Basic Books, 1953.

Kendall, Edward C. "The Development of Cortisone as a Therapeutic Agent." Nobel Lecture, December 11, 1950.

Lanier, Mark, and Richard Epstein, interviewed by Larry Kudlow, *Kudlow and Company.* CNBC, August 23, 2005.

Laporte, Joan-Ramón. *"Las Supuestas Ventajas de Celecoxib y Rofecoxib: Fraude Científico"* (editorial). *Butlletí Groc,* July–September 2002.

Martin, Jr., John S. "Report to the Special Committee of the Board of Directors of Merck & Co, Inc. Concerning the Conduct of Senior Management in the Development and Marketing of Vioxx."

McTavish, J. "What's in a Name? Aspirin and the American Medical Association." *Bulletin of the History of Medicine* 61 (1989): 364–65.

Merck outtake video, DVD, Tape "B25213 LAINE" by DWJ Television, Ridgewood, New Jersey.

Mukherjee, Debabrata, Steven E. Nissen, and Eric J. Topol. "Risk of Cardiovascular Events Associated with Selective COX-2 Inhibitors." *The Journal of the American Medical Association,* 286, no. 8 (2001): 954–59.

Nutton, Vivian. "The Drug Trade in Antiquity." *Journal of the Royal Society of Medicine* 78 (February 1985).

O'Rourke IV, James S. "Merck & Co., Inc.: Communication Lessons from the Withdrawal of Vioxx." *Journal of Business Strategy* 27 (2006): 11–22.

Pierson, Ransdell. "Merck's Vioxx Seen Facing FDA Scrutiny on Heart Attacks." Reuters, April 27, 2000.

Rubin, Rita. "FDA Action Could Give Boost to Celebrex, Vioxx." *USA Today,* February 6, 2001, http://www.usatoday.com/news/health/2001-02-06-hotdrugs.htm.

Schaefer, Naomi. "The Legacy of Nazi Medicine." *New Atlantis,* www.thenewatlantis.com/archive/5/schaefer.htm.

Schwartz, Stephan A. "Franklin's Forgotten Triumph: Scientific Testing." *American Heritage* (October 2004): 65–73.

Singh, Gurkipal. "2002 Study Submitted to FDA Showed Possible Heart Risks Related to Vioxx." *Medical News Today,* February 11, 2005.

Singh, Gurkirpal. Testimony, Senate Finance Committee, *FDA, Merck and Vioxx: Putting Patient Safety First.* November 18, 2004, http://finance.senate.gov/

hearings/testimony/2004test/111804dgtest.pdf; energycommerce.house.gov/reparchives/108/Hearings/02102005hearing1433/Singh.pdf.

Sofair, Andre N., and Lauris C. Kaldjian. "Eugenic Sterilization and the Qualified Nazi Analogy: The United States and Germany, 1930–1945." *Annals of Internal Medicine* 132 (2000): 312–19.

Stein, Jill. "Rofecoxib (Vioxx) Has Good Cardiovascular Safety Profile in Older Patients with Alzheimer's or Cognitive Impairment." November 20, 2002.

Stoltzenberg, Dietrich. "Scientist and Industrial Manager: Emil and Carl Duisberg." www.ciaonet.org/wps/std01/, March 1997.

Topol, Eric J. "Failing the Public Health—Rofecoxib, Merck, and the FDA." *The New England Journal of Medicine* 351(2004):1707–9.

"WAGA Show Helps Celeb Pitch Merck's Arthritis Drug." *Atlanta Journal-Constitution*, September 16, 2000.

Wollheim, F. "Second International Workshop on Cox-2: Cox in Paradise." *Rheuma 21st*, July 28–31, brochure and online report at www.rheuma21st.com.

Young, J. H. *The Toadstool Millionaires*, www.quackwatch.com.

Zhang, J. J., E. L. Ding, and Y. Song. "Adverse Effects of Cyclooxygenase 2 Inhibitors on Renal and Arrhythmia Events: A Class-Wide Meta-Analysis." *The Journal of the American Medical Association* 2006; 296.

INDEX